NUTSHELLS

Constitutional Law

THIRD EDITION

Round Hall's Nutshell, Nutcase, Exam Focus, and Legal Skills Series

NUTSHELL TITLES

Specially written for students of Irish law, each title in the **Nutshell Series** from Round Hall is an accessible review of key principles, concepts and cases. Nutshells are both the ideal introductory text, and the perfect revision aid.

- **Administrative Law** by Matthew Holmes
- **Company Law** – 4th edition
- **Constitutional Law** – 3rd edition by Fergus Ryan
- **Contract Law** by Fergus Ryan
- **Criminal Law** – 4th edition by Cecilia Ní Choileáin
- **Employment Law** – 2nd edition by Dorothy Donovan
- **Equity and Trusts** – 2nd edition by Miriam Dowling
- **EU Law** by Matthew Holmes
- **Evidence** by Ross Gorman
- **Family Law** by Louise Crowley
- **The Irish Legal System** by Dorothy Donovan
- **Land Law** – 2nd edition by Ruth Cannon
- **Succession Law** by Karl Dowling and Robert Grimes
- **Tort** – 2nd edition by Ursula Connolly

NUTCASE TITLES

Round Hall Nutcases are written to give you the key facts and principles of **important cases** in core legal subject areas. Straightforward, no-nonsense language makes Nutcases an easy way to understand and learn key cases.

- **Criminal Law** by Majella Walsh
- **Evidence** by Neil Van Dokkum
- **Tort** – 2nd edition by Val Corbett

EXAM FOCUS TITLES

The series is especially designed to support students in the weeks coming up to exams by providing a unique tutorial approach to answering questions.

- **Criminal Law** by Sarah Carew

LEGAL SKILLS TITLES

The Legal Skills Series helps students master the essential legal and research skills needed to succeed in their studies and in their future careers.

- **How to Think, Write and Cite: Key Skills for Irish Law Students**, 2nd edition by Jennifer Schweppe, Rónán Kennedy and Lawrence Donnelly.

NUTSHELLS

Constitutional Law

THIRD EDITION

ROUND HALL

 **THOMSON REUTERS**

Published in 2018 by
Thomson Reuters Ireland Limited
(Registered in Ireland, Company No. 416940. Registered Office
and address for service 12/13 Exchange Place, IFSC, Dublin 1)
trading as Round Hall.

Typeset by Carrigboy Typesetting Services

Printed and bound in the UK by
CPI Group (UK) Ltd, Croydon, CR0 4YY

ISBN 978-0-41406-097-5

A catalogue record for this book is available from the British Library.

All rights reserved. No part of this publication may be reproduced or transmitted in any form or by any means, or stored in any retrieval system of any nature, without prior written permission.

Thomson Reuters and the Thomson Reuters Logo are trademarks of Thomson Reuters. Round Hall is a registered trademark of Thomson Reuters Ireland Limited.

© Thomson Reuters Ireland Limited, 2018

Contents

Table of Cases xiii
Table of Legislation xxii

1. **Introduction** 1
   The purpose of a constitution 1
   Historical context—The Irish Free State 2
   The Constitution of Ireland 1937 2
   The ethos of the Constitution 3
   An evolving Constitution 3

2. **Constitutional Interpretation** 5
   Language 5
   Precedent and the Constitution 5
   Methods of interpretation 5
   The presumption of constitutionality 13
   The double construction rule 15
   Reaching the constitutional issue last 15

3. **Challenging the Constitutionality of State Conduct** 16
   General remarks 16
   Article 26 16
   Article 34 20
   Article 50 20
   Locus standi 21
   Immunity from constitutional review 23
   The effects of a finding of unconstitutionality 25
   Remedies for breach of the Constitution 28

4. **Articles 2 and 3—The Nation and the Position of Northern Ireland** 29
   The Irish Nation under the old Articles 2 and 3 29
   The Good Friday Agreement 29
   What do the new Articles 2 and 3 say? 30

5. **The Irish State** 31
   What is a state? 31

	Languages and flag	31
	The name of the State	31
	The State has separate legal personality	31
	The State is a democracy	32
	The State is described as a republic	32
	Is the State "independent"?	33
	Sovereignty	33
	The royal prerogative powers	34
6.	**Ireland in the International Order**	36
	The exclusive powers of the Government	36
	Dáil Éireann and foreign relations	37
	The impact of Article 29	38
	Ireland is a dualist state	39
	European Convention on Human Rights	41
	Extra-territoriality	42
	The position of the European Union under the Constitution	42
7.	**The Separation of Powers**	46
	Typically the powers of the State are divided between:	46
	The legislative role—making law	46
	The executive role—governing the State, administering the operation of laws	47
	The judicial role—interpreting and enforcing law	47
	Checks and balances	48
	Mandatory orders	48
	Money matters	49
8.	**The President**	51
	How long does a President serve?	51
	Electing the President	51
	The limited powers of the President	52
	Accountability and impeachment	55
	The Council of State	56
	Article 14	56
9.	**The Oireachtas**	57
	The exclusive powers of the Oireachtas: only the Oireachtas may make laws	57
	The Government's role in delegated legislation	59
	Changing, amending or repealing legislation	62

Delegated legislation and the implementation of EU law 63
Law-making by reference 64
The *Sheehan* principle: delaying the coming into force of
   legislation 65
Parliamentary privilege 65
The powers of Oireachtas committees 69

10. **The Dáil and the Seanad: Making Legislation** 71
   The Dáil 71
   The Seanad 74
   Making legislation 74
   "Money Bills" 75
   Government is responsible to the Dáil 76
   The role of Dáil Éireann in declarations of war 77

11. **The Government** 78
   An Taoiseach 78
   The appointment of Ministers 79
   The removal of Ministers 80
   Foreign affairs 80
   Cabinet confidentiality 81

12. **The Attorney General** 83
   Independence 83
   Prosecution of offences 84

13. **The Courts** 85
   The Supreme Court 85
   The Court of Appeal 86
   The High Court 86
   Other courts 86
   Judges 87
   The independence of the judiciary 87
   Removal of judges from office 89
   Justice to be administered in public 90
   Defining the judicial role 91
   Article 37 93

14. **Liberty and the Right to a Fair Trial** 96
   Rights on arrest 96
   The inviolability of the dwelling 97

       Fairness in the trial of offences. 98
       Unconstitutionally obtained evidence 106
       Criminal intent and the Constitution 107
       Trial by jury. 108

15. Equality 111
       Gender equality 112
       Equality in the political process 114
       Other examples 114
       Where the inequality may be justified on other grounds. 115

16. Personal Rights 117
       Some important examples of enumerated rights 117
       Unenumerated rights 118
       Some important examples of unenumerated rights 121
       Limitations and restrictions on constitutional rights 129

17. The Right to Life. 132
       The ban on the death penalty. 132
       Right to refuse medical treatment. 132
       The right to life of the unborn 133
       What was the "unborn" for this purpose? 134
       Where the unborn has little chance of survival. 134
       The freedom to travel and to information 135
       The repeal and replacement of the Eighth Amendment. 135

18. Freedom of Expression, Association and Assembly 137
       Overlap with the right to communicate 137
       Freedom of the press 138
       Examples of the right 138
       Freedom of expression is not absolute. 139
       Freedom of assembly. 141
       Freedom of association 141

19. The Family, Children, and Education 143
       The family. 143
       Marriage and the definition of "Family" 143
       The special position of marriage. 144
       Equality and marriage. 145
       The autonomy of the constitutional family 146
       Limitations on family rights 147

	Women and mothers	148
	Divorce	149
	The rights of non-marital parents and families	149
	Article 42 and the education of children	151
	Children's rights	152
20.	**Property Rights**	**155**
	The scope (and limits) of property rights	155
	An "unjust attack" on property rights	156
	The right to compensation	159
21.	**Freedom of Religion**	**160**
	Limits on the free practice of religion	160
	The establishment of religion	161
	The endowment of religion	161
	The ban on religious discrimination	162
	Support for the practice of religion	163
22.	**Amending the Constitution**	**165**
	How is the Constitution amended?	165
	What kind of amendments can the People make?	165
	Can an amendment be made contingent on events occurring? ..	166
	The conduct of a referendum	166
	The Amendments explained	167
	The failed amendments	168
Index	....	**169**

Preface to the Third Edition

Studying the Constitution of Ireland can be a daunting task. The sheer breadth of the subject can often seem overwhelming to scholars of the topic. This Nutshell therefore seeks to present Irish constitutional law in a manner that is accessible, informative, and succinct. Designed primarily with undergraduate students in mind, it aims to explain the key concepts and principles of constitutional law, alongside major decisions in the field, in a brief and easily comprehensible way. The Nutshell is framed with particular regard to students who seek a straightforward introduction to constitutional law, as well as those revising for exams.

Given the nature and scope of the subject matter, this text highlights the most significant and helpful examples of constitutional law. It does not, therefore, purport to be an all-encompassing, exhaustive review of the subject. Nonetheless, it is hoped that this Nutshell will be of use to those studying constitutional law, providing a sound basis for the further study of cases and commentaries, and clarifying the fundamental principles of law in this area.

Recent years have seen significant changes in Irish constitutional law, not least in the passage of constitutional amendments allowing same-sex couples to marry and removing the constitutional ban on abortion. New case law has also served to clarify important points of constitutional law. While certain well-established principles and precedents remain of relevance, this text has also sought to capture recent changes and new decisions that continue to shape the landscape of constitutional law.

The author has endeavoured to state the law as accurately as possible as of July 11, 2018. Nonetheless, constitutional law continues to evolve. In particular, future referendums are planned to delete Art.41.2 (on the role of women and mothers in the home), and to remove provisions mandating an offence of blasphemy (Art.40.6). An amendment to make it easier to divorce in Ireland has also been proposed, while measures to extend the right to vote to emigrants and to those aged 16 and over have been floated.

In completing this text, and previous editions, I am greatly indebted to a number of people. Sincere appreciation is due, in particular, to Adam Brophy, Thérèse Carrick, Catherine Dolan, Peter Donnelly, Frieda Donohue, Dave Ellis, Kristiina Kojamo, Pamela Moran, Martin McCann, Susan Rossney, Elina Talvitie, and all at Thomson Reuters/Round Hall for their great work on this and previous editions, and for their immense support and patience. I take sole responsibility, of course, for any errors and opinions herein.

As always, my heartfelt gratitude goes to my family, particularly José, and to my colleagues at Maynooth University, for their support and encouragement during the completion of this edition.

This edition is dedicated to the cherished memory of Bruce Carolan, my dear friend, former colleague, and original series editor of this collection of Nutshells. *Ar dheis Dé go raibh a anam dílis.*

Fergus Ryan
Maigh Nuad, Iúil 2018

Table of Cases

IRISH CASES

A. v Eastern Health Board [1998] 1 I.R. 464 . . . . 134, 135
A. v Governor of Arbour Hill Prison [2006] IESC 56 27
A.B. v C.D. [2016] IEHC 161 133
Ahern v Mahon [2008] 4 I.R. 704 67
An Blascaod Mór Teo v Commissioners for Public Works (No. 4)
   [2000] 3 I.R. 565. 67
Article 26 and Part V of the Planning and Development Act 1999,
   Re [2001] 1 I.L.R.M. 81 . . . . 17, 156
Article 26 and Part V of the Planning and Development Bill 1999,
   Re [2000] 2 I.R. 321. 159
Article 26 and Section 4 of the School Attendance Bill 1942, Re [1943] I.R. 334 . . . 17
Article 26 and Sections 5 and 10 of the Illegal Immigrants (Trafficking)
   Bill 1999, Re [2000] 2 I.R. 360. 127
Article 26 and the Employment Equality Bill 1996, Re [1997]
   2 I.R. 321 . . . . 107, 111, 131, 158
Article 26 and the Equal Status Bill 1997, Re [1997] 2 I.R. 387 . . . . 14, 18, 158
Article 26 and the Health (Amendment) (No. 2) Bill 2004,
   Re [2005] IESC 7. . . . . 18, 50, 60, 155, 157
Article 26 and the Matrimonial Home Bill 1993, Re [1994] 1 I.R. 305 146
Article 26 and the Regulation of Information Bill 1995,
   Re [1995] 1 I.R. 1. . . . . 17, 19, 120, 165
Attorney General (S.P.U.C.) v Open Door Counselling [1988] I.R. 593 135
Attorney General v Cunningham [1932] I.R. 28 98
Attorney General v Hamilton (No.1) [1993] 2 I.R. 250 . . . . 81, 83
Attorney General v Hamilton (No.2) [1993] 3 I.R. 227 68
Attorney General v Paperlink [1984] I.L.R.M. 373 . . . . 7, 123, 124, 129, 137
Attorney General v X [1992] 1 I.R. 1. . . . . 8, 59, 83, 133

B. v DPP [1997] 2 I.L.R.M. 118. 102
Bederev v Ireland [2016] IESC 34 60
Blake v Attorney General [1982] I.R. 117 . . . . 155, 158
Blascaod Mór v Commissioners for Public Works [2001] 1 I.L.R.M. 401 115
Blehein v Minister for Health [2004] IEHC 374; [2008] IESC 40. 126
Boland v An Taoiseach [1974] I.R. 388. . . . . 36, 47, 80
Brady v Donegal County Council [1989] I.L.R.M. 182 127
Breathnach v Ireland [2001] 3 I.R. 230. 71

Brennan v Attorney General [1984] I.L.R.M. 355 157
Buckley v Attorney General [1950] I.R. 67 .... 47, 87
Bula v Tara Mines (No. 6) [2000] 4 I.R. 412 103
Byrne v Ireland [1972] I.R. 241........................ 31, 32, 33, 34, 35, 126

C. O'S. v Judge Doyle [2013] IESC 60................................. 144
C.C. v Ireland [2006] IESC 33 ....27, 58, 108, 117
Callely v Moylan [2014] IESC 26 66
Campaign to Separate Church and State v Ireland
    [1998] 2 I.L.R.M. 181................................11, 152, 161, 164
Campus Oil v Minister for Industry and Energy (No. 2) [1983] I.R. 88.......... 43
Carmody v Minister for Justice [2010] 1 I.R. 635....................... 15, 128
Central Dublin Development Association v Attorney General (1975)
    109 I.L.T.R. 69 .... 94, 155, 159
Charlton v Ireland [1984] I.L.R.M. 39................................... 109
Cityview Press v An Comhairle Oiliúna (AnCO) [1980] I.R. 381............ 59, 60
Clinton v An Bord Pleanála [2005] IEHC 84........................ 156, 156
Cogley and Aherne v RTÉ [2005] IEHC 180 125
Commission to Inquire into Child Abuse, Re the Commission v Notice
    Party A [2002] 3 I.R. 459 127
Commissioners of Public Works [1994] 1 I.R. 101...................... 33, 35
Comyn v Attorney General [1950] I.R. 142.............................. 31
Conroy v Attorney General [1965] I.R. 411........................11, 108, 109
Cooke v Walsh [1984] I.R. 710... 62
Cooney, King, Riordan and the Minister for the Environment [2006] IESC 61..... 73
Corway v Independent Newspapers [2000] 1 I.L.R.M. 426 141
Coughlan v Broadcasting Complaints Commission [2000] 3 I.R. 1 .....73, 114, 167
Cox v Ireland [1992] 2 I.R. 503............................... 104, 124, 158
Creighton v Ireland [2010] IESC 50 130
Crotty v An Taoiseach [1987] I.R. 713 .... 23, 34, 37, 45, 47, 81
Crowley v Ireland [1980] I.R. 102....................................... 151
Cullen v Tóibín [1984] I.L.R.M. 577 138
Curtin v Dáil Éireann [2006] 2 I.R. 556................................. 89

D. v Health Service Executive (HSE) unreported, McKechnie J., 9 May 2007... 135
D.P.P. v Cunningham [2012] IECCA 64 28
D.P.P. v Kavanagh [2012] IECCA 65 28
Damache v DPP [2012] 2 I.R. 266..................................... 98
De Búrca v Attorney General [1976] I.R. 38..................... 11, 110, 111, 112
Deaton v Attorney General [1963] I.R. 170.......................... 92, 93
Dellway v NAMA [2011] IESC 4 155
Desmond v Glackin (No. 1) [1993] 3 I.R. 1.............................. 40
Dillane v Ireland [1980] I.L.R.M. 167 ....9, 111
Dillon v DPP [2008] 1 I.R. 383 138
Doherty v Government of Ireland [2011] 2 I.R. 222 .... 15, 32, 73
Donnelly v Ireland [1998] 1 I.R. 325.................................... 105

Douglas v DPP [2014] 1 I.R. 510 99
Doyle v Commissioner of An Garda Síochána [1999] 1 I.R. 249 40
DPP v Best [2000] 2 I.L.R.M. 1. 151
DPP v Doyle [2017] IESC 1 .... 97, 106
DPP v Gormley and White [2014] IESC 17 106
DPP v J.T. (1988) 3 Frewen 141 143
DPP v JC [2015] IESC 31. 106
DPP v Michael Delaney [1997] 3 I.R. 453 98
Draper v Attorney General [1984] I.R. 277. 71
Dreher v Irish Land Commission [1984] I.L.R.M. 94. .... 9, 159
Dublin Wellwoman Centre v Ireland [1995] 1 I.L.R.M. 408. 87
Dubsky v Government of Ireland [2005] IEHC 442 .... 47, 77
Dubsky v Ireland [2007] 1 I.R. 63. 37
Duggan v An Taoiseach [1989] I.L.R.M. 710 63

E.S.B. v Gormley [1985] I.L.R.M. 494 159
East Donegal Co-operative v Attorney General [1970] I.R. 317. 14
Educational Co. v Fitzpatrick (No. 2) [1961] I.R. 345 .... 119, 142
Emergency Powers Bill 1975, Re the [1977] I.R. 129 24
Employment Equality Bill 1996, Re the [1997] 2 I.R. 321. .... 14, 111, 131, 163
Equal Status Bill 1997, Re the [1997] 2 I.R. 387 18

F.N. v C.O. [2004] IEHC 60 153
Finn v Attorney General [1983] I.R. 514. .... 165, 166
Fitzpatrick v FK [2009] 2 I.R. 7. .... 132, 161
Fleming v Ireland [2013] IESC 19. .... 115, 133
Flynn v Power [1985] I.R. 648 163
Foley v Sunday Newspapers Ltd [2005] 1 I.R. 89 .... 10, 90, 138
Foy v An tArd-Chláraitheoir [2007] IEHC 470. 41
Foy v Governor of Cloverhill Prison [2010] IEHC 52 147

G. v An Bord Uchtála [1980] I.R. 32. .... 143, 149, 150, 152
Gallagher, Re [1991] 1 I.R. 31 92
Garvey v Ireland [1981] I.R. 75. 129
Geoghegan v Institute of Chartered Accountants [1995] 3 I.R. 86. 35
Gilligan v Ireland [2001] 1 I.L.R.M. 473 110
Gilligan v Special Criminal Court [2006] 2 I.R. 389 15
Glover v BLN Ltd. [1973] I.R. 388. 129
Goodman International v Hamilton (No. 1) [1992] 2 I.R. 542. 92
Governor of X. Prison v P.McD. [2015] IEHC 259 133
Grant v Roche Products [2009] 4 I.R. 679 127
Greene v Minister for Agriculture [1990] 2 I.R. 17 .... 43, 144

H. v DPP [2006] IESC 55. 102
Hall v Minister for Finance [2013] IESC 10. 21
Hanafin v Minister for the Environment [1996] 2 I.R. 321. 167

Hand v Dublin Corporation [1991] 1 I.R. 409 124
Hardy v Ireland [1994] 2 I.R. 550 .... 99, 100
Harvey v Minister for Social Welfare [1990] 2 I.R. 232.................... 13, 62
Haughey, Re [1971] I.R. 217 .... 15, 66, 92, 105, 108, 109, 118
Heaney v Ireland [1994] 3 I.R. 593.......................... 98, 104, 130, 137
Herrity v Associated Newspapers [2009] 1 I.R. 316........................ 125
Hoey v Minister for Justice [1994] 3 I.R. 329............................. 63
Holland v Governor of Portlaoise Prison [2004] 2 I.R. 573............... 129, 139
Holohan v Donohue [1986] I.R. 45...................................... 108
Horgan v An Taoiseach [2003] 2 I.L.R.M. 357 37
Horgan v Ireland [2003] 2 I.R. 468................................. 38, 47, 77
Housing (Private Rented Dwellings) Bill 1981 [1984] I.L.R.M. 246 158
Howard v Cahill v Sutton [1980] I.R. 269 21
Howlin v Morris [2004] 2 I.L.R.M. 53, [2006] I.L.R.M. 440 66

Iarnród Éireann v Ireland [1996] 3 I.R. 321 156
In the Matter of AB: Temple Street Hospital v CD [2011] 1 I.R. 665........... 160
In The Matter of Baby AB: Temple Street Hospital v CD [2011] IEHC 1........ 147
In the Matter of S.R. (A Ward of Court) [2012] IEHC 2..................... 133
Independent Newspapers v Anderson [2006] IEHC 62 90
IO'T v B [1998] 2 I.R. 321... 121, 125
Ireland v Mulvey, *Irish Times*, 11 November 1989 31
Irish Penal Reform Trust v Governor of Mountjoy Prison [2005] IEHC 305 23
Irish Times v Ireland [1998] 1 I.R. 359 .... 90, 137, 138

J.H., Re; K.C. v An Bord Uchtála [1985] I.R. 375......................... 153
JMcD v PL and BM [2009] IESC 81 .... 39, 41
JMcD v PL and BM [2010] 2 I.R. 199................................... 144
John Grace Fried Chicken Ltd. v. Catering J.L.C. [2011] IEHC 277............ 61
Jordan v Minister for the Environment [2015] 4 I.R. 232 167

K. v W. [1990] 2 I.R. 437.. 150
Kavanagh v Governor of Mountjoy Prison [2002] 3 I.R. 97 .... 39, 40
Kavanagh v Ireland [1996] 1 I.R. 321.................................. 110
Keady v Garda Commissioner [1992] 2 I.R. 197 91
Kelly v Minister for the Environment [2002] 4 I.R. 191.................. 73, 114
Kennedy v Ireland [1987] I.R. 587 .... 28, 119, 124
Kennedy, Re [1976] I.R. 382 140
Kenny v Dental Council [2004] IEHC 29................................ 124
Kerins v McGuinness [2017] IEHC 34 68
KI v Minister for Justice and Equality [2014] IEHC 83 150
King v Attorney General [1981] I.R. 233............................ 98, 115
King v Attorney General [1981] I.R. 83.................................. 21
Kinsella v Governor of Mountjoy Prison [2011] IEHC 235 122
Kinsella v Governor of Mountjoy Prison [2012] 1 I.R. 467 118

Kirwan v Minister for Justice [1994] 2 I.R. 417.......................... 128
Kostan v Ireland [1978] I.L.R.M. 12.................................. 109

Landers v Attorney General (1973) 109 I.L.T.R. 1........................ 123
Laurentiu v Minister for Justice, Equality and Law Reform [1999] 4 I.R. 26...... 61
Lavery v Member in Charge, Carrickmacross Garda Station
    [1999] 2 I.R. 390... 97
Lawlor v Hogan [1993] I.L.R.M. 607.................................. 102
LB v Ireland [2015] IESC 1.. 159
Lennon v Fitzgerald [1981] I.L.R.M 84................................ 128
Leontjava v DPP [2004] 1 I.R. 591.................................... 64
Lobe, Osayande and Others v Minister for Justice, Equality and Law Reform
    [2003] 1 I.R. 1... 148
Lovett v Minister for Education [1997] I.L.R.M. 89.................... 104, 158
Lowth v Minister for Social Welfare [1998] 4 I.R. 321......................113

M v Minister for Justice and Equality [2018] IESC 14............... 23, 134, 153
M. v An Bord Uchtála [1975] I.R. 81................................... 163
M. v An Bord Uchtála [1977] I.R. 287.............................. 14, 124
M., an infant, Re [1946] I.R. 334..................................... 152
M.R. v T.R. [2006] IEHC 359 160
Macauley v Minister for Post and Telegraphs [1966] I.R. 345 126
Madigan v Attorney General [1986] I.L.R.M. 136..................... 13, 156
Magee v Farrell [2009] I.R. 703 128
Magee v O'Dea [1994] 1 I.R. 500..................................... 103
Maguire v Ardagh [2002] 2 I.R. 385 .... 6, 11, 66, 69, 118, 129
Maher v Attorney General [1973] I.R. 140 .... 28, 58, 88
Maher v Minister for Agriculture [2001] 2 I.R. 139 .... 44, 64, 155
Mahon v Post Publications [2007] IESC 15 .... 137, 138
Mallon v Minister of Agriculture [1996] 1 I.R. 517......................... 109
Margine v Minister for Justice, Equality and Law Reform [2004] IEHC 127...... 148
McA. v McA. [2000] 2 I.L.R.M. 48..................................... 149
McCrystal v Minister for Children and Youth Affairs [2012] I.E.S.C. 53 167
McDaid v Sheehy [1991] 1 I.R. 1...................................... 61
McDonald v Bord na gCon (No. 2) [1965] I.R. 217..................... 15, 91
McDonnell v Ireland [1998] 1 I.R. 134 26
McGee v Attorney General [1974] I.R. 284............ 4, 5, 12–14, 120, 124, 146
McGimpsey v Ireland [1990] 1 I.R. 110 29
McGowan v Labour Court [2013] IESC 21.............................. 61
McGrath v Maynooth College [1979] I.L.R.M. 166....................... 163
McGrath v McDermott [1988] I.L.R.M. 647............................. 58
McInerney v DPP [2014] IEHC 101 99
McK v Information Commissioner [2006] IESC 2........................ 146
McKenna v An Taoiseach (No. 2) [1995] 2 I.R. 10 ....23, 32, 73, 114, 166
McKinley v Minister for Defence [1992] 2 I.R. 333.......................112

McLoughlin v Minister for Social Welfare [1958] I.R. 1..................... 83
McMahon v Attorney General [1972] I.R. 69 .... 11, 72
McMahon v Leahy [1984] I.R. 525 114
MD (A Minor) v Ireland [2012] IESC 10 113
Meagher v Minister for Agriculture [1994] 1 I.R. 329 .... 43, 44
Melling v Ó Mathghamhna [1962] I.R. 1............................. 11, 108
Melton Enterprises v Censorship of Publications Board [2004] 1 I.L.R.M. 260 ... 94
Meskell v C.I.É. [1973] I.R. 121 .... 28, 141
MhicMhathúna v Ireland [1995] I.L.R.M. 69 145
Moore v D.P.P. [2016] IEHC 244 115
Morris v Minister for the Environment [2002] 1 I.R. 326 166
Muckley v Ireland [1985] I.R. 782..................................... 26
Mulloy v Minister for Education [1975] I.R. 88 162
Murphy and McGrath v Minister for the Environment [2007] IEHC 185 72
Murphy v Attorney General [1982] I.R. 241 .... 13, 25, 115, 144
Murphy v British Broadcasting Corporation [2004] IEHC 440 .... 88, 110
Murphy v Dublin Corporation [1972] I.R. 215........................... 88
Murphy v Greene [1990] 2 I.R. 566 126
Murphy v I.R.T.C. [1999] 1 I.R. 12 .... 139, 161
Murphy v Independent Radio and Television Commission
 [1998] 2 I.L.R.M. 360 138
Murphy v IRTC [1997] 2 I.L.R.M. 467.................................. 41
Murray v Ireland [1985] I.R. 332, [1991] 1 I.L.R.M. 465 .... 125, 130, 143, 147
Murtagh Properties v Cleary [1972] I.R. 330 .... 119, 123

N. v Health Service Executive [2006] IESC 60........................... 153
NHV v Minister for Justice and Equality [2017] IESC 35 .... 28, 115, 123
Norris v Attorney General [1984] I.R. 36................. 21, 58, 63, 101, 113, 120
North-Western Health Board v H.W. [2001] 3 I.R. 622.................... 146

Ó Domhnaill v Merrick [1985] I.R. 151 40
Ó Láighléis, Re [1960] I.R. 93 40
O'B. v S. [1984] I.R. 316.................................. 10, 40, 115, 144
O'Brien v Clerk of Dáil Éireann [2017] IEHC 179......................... 68
O'Brien v Keogh [1972] I.R. 144....................................... 155
O'Byrne v Minister for Finance [1959] I.R. 1.......................... 7, 87
O'Callaghan v Clifford [1993] 3 I.R. 603............................... 102
O'Callaghan v Commissioners of Public Works [1985] I.L.R.M. 364 159
O'Donoghue v Legal Aid Board [2004] IEHC 413......................... 128
O'Donovan v Attorney General [1961] I.R. 114 .... 11, 72
O'Leary v Attorney General [1993] 1 I.R. 102........................ 99, 100
O'Malley v An Taoiseach [1990] I.L.R.M. 461............................ 55
O'Malley v Ceann Comhairle of the Dáil [1997] 1 I.R. 427.................. 66
O'Reilly v Limerick Corporation [1989] I.L.R.M. 181...................... 49
O'Shea v Ireland [2007] 2 I.R. 313.................................... 126

Oates v Browne [2016] IESC 7.. 89
OR v An tArd Chláraitheoir [2014] IESC 60 59
Osheku v Ireland [1987] I.L.R.M. 330.. 148
Osmanovic v DPP [2006] 3 I.R. 504... 93

People (Attorney General) v Dwyer [1972] I.R. 416..................... 132
People (Attorney General) v Edge [1943] I.R. 115....................... 98
People (Attorney General) v Kelly [1982] I.L.R.M. 1.................... 103
People (Attorney General) v Messitt [1972] I.R. 204.................. 102
People (Attorney General) v O'Brien [1965] I.R. 142.................. 107
People (Attorney General) v O'Callaghan [1966] I.R. 501.......... 100
People (Attorney General) v Singer [1975] I.R. 408.................... 103
People (D.P.P.) v Shaw [1982] I.R. 1... 132
People (DPP) v Finnerty [1999] 4 I.R. 364................................. 104
People (DPP) v Healy [1990] I.L.R.M. 313.................................. 97
People (DPP) v Kenny [1990] 2 I.R. 110 106
People (DPP) v Lynch [1982] I.R. 64.. 97
People (DPP) v McNally (1981) 2 Frewen 43............................. 97
People (DPP) v O'Shea [1982] I.R. 384...................................... 6
People (DPP) v S.M. [2003] 1 I.R. 606....................................... 86
People (DPP) v Shaw [1982] I.R. 1 .... 9, 10, 97, 130
People (DPP) v Walsh [1980] I.R. 294....................................... 96
People v Tobin [2001] 3 I.R. 469 103
Pok Sun Shum v Ireland [1986] I.L.R.M. 593............................ 148
PP v HSE [2014] IEHC 622 135
Prendergast v HEA [2008] IEHC 257... 35
Pringle v Ireland [2013] 3 I.R. 1 .... 34, 37, 81

Quinn's Supermarket v Attorney General [1972] I.R. 1 .... 111, 162, 163

R. Ltd, Re [1989] I.R. 126... 90
Redmond v Minister for the Environment [2001] 4 I.R. 61 72
Regulation of Information Bill 1995, Re [1995] 1 I.R. 1 .... 13, 120
Ring v Attorney General [2004] I.R. 185................................... 73
Riordan v An Tánaiste [2005] 3 I.R. 62..................................... 121
Riordan v An Taoiseach (No. 2) [1999] 4 I.R. 343 166
Riordan v An Taoiseach (No. 5) [2001] 4 I.R. 463 23
Riordan v An Taoiseach [2006] IEHC 312 23
Riordan v Ireland (No. 4) [2001] 3 I.R. 365................................ 23
Roche v Roche [2006] IEHC 359 134
Roche v Roche [2009] IESC 82; (2010) 114 B.M.L.R. 1 .... 7, 11
Rock v Ireland [1997] 3 I.R. 484... 104
Ryan v Attorney General [1965] I.R. 294.......................... 6, 118, 121
Ryan v DPP [1989] I.R. 399... 100

S.M. v Ireland [2007] IEHC 280 112
S.P.U.C. v Coogan [1989] I.R. 734 .... 23, 135
S.P.U.C. v Grogan [1989] I.R. 753 135
Simpson v Governor of Mountjoy Prison [2017] IEHC 561 125
Sinnott v Minister for Education [2001] 2 I.R. 545 .... 32, 49, 151
Sinnott v Minister for the Environment, Community and Local Government
 [2017] IEHC 214. 72
Slattery v An Taoiseach [1993] 1 I.R. 286. 166
Solicitors' Act 1954, Re the [1960] I.R. 239 .... 91, 94
Somjee v Minister for Justice [1981] I.L.R.M. 324 113
State (Buchan) v Coyne (1936) 70 I.L.T.R. 185 103
State (Byrne) v Frawley [1978] I.R. 326 26
State (C) v Frawley [1976] I.R. 365 122
State (DPP) v Walsh [1981] I.R. 412 .... 112, 145
State (Gilliland) v Governor of Mountjoy Prison [1987] I.R. 201 38
State (Healy) v Donoghue [1976] I.R. 325 .... 5, 12, 97, 106, 127
State (Lynch) v Cooney [1983] I.L.R.M. 89. 140
State (M.) v Attorney General [1979] I.R. 73 .... 120, 128
State (McEldowney) v Kelleher [1983] I.R. 289 89
State (Murphy) v Johnston [1983] I.R. 235. 58
State (Murray) v McRann [1979] I.R. 133. 94
State (Nicolaou) v An Bord Uchtála [1966] I.R. 567 .... 143, 150
State (O.) v O'Brien [1973] I.R. 50 92
State (O'Connell) v Fawsitt [1986] I.L.R.M. 639 101
State (O'Rourke) v Kelly [1983] I.R. 58 93
State (Pheasantry) v Donnelly [1982] I.L.R.M. 512 109
State (Quinn) v Ryan [1965] I.R. 70 5
State (Richardson) v Mountjoy Prison [1980] I.R. 82 122
State (Sheehan) v Government of Ireland [1987] I.R. 550 65
State (Sheerin) v Kennedy [1966] I.R. 379. 92
State (Walshe) v Murphy [1981] I.R. 275 .... 52, 55
Sullivan v Boylan (No 2) [2013] IEHC 104 118

T.D. v Minister for Education [2001] 4 I.R. 259 .... 22, 28, 48, 50, 78, 121
T.F. v Ireland [1995] 1 I.R. 321 160
T.O'G. v Attorney General [1985] I.L.R.M. 61 112
Tilson, Re [1951] I.R. 1. 145
Tormey v Ireland [1985] I.R. 289 8
Tuohy v Courtney [1994] 3 I.R. 1 .... 127, 130

W v W [1993] 2 I.R. 476 112
W.O'R. v E.H. [1996] 2 I.R. 248 .... 144, 150
Wansboro v D.P.P. [2017] IEHC 391 28
Ward of Court, Re a (Withdrawal of Medical Treatment)
 [1996] 2 I.R. 79. .... 122, 132, 133

Webb v Ireland [1988] I.R. 353. . . . . 34, 35
Whelan and Lynch v Minister for Justice, Equality and Law Reform
 [2012] 1 I.R. 1. 93
White v Bar Council of Ireland [2016] IECA 363. 124
White v Dublin City Council [2004] 1 I.R. 545. 127

Zappone v Revenue Commissioners [2006] IEHC 404 . . . . 126, 145

OTHER CASES

Costa v ENEL [1964] E.C.R. 585 43

Goodwin v United Kingdom [2002] 35 E.H.R.R. 18 41

Heaney v Ireland (2001) 33 E.H.R.R. 264 104
Hirst v United Kingdom (No. 2) (2006) 42 E.H.R.R. 41 71

Lotus Case (1927) P.C.I.J. Ser. A., No. 10 42

Norris v Ireland (1989) 13 E.H.R.R. 186. 40

Sutter v Switzerland (1984) 6 E.H.R.R. 272. 90

Table of Legislation

CONSTITUTIONAL PROVISIONS

Bunreacht na hÉireann.... 1–20, 22, 24–30, 32– 34, 35, 37, 38, 40–49, 51, 52, 54, 55, 57, 60, 65, 66, 69, 70– 72, 74, 75, 77, 78, 80–83, 85, 88, 90, 101, 107, 108, 112, 117, 118–122, 128, 129, 132–134, 136–141, 143–149, 152, 156, 159–162, 165–168

- Art.1 .... 2, 33
- Art.2 .... 2, 3, 29, 30, 166
- Art.3 .... 2, 3, 29,30, 166
- Art.4 31
- Art.5 .... 32, 35
- Art.6 .... 2, 33, 34, 35, 46
- Art.7 31
- Art.8 31
- Art.9
  - 9.3 129
- Art.10 35
- Art.12 51
  - 12.3 .... 51, 85
  - 12.4 .... 51, 52
  - 12.10 .... 51, 55, 89
- Arts 12–37 1
- Art.13
  - 13.1.1° 48, 53, 76, 78
  - 13.1.2° 48, 79
  - 13.2 54
  - 13.2.1° 53
  - 13.2.2° 53, 54, 79
  - 13.4 53
  - 13.6 93
  - 13.7 54
  - 13.8 55
  - 13.9 .... 48, 52
  - 13.11 .... 52, 53
- Art.14 .... 52, 56
- Art.15 68
  - 15.2 .... 44, 46, 57, 59, 63, 64
  - 15.4 .... 13, 25
  - 15.5 99

15.5.2°	24, 132
15.6	77
15.10	65, 66, 67
15.12	65, 67, 68
15.13	65, 67, 68, 69
Art.16	71, 73
16.2	72, 73
16.7	72
Art.17	21
17.2	49
Art.18	
18.3	79
Art.21	75, 76
Arts 21–22	54
Art.22	75, 76
Art.23	54, 74, 75, 77, 165
Art.24	54
Art.25	
25.5.4°	5
Art.26	8, 14, 24, 52, 54, 85, 156
26.2.2°	18
Art.27	54, 55
Art.28	36, 37
28.1	78
28.3	23, 132
28.3.1°	77
28.4	48, 76
28.4.2°	81
28.4.3°	47, 82
28.5.2°	79
28.6.1°	79
28.7	75, 76
28.7.1°	80
28.7.2°	80
28.9.3°	80
28.9.4°	53, 79, 80
28.10	48, 76, 79
28.11	48, 76, 79
Art.29	33, 36, 38, 39
29.1–29.3	38, 39
29.4	36, 63
29.4.3°	45
29.4.6°	24, 25, 43, 44, 57, 64
29.4.9°	77
29.5	38
29.6	39, 57

Bunreacht na hÉireann (*continued*)
- 29.7 ... 29
- 29.8 ... 42
- Art.30 ... 84
- 30.2 ... 53, 79
- 30.3 ... 84
- 30.4 ... 83
- 30.5 ... 53
- Art.31 ... 56, 79
- 31.3 ... 55
- Arts 31–32 ... 54
- Art.32
- Art.34 ... 6, 16
- 34.1 ... 47, 90
- 34.3 ... 86
- 34.3.1° ... 8
- 34.3.2° ... 20
- 34.3.3 ... 18
- 34.3.4° ... 8
- 34.4.3° ... 6, 86
- 34.6 ... 87
- Art.35
- 35.1 ... 48, 53, 87
- 35.2 ... 47, 48, 87
- 35.4 ... 89
- 35.4.1° ... 89
- 35.5 ... 7, 87
- 35.5.2° ... 87
- Art.37 ... 47, 85, 91, 93, 94, 95
- Art.38 ... 1
- 38.1 ... 98, 99, 107
- 38.2–38.4 ... 108
- 38.3 ... 86, 109
- 38.5 ... 88
- Art.40 ... 27, 108, 117
- 40.1 ... 9, 10, 99, 107, 110, 111, 115, 123, 145
- 40.3 ... 6, 9, 117, 118, 119, 126, 129, 130, 137, 144, 149, 150, 155, 157
- 40.3.1° ... 7, 123, 149, 150, 152
- 40.3.2° ... 7, 9, 70, 117, 118, 132, 139, 155, 156
- 40.3.3° ... 11, 133, 134, 136
- 40.4 ... 99, 117
- 40.4.1° ... 96, 99
- 40.4.2 ... 22
- 40.4.6° ... 101
- 40.5 ... 97, 118
- 40.6 ... 104, 129, 138, 139, 141, 142

40.6.1°.	117, 138
40.6.1.i.	137
Arts 40–44.	1
Arts 41–44.	3
Art.41	10, 12, 25, 115, 120, 143, 144, 145, 146, 149, 150, 151
41.2.	148
41.3.	144
41.3.1°.	115, 143
41.3.2°.	149, 159
41.4.	126, 145
Art.42	12, 143, 146, 151
42.4.	151, 152, 164
Art.42A	10, 13, 134, 146, 147, 149, 152, 153, 154
42A.2.	152
42A.2.1°.	151
Art.43	9, 12, 120, 155, 157
43.2.	155
Art.44	117, 119, 160, 161
44.1.	160
44.2.2°.	161
44.2.3°.	161, 162
44.2.4°.	147, 161, 162
44.2.5	163
44.2.6°.	159
Art.45	119, 123
Art.46	165
Art.47	165
Art.50	3, 16

AMENDMENTS

Third	45, 167
Fifth	160, 167
Seventh	74
Eighth	7, 11, 133, 134, 135, 168
Ninth	71
Tenth	167
Eleventh	167
Twelfth	134, 168
Thirteenth	135, 168
Fourteenth	135, 168
Fifteenth	149, 168
Sixteenth	101
Seventeenth	82
Eighteenth	167

Nineteenth 30, 166, 168
Twenty-first 132, 149, 152, 168
Twenty-second 168
Twenty-fourth 126, 145, 168
Twenty-fifth 134, 168
Twenty-sixth 135, 136, 168
Twenty-seventh 2
Twenty-eighth 167
Twenty-ninth 11, 87
Thirtieth 70
Thirty-second 168
Thirty-third 20, 85, 86
Thirty-fifth 168
Free State Constitution 1922 . . . . 2, 11, 35
Art.2 35

Irish Statutes

Adoption (Amendment) Act 2017 153
Adoption Act 1952 163
Adoption Act 2010 150
 s.54 153
Aliens Act 1935 . . . . 61, 64

Bail Act 1997 101
 Sch 101
Broadcasting Act 1960
 s.31 140

Child Care Act 1991 147
Civil Legal Aid Act 1995 128
Civil Liability Act 1961
 s.12(1) 156
 s.60 65
Criminal Evidence Act 1992 105
Criminal Justice Act 1951 96
 s.23 93
Criminal Justice Act 1984
 s.4 96
 s.18 104
 s.19 104
Criminal Justice Act 1990 132
Criminal Justice Act 2007 104
 s.30 105

Criminal Justice (Drug Trafficking) Act 1996
    s.2 96
Criminal Justice (Public Order) Act 1994
    s.6 140
Criminal Law (Sexual Offences) Act 1993 40
Criminal Law (Sexual Offences) Act 2006
    s.5 113
Criminal Procedure Act 2010 .... 6, 96

Defamation Act 2009 .... 118, 139
    s.36 141
Defence Acts 1954–1998 108

Electoral Act 1992 73
Electoral (Amendment) Act 2006 71
Emergency Powers Act 1976 24
European Communities Act 1972 .... 43, 44, 57
    s.2 43
    s.3 .... 44, 63
        (2) 63
European Communities Act 2007 63
European Convention on Human Rights Act 2003 .... 15, 40, 41
    s.2 41
    s.3 41
    s.4 41
    s.5 41
Executive Authority (External Relations) Act 1936 2

Farm Tax Act 1985 63
Fines Act 2010 109

Gender Recognition Act 2015 41

Health Act 1970 62
Houses of the Oireachtas (Inquiries, Privileges and Procedures) Act 2013 70
Human Rights and Equality Act 2014
    s.41 22

Immigration Act 1999
    s.2 64
Industrial Relations Act 1946
    Pt III 61
Industrial Training Act 1967 59

Juries Act 1927 .... 110, 112

Marriage Act 2015 .... 126, 145
Mental Treatment Act 1945 126
   s.260 126
Misuse of Drugs Act 1977 60

Offences Against the Person Act 1861
   s.62 .... 112, 113
Offences Against the State Act 1939 40
   s.29(1) 98
   s.30 96
   Part V 110

Prosecution of Offences Act 1974 84
Protection of Life During Pregnancy Act 2013 134
Protection of Young Persons in Employment Act 1996 123

Referendum Act 1994 167
Regulation of Information Act 1995 135
Republic of Ireland Act 1948 .... 3, 32
   s.2 31
   s.3 36

Sexual Offences (Jurisdiction) Act 1996 42
Sinn Féin Funds Act 1947 87
Statute Law Revision Acts 1861–2015 20
Status of Children Act 1987 .... 10, 115, 145, 149, 152
Statute of Limitations 1957 21
Statutes of Limitations 1957–2000 127
Succession Act 1965 .... 40, 145

Tribunals of Inquiry (Evidence) Acts 1921 to 2004 91

Vagrancy Act 1847 138

Irish Bills

Electoral (Amendment) Bill 1983 18
Employment Equality Bill 1996 .... 14, 18
Equal Status Bill 1997 18

Health (Amendment) (No. 2) Bill 2004 .... 18, 19
Housing (Private Rented Dwellings) Amendment Bill 1982 18

Matrimonial Home Bill 1993 18

School Attendance Bill 1942 18

UK Legislation

Bill of Rights 1689. 65

European Union Legislation

Single European Act 1986 . . . . 44, 81

Treaty of Amsterdam 1997 44
Treaty of Lisbon 2007. 44
Treaty of Maastricht 1992. 44
Treaty of Nice 2001 44

Other

Anglo-Irish Treaty of 1921 2

European Convention on Human Rights 40
    Art.6 104
    Art.8 . . . . 40, 41

Introduction

The Constitution of Ireland 1937 (Bunreacht na hÉireann) came into force on 29 December 1937, replacing the preceding Constitution of the Irish Free State 1922. It was approved by the People of Ireland in a public vote (plebiscite) on 1 July 1937. It is a vitally important legal document with which the institutions of the Irish State are required to comply in the conduct of their functions. It prevails over all other forms of law, other than EU law, and may be invoked to invalidate conflicting laws.

THE PURPOSE OF A CONSTITUTION

A constitution sets out the core rules for the running of a state. It typically consists of a series of general principles and rules requiring the state to conduct its affairs in a particular manner. Ordinarily, it seeks to lay down a framework for the governance of a territory by establishing a set of institutions with responsibility for assigned tasks. Typically, constitutions also guarantee to protect certain rights and liberties. Constitutions, however, tend in the main to be relatively brief and general, leaving the fine detail of legal regulation to be addressed in legislation passed by a parliament.

Articles 12–37 of the 1937 Constitution establish a variety of offices and institutions amongst which the Constitution divides the powers of the State. The Constitution thus creates a national parliament (the Oireachtas). The Constitution provides for the appointment of the Government (Executive), which is led by An Taoiseach, the Prime Minister. It also provides for the election of a head of state, the President, and a system of courts, presided over by judges.

The Constitution gives each of these functionaries and institutions exclusive tasks. Only the functionary or institution to which the Constitution assigns a particular task may perform that function. Furthermore, these institutions must perform their assigned tasks in compliance with the Constitution. For instance, Art.15.4 of the Constitution deems a law passed by the Oireachtas to be invalid to the extent that it is repugnant to the Constitution.

The Irish Constitution also serves to regulate the relationship between the State and those resident therein, in particular by guaranteeing certain human rights to those residents. Thus, in Art.38 and Arts 40–44, the Constitution outlines a series of fundamental rights and freedoms enjoyed by citizens and other residents of the State. This effectively limits the power of the State by restricting the State from acting in contravention of these rights and freedoms.

HISTORICAL CONTEXT—THE IRISH FREE STATE

From 1801 to 1922, Ireland was part of the United Kingdom of Great Britain and Ireland, with Ireland and Great Britain ruled by a common Parliament in Westminster, London. Following the Easter Rising of 1916 and the War of Independence (1919–21), the British Government and the breakaway Provisional Government of Ireland signed the Anglo-Irish Treaty of 1921. This allowed for the creation of the Irish Free State, a self-ruling dominion governed by the Treaty and the Constitution of the Irish Free State of 1922. The new State had its own Parliament, Government, and judicial system. Nonetheless, the British monarch (the King) retained a formal role, particularly as Head of State and formal holder of executive power in Ireland. The Treaty gave Northern Ireland the right to opt out of the new Free State. It did so, meaning that the Free State comprised 26 of the 32 historic counties of Ireland.

THE CONSTITUTION OF IRELAND 1937

The main architect of the new Constitution of Ireland 1937 (Bunreacht na hÉireann) was Éamon de Valera, a leading figure in the 1916 Rising and the Irish War of Independence. In 1932, De Valera was elected President of the Executive Council (Prime Minister) of the Irish Free State. De Valera wanted to tear up the Constitution of 1922 and the Anglo-Irish Treaty of 1921 on which it was based. He objected, in particular, to the role that the King had under that Treaty and to the partition of Ireland effected thereby. He wanted a United Ireland, North and South, fully independent from the United Kingdom, at least in its internal affairs. Thus the 1937 Constitution, as initially drawn up in 1937, contained a claim over the territory of Northern Ireland (Arts 2 and 3—see Ch.4 below), though this claim has since been removed.

The main aim of the Constitution was to assert Ireland's full sovereignty and control over its own destiny. (See, for instance, Arts 1 and 6). The Constitution, in particular, asserted Ireland's right to govern itself, and allowed for the election of a President of Ireland. The Constitution (Amendment No. 27) Act 1936 and the Executive Authority (External Relations) Act 1936 had already confined the King to a purely ceremonial role in respect of Irish foreign relations, removing him from any role in the internal governance of Ireland. The King retained this limited, purely formal foreign affairs role in respect of Ireland until 1949. That year, Ireland formally declared itself a Republic.

The Republic of Ireland Act 1948 transferred the ceremonial responsibility for foreign relations to the President, thus ending the last remaining vestiges of the King's role in the State.

THE ETHOS OF THE CONSTITUTION

Indicative of the dangerous times in which it was drafted, the Constitution reflects a concern to preserve and nurture democratic values and the protection of human rights. The role of the President, for instance, is significantly limited (the concern being to prevent facilitating dictatorship), while various human rights are expressly and implicitly guaranteed. The Constitution emphasises the sovereignty of the People. From 1941 onwards, the right of constitutional amendment was reserved to the People alone, although the sole power to initiate a proposal to amend the Constitution lies with the Dáil. The Constitution carefully balances the powers of the various institutions of State, ensuring a delicate system of checks and balances. In particular, it gives judges powers to ensure that the organs of State comply with the Constitution, and to declare conflicting legislation unconstitutional.

While the Constitution of 1937 is liberal-democratic in its basic leanings, it also bears the hallmark of Roman Catholic social teaching, particularly in Arts 41–44. The Christian ethos is notable, in particular, in the Preamble (the Constitution's introduction) which invokes the "Name of the Most Holy Trinity" and acknowledges "all our obligations to our Divine Lord, Jesus Christ". The document includes frequent references to God, including in the oath of office taken by the President and by judges. As originally conceived, the Constitution included a clause acknowledging the "special position" of the Roman Catholic Church and a ban on divorce, both of which provisions have since been removed. The words "Dochum Glóire Dé agus Onóra na hÉireann" ("For the Glory of God and the Honour of Ireland") appear after Art.50.

AN EVOLVING CONSTITUTION

The Constitution, however, is not frozen in time. Despite coming into force in 1937, it has tracked at least some of the social and political changes that have occurred in Ireland in the intervening period. It has been amended on 30 separate occasions—twice by the Legislature (1939 and 1941 respectively) and 28 times by referendums approved by the People. (See Ch.23 below). The contentious legal claim over Northern Ireland, in Arts 2 and 3, for instance, has been dropped (by referendum) in the context of the Good Friday Agreement. (See Ch.4 below). The special position of the Roman Catholic

Church and the ban on divorce have met a similar fate at the hands of the People in referendum, while a constitutional amendment to extend marriage to same-sex couples was approved in 2015.

The courts have also acknowledged that, even without a referendum, the interpretation (meaning) of the Constitution is capable of changing with the times. It is a dynamic document, which must be interpreted (read) by the courts in the light of prevailing ideas of what is consistent with the common good. For instance, in *McGee v Attorney General* [1974] I.R. 284, the Supreme Court declared laws banning the importation of artificial contraception to be unconstitutional. This legislation had been passed in 1935, a mere two years before the Constitution was enacted. Walsh J., in particular, noted that the Constitution had to be read in an "updating" manner, in line with current views of prudence, justice and charity (and not those prevalent in 1937).

In recent decades there has been considerable discussion of reform to the Constitution. In particular, the *Report of the Constitution Review Group* (1996), the Constitutional Convention (2012–2014) and the Citizens' Assembly (2016–2018) have set out various proposals for the amendment of the Constitution. The Government plans a suite of referendums over the course of 2018–2020 to amend various parts of the Constitution.

Constitutional Interpretation

The interpretation or "construction" of the Constitution is a process best described as a search for the true meaning of the Constitution. The role of interpreting the Constitution falls exclusively to the judges; the determination of the correct meaning of the text is a matter for the courts. There is, however, no single definitive method of interpreting the Constitution, the courts having adopted several different approaches to the issue.

Language

The Constitution is written in both Irish and English. Both texts are official texts of the Constitution and a court may proceed by reference to either. In cases of conflict between the two texts, however, the Irish text prevails, in that where the Irish and English texts differ in meaning, it is the meaning in the Irish text that is to be preferred (Art.25.5.4°). Nonetheless, the courts tend to read the two texts harmoniously, and try to avoid conflicting interpretations. The courts have often used the Irish text to clarify the meaning of the English text.

Precedent and the Constitution

The courts have confirmed that the Constitution is a dynamic document, and its interpretation is capable of changing with the times in line with prevailing conceptions of "prudence, justice and charity" (see *McGee v Attorney General* [1974] I.R. 284 and *State (Healy) v Donoghue* [1976] I.R. 325). As such, while the Supreme Court generally follows precedent in constitutional cases, it may decline to follow its own prior decisions if there is good reason to depart from those rulings. In *State (Quinn) v Ryan* [1965] I.R. 70, for instance, the Supreme Court ruled definitively that it is entitled, in appropriate cases, to overrule its own prior decisions on constitutional matters.

Methods of Interpretation

The courts have adopted a variety of methods of interpretation, sometimes conflicting, to determine the meaning of constitutional provisions.

Literal interpretation

Adopting a "literal interpretation" of the Constitution presupposes that the courts will give the words of the Constitution their ordinary, plain or basic meaning. A literal interpretation thus requires that the straightforward meaning of the words will prevail. It ensures that the courts keep faith with the plain intention of the People in adopting the Constitution.

For instance, in *People (DPP) v O'Shea* [1982] I.R. 384, the Supreme Court had to consider whether the State could appeal where the High Court had acquitted a suspect on criminal charges. Although the common law rule against double jeopardy normally prevented the appeal of an acquittal to a higher court, a majority of the Supreme Court concluded that the literal meaning of Art.34.4.3° (as it stood at that time) prevailed over this rule. That Article, at that time, allowed all decisions of the High Court to be appealed to the Supreme Court, subject to legislation limiting this right (which, in this case, had not occurred). Although the double jeopardy rule is well established and well respected in common law, the Supreme Court nonetheless concluded that it could not argue with the plain meaning of Art.34. (Since this decision, the Criminal Procedure Act 2010 has altered the law on the appeal of acquittals; such appeals may only take place, however, in exceptional cases where new and compelling evidence emerges).

In *Ryan v Attorney General* [1965] I.R. 294, Kenny J. in the High Court employed a literal or grammatical approach to the interpretation of Art.40.3, concluding that the use of the phrase "in particular" in reference to certain specified rights necessarily implied that these specified rights were not the only ones protected by the Constitution.

It would be near impossible to deviate from a literal interpretation of some of the more precise requirements of the Constitution (for instance, that the Seanad must comprise 60 members). Nonetheless, the Constitution often speaks in general and sometimes rather vague terms. As a result, the courts often avoid a strictly literal constitutional interpretation in favour of other methods.

Broad/purposive interpretation

A broad or purposive approach to constitutional interpretation requires that the court read the Constitution in the light of its overall purpose or aims. Here it is the spirit rather than the strict letter of the law that counts. The precise words that are used are not nearly as important as the broad sentiment underlying the Article. As Keane C.J. observed in *Maguire v Ardagh* [2002] 2 I.R. 385: "The Constitution is a political charter, using the adjective in its broadest sense. One does not expect to find in it the level of detail which, in our legislative tradition, we associate with Acts, regulations and by-laws." Indeed, because the Constitution is a general (and sometimes vague) document it is often more appropriate to forego a very close parsing of the words in favour of a broader approach to its meaning.

In *Attorney General v Paperlink* [1984] I.L.R.M. 373 Costello J. rejected an argument that certain semantic differences in wording as between Art.40.3.1° and Art.40.3.2°, both of which relate to the various personal rights of citizens, meant that the level of protection afforded by each was different. Article 40.3.1°, for instance, requires the State to "respect", "defend" and "vindicate" such rights. Article 40.3.2° mandates the State to "protect" and "vindicate" certain specified rights. Costello J. nonetheless ruled that these various words offered similar levels of protection for the personal rights covered by each sub-section. He observed that the Constitution is a political as well as a legal document, and thus contains many relatively broad statements of a general, rhetorical nature. Thus, he concluded, the courts should not read the Constitution too literally.

In *O'Byrne v Minister for Finance* [1959] I.R. 1, the Supreme Court had to consider the requirement in Art.35.5 that a judge's remuneration "shall not be reduced" during his or her tenure in office. (Since the Twenty-ninth Amendment of the Constitution of 2011, Art.35.5 now allows judicial salary reductions in specific cases). The plaintiff, who was the widow of a deceased judge, claimed that the taxation of her husband's salary while he was alive breached this requirement. On a literal basis, one might argue that the imposition of tax "reduces" one's take-home pay, but the Supreme Court adopted a more purposive interpretation. It concluded that the purpose of Art.35.5 was to protect the independence of the judiciary, in particular, to prevent the State from attempting to influence a judge's behaviour by threatening to cut his or her salary. The imposition of tax equally applicable to all was not an attack on judicial independence. The Court therefore ruled that the application of general taxation to judges' salaries did not breach Art.35.5.

The decision in *Roche v Roche (M.R. v T.R.)* [2006] IEHC 359, [2009] IESC 82 illustrates the use of the purposive approach in the interpretation of constitutional amendments. The Eighth Amendment to the Constitution (passed in 1983) purported to protect the right to life of the unborn. In this case, McGovern J. in the High Court, and some of the Supreme Court judges looked, in part, to the context in which the Eighth Amendment was passed in determining whether the term "unborn" included an embryo created outside the womb and not yet implanted therein. In concluding that it did not, McGovern J. and several of the Supreme Court judges looked to the purpose to which the Amendment was primarily directed: the prevention of abortion. The term "unborn" was therefore read as being restricted to an embryo created outside the womb only after it is implanted in the womb and not before.

Harmonious interpretation

The harmonious method of interpretation underlines the point that different parts of the Constitution should not be read in isolation from each other. Instead, they should be read as a set of complementary principles that fall to be interpreted in the light of the whole constitutional document.

For instance, in *Tormey v Ireland* [1985] I.R. 289, the Supreme Court favoured a harmonious interpretation over a strictly literal interpretation of Art.34.3.1°, which gives the High Court full original jurisdiction to hear all cases. The plaintiff in this case challenged the constitutionality of legislation confining jurisdiction in relation to some serious offences to the Circuit Court. In the Supreme Court, Henchy J. noted that the Constitution "... must be read as a whole ... its several provisions must not be looked at in isolation, but treated as interlocking parts of the general constitutional scheme." He added:

> "Any single constitutional right or power is but a component in an ensemble of interconnected and interacting provisions which must be brought into play as part of a larger composition, and which must be given such an integrated interpretation as will fit it harmoniously into the general constitutional order and modulation. It may be said of a constitution, more than of any other legal instrument, that 'the letter killeth, but the spirit giveth life'".

Thus, where it was possible, reading the Constitution as a whole, to find two different meanings of a provision, the interpretation favouring "the smooth and harmonious operation of the Constitution" should be preferred. In this case, the Supreme Court noted that the Constitution in several places limits the role of the High Court (e.g. in Article 26 references) and allows other courts (such as the Special Criminal Court and military courts) special powers that effectively oust the High Court's jurisdiction in certain contexts. Article 34.3.4°, moreover, allows for the setting up of courts of local and limited jurisdiction, a statement that implied, the court ruled, that the Constitution did not require that all cases be heard at first instance in the High Court. Notably, the High Court retained oversight of lower court decisions through its power of judicial review and constitutional oversight.

Likewise, in *Attorney General v X* [1992] 1 I.R. 1 Finlay C.J. in the Supreme Court invoked the doctrine of harmonious interpretation in the context of a girl who sought an abortion. The Court thus had to consider "... the position of the mother within a family group, with persons on whom she is dependent, with, in other instances, persons who are dependent upon her and her interaction with other citizens and members of society in the areas in which her activities occur." Weighing these various matters, the Court concluded that the girl would be entitled to an abortion where there was a real and substantial risk to her life that could only be avoided by terminating the pregnancy.

The courts have frequently suggested that measures permitted by one section of the Constitution may correspondingly be justified generally for the purpose of other sections of the Constitution. For instance, in *Dreher v Irish Land Commission* [1984] I.L.R.M. 94 the Supreme Court noted that a measure found to be justified by Art.43 (protecting the general right to property), cannot simultaneously be deemed an "unjust attack" on individual property rights under Art.40.3. Similarly, in *Dillane v Ireland* [1980] I.L.R.M. 167 the Supreme Court considered a measure preventing an accused person (found not guilty at trial) recouping his costs from a Garda who took a prosecution against him, in circumstances where a private person taking such a prosecution would not have been so exempted. The Supreme Court reasoned that the special treatment of Gardaí in this instance was justified under Art.40.1 (which generally requires equal treatment before the law) as Gardaí hold a different social function to lay litigants (see below at p.111). Having so concluded, the Court declined to rule that the special treatment of Gardaí constituted an unjust attack on the plaintiff's property rights contrary to Art.40.3. As the difference of treatment was "... categorically permitted by Article 40.1, so it cannot be part of the injustice which Article 40.3.2 was designed to prevent".

HIERARCHICAL INTERPRETATION

The hierarchical method of interpretation presupposes that some constitutional values are more important than others. While there is no definitive list prioritising certain rights, some clearly rank higher than others. As Griffin J. observed in *People (DPP) v Shaw* [1982] I.R. 1, "[i]f possible, fundamental rights under a Constitution should be given a mutually harmonious application, but when that is not found possible, the hierarchy or priority of the conflicting rights must be examined, both as between themselves and in relation to the general welfare of the society." This may result, he added, in the "toning down or even the putting into temporary abeyance of a particular guaranteed right so that, in a fair and objective way, the more pertinent and important right in a given set of circumstances may be preferred and given application." In the same case Kenny J. remarked that "[t]here is a hierarchy of constitutional rights, and, when a conflict arises between them that which ranks higher must prevail." When such a conflict arises, he said, the court must resolve it by looking to "(a) the terms of the Constitution, (b) the ethical values which all Christians living in the State acknowledge and accept, and (c) the main tenets of our system of constitutional parliamentary democracy."

Thus where there exists a straightforward conflict between the terms of one right and those of another, or between the respective rights of two individuals, the court may decide that one right takes priority over the other. The best example is the right to life, which (while not absolute) has consistently prevailed over lesser rights in the constitutional scheme. Similarly, the courts have generally subordinated the requirement of non-discrimination on religious grounds in favour of supporting the free practice of religion as a superior right, both being guaranteed by Art.44.

In the *People (DPP) v Shaw* [1982] I.R. 1, the Gardaí arrested a person suspected of kidnapping a woman. They detained him beyond the time at which he they should either have brought him before the District Court or released him. The Supreme Court nonetheless found that this detention was constitutionally permitted on the grounds that the Gardaí had acted with a view to saving the life of the kidnapped woman. Although the woman in question was not found alive, the Court ruled that the Gardaí's concern to vindicate the right to life of the woman justified the breach of the defendant's right to liberty. Similarly in *Foley v Sunday Newspapers Ltd* [2005] 1 I.R. 89, Kelly J. noted that however important freedom of the press might be, it cannot equal or exceed the protection afforded to the right to life. Thus if there was sufficiently compelling evidence that media coverage of a trial would endanger the life of any person, the court would restrict such coverage. *Foley* illustrates, however, that it is not enough simply to assert the superior right—the risk to life must be established.

In *O'B. v S.* [1984] I.R. 316 the Supreme Court decided that discrimination against the children of unmarried parents was justified by the constitutional preference for marriage in Art.41. The defendant's father had died without making a will. However, as her parents had not been married to each other, she was not (at that time) entitled to a share in his estate. Had her parents been married to each other, by contrast, she would have been entitled to succeed to his property. The daughter claimed that this infringed Art.40.1, the equality guarantee. Nonetheless, Art.40.1, the judges said, had to be read in the light of the constitutional preference for marriage contained in Art.41. This, they concluded, justified the discrimination of which she complained. The distinction, therefore, was constitutionally permitted, though not mandated by the Constitution. (The Status of Children Act 1987 subsequently removed this discriminatory provision. It is at least arguable that such a distinction might today fall foul of Art.42A of the Constitution).

The hierarchies of the Constitution are not always easily explained. They arguably involve the courts in making value judgments about the relative importance of constitutional principles. In *O'B. v S.* the protection of marriage prevailed over the principle of equality, even where children were involved. Could the courts not have concluded that the marriage clause was subject to an overriding requirement of equal treatment, at least in relation to children?

Historical interpretation

The courts often look to the state of the law or public opinion at the time that the Constitution was enacted as a guide to its meaning. In particular, if a specific practice was commonplace before 1937, and the Constitution did not expressly prohibit it, it might be reasonable to assume that it was intended to continue that practice. On the other hand, where something expressly provided for in the Constitution of 1922 or preceding law is not expressly provided for in the current Constitution, an inference may be drawn that it was not intended to be allowed.

In *Conroy v Attorney General* [1965] I.R. 411, the Supreme Court had to consider whether an offence was or was not a "minor" offence: an offence that could be tried without a jury (see below at pp.108–110). In deciding that it was a "minor offence", the Court took into account the fact that at the time of enactment of the Constitution the relevant offence was treated as minor in nature. Similarly, in *Melling v Ó Mathghamhna* [1962] I.R. 1, the Supreme Court looked to the state of law in 1937 in determining the intended scope of the words "minor offence".

The courts have also referred to 19th- and 20th-century developments in education in the *Campaign to Separate Church and State v Ireland* [1998] 2 I.L.R.M. 181 in interpreting the "endowment" of religion prohibited by Art.44. Similarly, in *Maguire v Ardagh* [2002] 1 I.R. 385, the Supreme Court had regard to the historical context in which the 1922 and 1937 Constitutions were enacted in deciding that the Oireachtas did not have an inherent power to establish investigative committees.

In *Roche v Roche* [2006] IEHC 359 the High Court and some Supreme Court judges looked to the context in which the Eighth Amendment to the Constitution was passed in 1983 to determine the meaning of "unborn" as used in Art.40.3.3°. Looking to the historical context in which the referendum was proposed—the primary concern being to restrict the termination of pregnancies (abortion)—McGovern J. concluded that the term "unborn" meant only an embryo within the womb and not an embryo not yet implanted in the womb.

IS AN UPDATING CONSTRUCTION (INTERPRETATION) PERMITTED?

It is clear, however, that history does not provide a watertight defence. In several cases, the courts have rejected the proposition that because certain practices pre-dated the passage of the Constitution, that they were therefore constitutionally valid. The fact that a particular practice or approach is well established and has never previously been challenged does not mean that it is immune from being found unconstitutional. (See *de Búrca v Attorney General* [1976] I.R. 38, *McMahon v Attorney General* [1972] I.R. 69, and *O'Donovan v Attorney General* [1961] I.R. 114.)

There is clearly some logic, in determining the meaning of the Constitution, in examining the intention of the drafters and the historical context in which the Constitution was passed. Nevertheless, this tendency must be used cautiously. JM Kelly has suggested that a distinction should be made between technical matters, where a historical approach is appropriate, and matters of values, where the Constitution should be interpreted in a dynamic fashion, by reference to contemporary standards and views. The danger otherwise arises that the Constitution will become frozen in time, framed by reference to the values of an era very different from our own. On several occasions the courts have noted that the Constitution is a "dynamic" document, capable of changing with the times (see per O'Higgins C.J. in *State (Healy) v Donoghue* [1976] I.R. 325). In *McGee v Attorney General* [1974] I.R. 284, for instance, a majority of the Supreme Court ruled that a ban on the importation of contraception infringed the constitutional right to marital privacy. This was despite the fact that this ban was introduced only two years before the Constitution was enacted and with apparently little substantive opposition. In the Supreme Court, Walsh J., in particular, noted that the Constitution should be interpreted by reference to the concepts of prudence, justice and charity, viewed in the light of contemporary mores and values.

THE NATURAL RIGHTS APPROACH

The Constitution has sometimes been read, particularly where a court seeks to identify certain rights, by reference to what is called "natural law". Natural law is said to be a type of universal law that exists independently of laws made by humans and human institutions. Natural law is considered by some, moreover, to be God's plan for the universe revealed to us through the use of human reason. It is said that we as humans can determine certain universal truths or "laws" through the use of reason, in particular by observing human nature and learning from the natural order of things.

Some, like the great philosopher and jurist Jeremy Bentham, considered such theories to be "nonsense upon stilts". It is not easy to disagree, moreover, with those who suggest that natural law reasoning can potentially be used to support whatever conclusion a judge considers appropriate in a given case. That said, natural law reasoning in the past proved quite popular amongst Irish judges. For instance, in *McGee v Attorney General* [1974] I.R. 284, Walsh J. observed that the Constitution in Arts 41, 42 and 43 alike expressly refers to certain rights and duties as being "natural" and, moreover, as existing independently of any positive law. These rights are, furthermore, said to be "antecedent [prior to] and superior" to human laws. The Constitution nonetheless protects such rights as universal human rights, notwithstanding the fact that at least some of these rights are not even mentioned in the Constitution.

In more recent years, however, judges have become more reticent about using natural law reasoning and it has, accordingly, fallen out of favour. In particular, the natural rights approach cannot be used to frustrate the will of the people clearly expressed in a referendum. In the Article 26 reference of the *Regulation of Information Bill 1995* [1995] 1 I.R. 1 the Supreme Court rejected the contention that an Amendment to the Constitution that infringed the natural law would be unenforceable. The sovereignty (supreme power) of the People in referendum permits them, the Court reasoned, to amend the Constitution in any way they wish (though the initiative for a referendum lies solely with the Dáil). Even if such an amendment infringed natural law it would nonetheless be constitutionally sound. Since that decision, the courts have become more reluctant to rely on natural law as a source of rights. That said, Art.42A, inserted into the Constitution in 2015, references the "natural and imprescriptible rights" of children, illustrating that the concept has not entirely fallen from grace.

THE PRESUMPTION OF CONSTITUTIONALITY

The law often allows judges to "presume" certain things, until the contrary is proved. For instance, an accused person in a criminal trial is presumed innocent until his or her guilt is proved beyond a reasonable doubt. This is also called the "onus" or "burden" of proof. Similarly, where the Oireachtas creates a law it is generally presumed, until the contrary is proved, that the legislation is constitutional. The burden of proving that the legislation is unconstitutional is placed upon the person who makes this allegation.

Article 15.4 states that the Oireachtas shall not enact laws that are contrary to the Constitution. Because of the respect that each institution of State has for the others, the courts must not assume too readily that the Oireachtas has acted in contravention of the Constitution. In fact, flowing from the separation of powers, there is a strong tendency among some judges to defer to the Oireachtas in relation to legislation, particularly where the subject matter is controversial. That said, the presumption of constitutionality does not prevent a law from being found unconstitutional. It simply makes it harder to prove such an allegation.

SOME ASPECTS OF THE PRESUMPTION

- In relation to tax and social welfare legislation, it appears from case law that the presumption of constitutionality applies with particular rigour. The courts tend to be reluctant to negate legislative decisions relating to the imposition of taxes and the distribution of social welfare payments. In *Madigan v Attorney General* [1986] I.L.R.M. 136, O'Hanlon J. noted that the presumption of constitutionality is particularly strong in relation to taxation statutes. Nonetheless, in appropriate cases the courts have declared such laws to be unconstitutional (see, for instance *Murphy v Attorney General* [1982] I.R. 241 and *Harvey v Minister for Social Welfare* [1990] 2 I.R. 232).

- On the other hand, in some cases, the breach of the Constitution will be so obvious that the presumption may not be particularly strong. In *M. v An Bord Uchtála* [1977] I.R. 287, for instance, the High Court declared that a provision that prevented couples of mixed religion from adopting children was unconstitutional. This measure being so very obviously contrary to freedom of religion, Pringle J. felt that the presumption was especially weak in this case.
- Analogous principles apply where a piece of legislation contains a provision that is substantially similar to one previously deemed unconstitutional by the courts. In *Re Article 26 and the Equal Status Bill 1997* [1997] 2 I.R. 387, the Supreme Court declined to apply the presumption of constitutionality to a measure that was identical in substance to a provision of the Employment Equality Bill 1996 which had earlier been found to be unconstitutional. (*Re Article 26 and the Employment Equality Bill 1996* [1997] 2 I.R. 321.)
- The presumption does not apply to Acts passed or laws that came into being before 1937. Logically, one cannot presume that a piece of legislation passed before the 1937 Constitution was created with the Constitution's terms in mind. See, for example, *McGee v Attorney General* [1974] I.R. 284, where the Supreme Court ruled that the presumption of constitutionality did not apply to an Act of Parliament passed in 1935. By the same token, Acts passed by the British Parliament before 1922 cannot be presumed to have been enacted in compliance with the 1937 Constitution.
- The presumption, however, does apply to Bills passed by the Oireachtas and referred to the Supreme Court under Art.26, even though such Bills are not yet "law". Although it is not yet an enforceable "law", one must assume that the Houses of the Oireachtas would not intentionally have passed unconstitutional legislation.
- As a corollary to the presumption, where a body or person is given a power or discretion under law, it must be assumed that that body or person is required to exercise that power or discretion in compliance with the Constitution and the requirements of constitutional justice (see *East Donegal Co-operative v Attorney General* [1970] I.R. 317).

THE DOUBLE CONSTRUCTION RULE

Take the situation where there are two or more possible interpretations (meanings) of legislation open to a court, one of which would render the legislation constitutional and the others unconstitutional. In such a case, the double construction rule dictates that the interpretation that renders the legislation constitutional is to be preferred. This practice is sometimes called "reading down", the aim being to interpret the legislation in conformity with the

Constitution. In *McDonald v Bord na gCon* [1965] I.R. 217, Walsh J. referred to the presumption of constitutionality and remarked:

> "One practical effect of this presumption is that if in respect of any provision or provisions of the Act two or more constructions are reasonably open, one of which is constitutional and the other or others are unconstitutional, it must be presumed that the Oireachtas intended only the constitutional construction and a Court ... should uphold the constitutional construction. It is only when there is no construction reasonably open which is not repugnant to the Constitution that the provision should be held to be repugnant."

(See for instance, in *Re Haughey* [1971] I.R. 217 and *Doherty v Government of Ireland* [2011] 2 I.R. 222). In interpreting the Act, however, one cannot "do violence to the plain meaning of the words" (per Ó Dálaigh C.J. in *Re Haughey*) with a view to finding the legislation constitutional. The implication here is that the double construction rule is only helpful where a constitutionally valid interpretation is in fact open to the court.

REACHING THE CONSTITUTIONAL ISSUE LAST

The courts will generally avoid making a finding based on the Constitution if it is possible to resolve the dispute without relying on the Constitution. The principle here is that the court should "reach the constitutional issue last". If it is possible to decide the case on non-constitutional grounds, this approach is to be preferred (see *Gilligan v Special Criminal Court* [2006] 2 I.R. 389, per Denham J. at p.407). An exception to this rule arises, however, where a challenge under the European Convention on Human Rights Act 2003 is made claiming that Irish law is incompatible with the Convention; in such a case, the constitutional challenge is heard before the Convention is considered. (*Carmody v Minister for Justice* [2010] 1 I.R. 635).

3 Challenging the Constitutionality of State Conduct

GENERAL REMARKS

The Constitution is not merely a set of guidelines. It mandates the institutions of State to carry out their functions in compliance with the Constitution. Where they act in contravention of the Constitution, the institutions of State can be held to account in the courts, on the initiative of those adversely affected by the State's actions. Where the High Court, Court of Appeal, or Supreme Court find that legislation, or any part of such legislation, infringes a provision of the Constitution, that court is empowered to declare such unconstitutional provisions to be null and void. This means that the provisions are deemed to be unlawful and of no legal effect.

There are several different procedures for declaring legislation to be unconstitutional, each concerning different types of law. Different provisions apply depending on whether the challenged measure is yet an enforceable law and, if it is, whether it was enacted or became law before or after 1937. These procedures are set out in Arts 26, 34 and 50 respectively.

ARTICLE 26

A special provision of the Constitution, Art.26, allows the Supreme Court to assess the constitutionality of a Bill before the President signs the Bill into law. In practice, however, Art.26 is very rarely used. It has only been invoked 15 times in total and only once since 2000. This may reflect a concern about the implications of a finding under Art.26.

- **Who can use Art.26?** Only the President of Ireland may invoke Art.26. When the Dáil and Seanad pass a Bill, it must, to become a law, be signed by the President. Usually, this is simply a formality. The President normally has no right to reject the Bill, or to demand its amendment. Under Art.26, however, the President may refer the Bill to the Supreme Court to test whether it is constitutional or not. No other person or body may make an Article 26 reference.

- **What does Art.26 do?** Article 26 allows the President to refer a Bill (or a part of such a Bill) to the Supreme Court. The purpose of such a reference is to test whether the Bill, or any specified part of it, is unconstitutional.
- **What is a "Bill" for these purposes?** For the purposes of Art.26, a Bill is a piece of legislation passed (or deemed to have been passed) by both Houses of the Oireachtas but not yet signed by the President. The President, however, cannot refer a Bill proposing a change to the Constitution or a "Money Bill" (a Bill addressing issues such as the raising of taxes or the allocation of state funds).
- **Can the President refer only a part of a Bill?** While most Article 26 cases concern entire Bills, the President is free to refer only a section or part of a Bill, as he or she sees fit. *Re Article 26 and Section 4 of the School Attendance Bill 1942* [1943] I.R. 334 and *Re Article 26 and Part V of the Planning and Development Act 1999* [2001] 1 I.L.R.M. 81, are noteworthy, involving, as they did, the referral of only a portion (and not the whole) of a Bill. Yet even if the President refers only a section or part of a Bill and the Court finds that section or part alone to be unconstitutional, no part of that Bill may become law. The President in such circumstances cannot sign any part of the Bill into law.
- **Does the President act alone in making the reference?** Before referring a Bill, the President must first consult with the Council of State, a body that advises the President on the performance of his or her functions. While the President is obliged to seek the Council's prior advice, he or she, however, may choose to ignore its advice.
- **Who hears such a case?** The President refers the Bill directly to the Supreme Court, by-passing all lower courts. At least five judges of the Supreme Court must hear such a reference.
- **Do they hear argument first?** Yes. The Attorney General usually selects two barristers to argue for the validity of the Bill. The Court will generally appoint a similar number of barristers to argue against its validity. It is possible for the Court to appoint different teams of barristers to argue against the Bill from conflicting perspectives as in *Re Article 26 and the Regulation of Information Bill 1995* [1995] 1 I.R. 1. This Bill concerned the issue of information facilitating a termination of pregnancy abroad. While the Supreme Court ultimately found that the Bill was constitutional, the Court appointed two groups of counsel to argue against the Bill, one set representing the interests of the unborn, the other set representing the perspective of a mother contemplating an abortion.
- **Does the presumption of constitutionality apply to such Bills?** Yes. Even though the Bill is not yet "law", the Court presumes that Parliament did not act contrary to the Constitution in enacting its provisions. This presumption can be rebutted (overturned) by evidence showing that the

Bill (or part thereof) is unconstitutional. The only exception arises where the Court has already found a measure similar to the one in the Bill to be unconstitutional in a previous case. Thus, in *Re Article 26 and the Equal Status Bill 1997* [1997] 2 I.R. 387, the Supreme Court refused to apply the presumption in circumstances where the Bill replicated provisions that the court had previously found to be unconstitutional in *Re Article 26 and the Employment Equality Bill 1996* [1997] 2 I.R. 321.

THE OUTCOME OF AN ARTICLE 26 REFERENCE

- Article 26.2.2° requires the Supreme Court to issue only one judgment, representing the opinion of the whole court. Even if individual judges disagree with the decision, they cannot openly express such dissent.
- If the Court finds that *no* part of the Bill is unconstitutional, the President must sign the Bill into law. Once signed by the President, the Bill becomes an Act of Parliament. The Act (or parts of the Act) that were the subject of the Article 26 reference subsequently enjoy immunity from further constitutional challenge. No person may subsequently challenge an Act or part of an Act that was declared to be constitutional in an Article 26 reference. If the Court was only considering a part of a Bill, only that part enjoys constitutional immunity after the Bill becomes an Act (see Art.34.3.3°).
- If the Court finds *any* part of the Bill to be unconstitutional, however, the President must not sign the Bill into law. No part of the Bill can become law, even those parts that are found to be constitutional. For example, in *Re Article 26 and the Health (Amendment) (No. 2) Bill 2004* [2005] IESC 7, the President could not sign the Bill into law even though some of its provisions (those that were not retrospective) had expressly been found to be constitutionally valid, because other provisions were unconstitutional.
- Notably, it is not possible to sever the offending portions and pass the rest of the Bill into law. The entirety of the Bill either stands or falls. It is also important to note that while Parliament may sometimes introduce a new Bill with similar provisions (absent those found to be unconstitutional), the Supreme Court never "refers back" legislation to Parliament.

In all, various Presidents have referred 15 separate Bills to the Supreme Court, seven of which the Court has deemed unconstitutional in whole or in part:

- The School Attendance Bill 1942
- The Housing (Private Rented Dwellings) Amendment Bill 1982
- The Electoral (Amendment) Bill 1983
- The Matrimonial Home Bill 1993
- The Employment Equality Bill 1996
- The Equal Status Bill 1997
- The Health (Amendment) (No. 2) Bill 2004

Advantages of the Article 26 procedure

- Article 26 allows the President to test a Bill in court before it causes any harm to a member of the public. Thus, the Court may identify problems with the Bill before it has breached any individual's constitutional rights. This can be useful where the consequences of a constitutional breach would be serious or expensive.
- In some cases, it may not be possible, either for financial or practical reasons, for a person whom legislation affects to take a case concerning its provisions. A good example would be a baby in the womb, who would clearly not be in a position to challenge laws that potentially infringe its rights (see, for instance, the reference of the *Regulation of Information Bill 1995* [1995] 1 I.R. 1). An Article 26 reference would also be useful where the Bill purports to infringe the rights of vulnerable persons who might not be in a position to afford to sue the State, such as in the reference of the Health (Amendment) (No. 2) Bill 2004.
- From the State's perspective, it knows that if a Bill passes the Article 26 test, no one can challenge it again in court once it becomes an Act.

Disadvantages of the Article 26 procedure

- Only the President may refer a Bill under Art.26. Other concerned citizens may not do so. Moreover, no one can force the President to take such a case, even if it is obvious that a Bill is unconstitutional.
- As there are no "real people" in court claiming that their rights have been breached, the lawyers have to make moot arguments and imagine hypothetical scenarios in which the Bill may infringe the rights of an individual. It is not beyond the realms of possibility that the lawyers involved may not envision the full implications of a Bill and miss out on significant constitutional flaws.
- Where the Court finds a Bill to be constitutional, no person may challenge its constitutionality again. This remains the case even if it subsequently becomes clear that the law in fact infringes constitutional rights. It may be prudent to avoid giving a law perpetual constitutional immunity, particularly if the law is complex.
- The time for judicial consideration of Bills is comparatively short. The court must report to the President within 60 days of the referral. Hence, if the matter under scrutiny proves particularly complex, the court may not have sufficient time to consider it.
- Even if the Court finds only one, short section of a lengthy Bill to be unconstitutional, no part of the Bill may become law. The remainder of what might otherwise be a good Bill falls by the wayside just because one article is defective.

Article 34

Where the State passes legislation or takes an action after the coming into force of the Constitution, Art.34.3.2° applies. This allows the High Court (and on appeal the Court of Appeal and Supreme Court) to assess the constitutional validity of any provision of law. Where the court is considering a law passed by the Oireachtas after 1937, the presumption of constitutionality applies (see above at pp.13–14). Where such a law is found to be unconstitutional, it is null and void and of no legal effect. It is important to note that where a court declares a section or part of an Act unconstitutional, only that section or part is unlawful, the remainder of the Act retaining its legal force (see, however, the discussion of severance below, at p.28).

Formerly, where the Supreme Court was considering the constitutionality of a law passed by the Oireachtas since 1937, it was required to hand down only one single judgment, i.e. that of the court. It was not possible for any other judgment, dissenting or otherwise, to be expressed. The Thirty-third Amendment to the Constitution, however, has deleted this one-judgment rule, allowing a diversity of views on the point to be expressed at Supreme Court level.

Article 50

Special considerations apply to laws already in force before the Constitution was enacted. Such laws are "carried over" into the laws of the new State subject to two conditions:

- The law must have been in force on 29 December 1937, the date on which the Constitution came into force; and
- The law must be consistent with the Constitution.

Where a legislative provision has been repealed prior to the enactment of the Constitution, it cannot be carried over. It is possible, also, to repeal such legislation after the passage of the Constitution. Indeed, the Statute Law Revision Acts 1861–2015 have abolished many legislative Acts passed in respect of Ireland before 1922, though some pre-1922 Acts have been expressly retained in force.

Where a court declares that a specific pre-1937 provision is inconsistent with the Constitution, it is deemed not to have been carried over into the law of the new State though only to the extent to which it is repugnant to the Constitution. The presumption of constitutionality does not apply to measures passed before 29 December 1937.

Locus standi

"Locus standi" is a Latin phrase meaning a person's legal "standing" or right to sue. A person ordinarily has locus standi to challenge the constitutionality of State conduct only if he or she has been or stands to be directly and adversely affected by such conduct. The litigant must ordinarily demonstrate that the measure directly and personally affects or will affect their interest and that his or her rights are directly infringed or threatened.

For instance, one cannot generally complain that a statute is unconstitutional simply because it affects the rights of people other than the person making the complaint, what is called a "ius tertii" complaint. In *Cahill v Sutton* [1980] I.R. 269, the plaintiff claimed she had been injured as a result of a doctor's alleged negligence. She lost the right to sue in respect of her injuries, because she had not commenced proceedings within the time period laid down by the Statute of Limitations 1957. She alleged that this Act infringed the constitutional right of access to the courts of those who did not discover their injuries until after the limitation period had expired. Yet, as the plaintiff herself had known of her injuries long before the period of limitation ran out, she did not have locus standi to make this argument. The Supreme Court noted that in order to challenge a legal rule one must show that it adversely affected or endangered the personal interests of the party challenging the rule. The Supreme Court ruled that she could not invoke in her favour the fact that a law breached the rights of a third party.

In *King v Attorney General* [1981] I.R. 83, the plaintiff was allowed only to challenge parts of legislation under which he had been convicted, and not those parts that were not relevant to his specific situation. Likewise, in *Hall v Minister for Finance* [2013] IESC 10, the plaintiff, a citizen and taxpayer, had sought to challenge the process by which the Minister for Finance had issued promissory notes to various banks during the financial crisis. Mr Hall alleged that the financial support to the banks had not been approved by Dáil Éireann, as required by Art.17. The High Court concluded that he lacked standing to take the case; it would have been more appropriate for a member of the Dáil to take the case. Mr Hall had suffered no particular loss that was unique to him or that distinguished him from other members of the public. The Court acknowledged that the strict locus standi rules might be overlooked where there was a "transcendent need" to allow the challenge, but this was not such a case. In particular, there were other potential litigants (members of Dáil Éireann) who were in a better position to take such a case.

In *Norris v Attorney General* [1984] I.R. 36, the plaintiff (an unmarried gay man) had alleged that a legislative ban on anal intercourse infringed the marital privacy rights of married persons. As the plaintiff was not married, a majority of the Supreme Court ruled that he was not entitled to make this argument on behalf of married persons. The Court, however, allowed him to submit arguments alleging that the legislation breached his own personal rights because it criminalised consensual homosexual acts. The fact that the State had never prosecuted, accused or threatened to prosecute the plaintiff under this legislation did not prevent him from having locus standi to challenge it on the basis of his own personal circumstances. As O'Higgins C.J. commented, "as long as the legislation stands and continues to proclaim as criminal the conduct which the plaintiff asserts he has a right to engage in, such right, if it exists, is threatened and the plaintiff has standing to seek the protection of the Court." A litigant does not necessarily have to wait to be injured if he or she is threatened with a breach of rights.

EXCEPTIONS TO THE NORMAL LOCUS STANDI RULE

In some cases, the law expressly allows a person take a court case based on third party rights. For instance, under Art.40.4.2°, any person may complain about the unlawful detention of another person in what are called "habeas corpus" proceedings. Likewise, the Irish Human Rights and Equality Commission may institute court proceedings to obtain a declaration (or other relief) concerning the human rights of any person or class of persons. This includes a declaration of unconstitutionality. (See s.41 of the Irish Human Rights and Equality Act 2014).

The locus standi rule has also been relaxed in some constitutional cases to allow constitutional challenges to proceed even where the parties cannot show that they are directly and personally affected by a breach of the Constitution. Where a measure potentially affects the public at large, rather than one specific person or group of people, the litigant may nonetheless be allowed to take a case even though she cannot differentiate herself from other citizens. This is more likely to happen where the court cannot identify any person better placed to take such a case. In particular, in *T.D. v. Minister for Education* [2001] 4 I.R. 259 at 282, Keane C.J. observed that the strict locus standi rule:

> "... [M]ust on occasions yield to the overriding necessity that laws passed by the Oireachtas or acts and omissions of the executive should not go unchallenged, simply because it is difficult, if not impossible, for individual citizens or groups to establish that their individual rights are affected ...".

Thus, for instance, actions have been allowed to proceed in cases where the litigant may not have had locus standi in the strict sense of the term.

- *The "bona fide" interest group.* A body of persons may plead a breach of the Constitution where that organisation has a genuine concern in seeing that the State upholds the Constitution. In *S.P.U.C. v Coogan* [1989]

I.R. 734, for instance, the Supreme Court allowed a group interested in protecting the lives of the unborn to plead that the defendants' actions had endangered those lives. This was despite the clear fact that none of the plaintiffs were themselves unborn or endangered in any way. The argument might be made that there was unlikely to be a better placed litigant willing to take the case. Likewise, in *Irish Penal Reform Trust v Governor of Mountjoy Prison* [2005] IEHC 305 the plaintiff was permitted to make arguments relating to the rights of psychiatrically ill prisoners. Gilligan J. reasoned that if the Irish Penal Reform Trust were denied locus standi, the interests of such prisoners might not be effectively represented.

- *The "actio popularis".* A person may also take a case where it affects the interests and rights of the public as a whole although no one person stands individually to be affected more than another person. For instance, in *Crotty v An Taoiseach* [1987] I.R. 713, the Supreme Court allowed a concerned citizen to plead that the terms of the Single European Act undermined the exclusive right of the State to determine its own foreign policy. This was despite the fact that Mr Crotty was no more likely to suffer under the Treaty than any other member of the population. Likewise in *McKenna v An Taoiseach (No. 2)* [1995] 2 I.R. 10 a broad approach was taken in allowing the plaintiff to challenge State funding in favour of a "Yes" vote in the second divorce referendum.

Restrictions may, however, be placed on locus standi with a view to protecting the courts from what is seen as an abuse of the judicial process or from frivolous or vexatious claims (claims without foundation or designed primarily to stir up trouble). (See *Riordan v Ireland (No. 4)* [2001] 3 I.R. 365, *Riordan v An Taoiseach (No. 5)* [2001] 4 I.R. 463, and *Riordan v An Taoiseach* [2006] IEHC 312.) The courts will also strain against hearing cases that are strictly moot, in that a decision on the point is merely hypothetical and not relevant to the dispute between the parties (or no longer relevant). Nonetheless, there are exceptions to this rule, as in *M v Minister for Justice and Equality* [2018] IESC 14 where the High Court and Supreme Court considered a case involving the rights of the unborn even after the child in question was born. As Humphreys J. remarked in the High Court, "[a] court can proceed to determine an issue that is strictly moot if the interests of justice so require".

IMMUNITY FROM CONSTITUTIONAL REVIEW

EMERGENCY POWERS—ARTICLE 28.3

Certain types of law are immune from constitutional challenge. Legislation passed under the provisions of Art.28.3 is immune, even if such legislation clearly infringes the Constitution. Notably, however, Art.15.5.2° precludes the State from using Art.28.3 to impose the death penalty, even in times of emergency.

Article 28.3 applies to specified legislation enacted in times of war or armed rebellion. Legislation "expressed to be for the purpose of securing the public safety and the preservation of the State in time of war or armed rebellion" cannot be found unconstitutional. Such times of war or armed rebellion may include situations in which the State is not directly a participant, for example World War II (where Ireland was technically neutral) and the former "Troubles" in Northern Ireland. Where there is an armed conflict in which the State is not a participant, a declaration must be passed by both Houses of the Oireachtas to the effect that "a national emergency exists affecting the vital interests of the State". Again, such legislation will only be immune from constitutional challenge where it is "expressed to be for the purpose of securing the public safety and the preservation of the State in time of war or armed rebellion". After the termination of such war, conflict or armed rebellion, a state of emergency will continue in force until each House of the Oireachtas passes a resolution to the effect that the situation of peril has ceased to exist. Two such states of emergency have been declared, once in 1939 on the outbreak of World War II (formally ending in 1976), and a second in 1976, relating to the Troubles in Northern Ireland (ending in 1995).

To qualify for the exemption under Art.28.3, the legislation in question must expressly invoke that Article. One such piece of legislation was the Emergency Powers Act 1976. This provision, before it became an Act, was the subject of an Article 26 reference (*Re the Emergency Powers Bill 1976* [1977] I.R. 129). In the course of its judgment, the Supreme Court made the following points:

- Acts passed under Art.28.3 cannot be challenged on the basis of the unconstitutionality of their substantive content;
- The courts may, however, check that any legislation passed under Art.28.3 complies with the procedures for the adoption of such legislation as laid out in that Article;
- Even though the Constitution cannot be invoked to invalidate such legislation, it is not to be assumed too readily that the legislation necessarily displaces constitutional rights. To the extent that it is possible to do so, the legislation must be read in light of the Constitution's requirements.

European Union law

Measures passed by the institutions of the European Union are exempted by Art.29.4.6° from constitutional scrutiny. This means that laws adopted by the EU can become part of Irish law without having to comply with the Constitution. Article 29.4.6°, moreover, exempts from constitutional scrutiny any measure adopted by the State that is "necessitated by the obligations of membership" of the Union. The meaning of this phrase and the implications of Art.29.4.6° generally are examined further below in Ch.6.

THE EFFECTS OF A FINDING OF UNCONSTITUTIONALITY

It is well established that where a court finds that a piece of legislation is unconstitutional, that provision is said to be null and void and of no legal effect. For instance, Art.15.4 declares that laws passed by the Oireachtas are invalid to the extent that they are repugnant to the Constitution. The laws are invalid, however, only to the extent that the measure infringes the Constitution. The infringing provisions may be severed (cut) from the legislation, provided that what remains still reflects the intention of Parliament and is not unconstitutional. Severance is not possible, however, if what is left behind would alter the original intention of Parliament.

In strict theory, such unconstitutional legislation is said to be invalid with "retrospective" effect, void "ab initio" and not just from the date of the court's declaration of unconstitutionality. An Act that is unconstitutional is technically considered invalid from the date of its enactment, or, if it was passed before 1937, the date of the enactment of the Constitution. For instance, if an Act was passed in 1968 and found to be unconstitutional by a court in 2000, the view is taken that the Act is deemed to have been invalid from its very inception in 1968.

Nonetheless, the full force and logic of this approach has been substantially challenged and qualified in the courts. In practice, the courts have always found ways to limit the consequences of a finding of unconstitutionality. There are now significant limits on the extent to which a person may claim retrospective relief where a law is found to be unconstitutional, the key concern being the need to maintain order, certainty, and finality in respect of judicial decisions and other matters. For instance, there would be chaos if a finding of unconstitutionality in respect of the process of elections or the system of selecting juries rendered all prior elections or jury decisions invalid; for that reason, the courts often decline to upset prior decisions and actions, even where there has been a finding of unconstitutionality.

LIMITS ON THE RIGHT TO RECOUP OVERPAID TAXES

In *Murphy v Attorney General* [1982] I.R. 241, the Supreme Court examined the retrospective effect of a finding of unconstitutionality. In that case, the Supreme Court declared that provisions of the tax code that potentially taxed married couples more than unmarried couples with similar living arrangements constituted an unjust attack on the institution of marriage contrary to Art.41.

The Court confirmed that such laws were unconstitutional with retrospective effect. The relevant sections were void from their creation and never had the force of law. It nonetheless ruled that the surplus taxes collected under these laws would only have to be refunded to those who had already commenced proceedings at the date of the judgment. Even in those cases, the parties would be entitled to reclaim the excess taxes paid only in respect of the financial years succeeding that in which they had commenced proceedings against the State.

The reasoning of the Court was as follows: the State was entitled to assume, where people had paid their taxes without protest, that the tax had been validly imposed and collected and that the money could be used by the State. The State having spent the money that was collected in good faith, it could not now be ordered to repay that money. Thus, it was only where the taxes had been paid pending legal proceedings that the State could be obliged to repay the surplus monies collected. In making this decision, the Court had particular regard to the then precarious financial position of the State. (See, however, *Muckley v Ireland* [1985] I.R. 782).

THE RIGHTS OF PRISONERS CONVICTED UNDER LAWS SUBSEQUENTLY DEEMED UNCONSTITUTIONAL

Difficult questions arise where a person is convicted of a crime and imprisoned under a law subsequently found to be unconstitutional. Although the law is deemed retrospectively to be invalid, this does not necessarily mean that previous convictions under that law will be quashed.

The *State (Byrne) v Frawley* [1978] I.R. 326 concerned an accused man who was tried before a jury that had been selected in an unconstitutional manner. Although the accused was aware of this illegality at the time of the trial, he chose not to complain about it until after he had been convicted. The Supreme Court ruled that as he did not object to the method of jury selection at the time of his trial, he could not subsequently object to the jury that he had accepted. He had effectively waived his right to complain. As Henchy J. remarked, "[b]ecause the prisoner freely and knowingly elected at his trial to accept the empanelled jury as competent to try him, I consider that he is now precluded by that election from claiming that the jury lacked constitutionality." Notably, he went on to note that "it does not necessarily follow that court orders lack binding force because they were made in proceedings based on an unconstitutional statute."

Similarly, in *McDonnell v Ireland* [1998] 1 I.R. 134, the Supreme Court refused to compensate a postman who lost his job as a result of a criminal law measure subsequently found to be unconstitutional. The Court concluded that the postman had delayed in taking action, and should thus be denied relief. O'Flaherty J., however, expressed the view that "laws must be observed until struck down as unconstitutional". Once an Act is passed, citizens and the State alike were obliged to follow the law. As such, taking into account "the requirements of an ordered society", O'Flaherty J. suggested that the State could not be faulted for following a law that had not yet been found unconstitutional. This was particularly so where the person seeking relief had not sought to challenge the measure before it was found to be invalid.

In *C.C. v Ireland* [2006] IESC 33, the Supreme Court declared unconstitutional part of a 1935 Act banning unlawful carnal knowledge of (sexual intercourse with) a girl under the age of 15. As the Act did not afford a defence of genuine mistake as to the alleged victim's age, the Supreme Court concluded that the law infringed the right to liberty under Art.40 of the Constitution. In *A. v Governor of Arbour Hill Prison* [2006] IESC 56, a man who had been convicted of unlawful carnal knowledge of a 12-year-old girl, claimed the benefit of the decision in *C.C.* As he had been convicted under a provision found to be unconstitutional, he was (he claimed) entitled to be released. In the High Court, Laffoy J. concluded that, because the 1935 provision was retrospectively deemed invalid, it had never been carried over into the law of the State in 1937. The offence, she claimed, had stopped being an offence in 1937. Therefore, she concluded, Mr A was entitled to be released.

On appeal, however, the Supreme Court overturned the High Court verdict and ordered that Mr A be returned to prison. In a ruling that greatly limits the impact of a finding of unconstitutionality, the Supreme Court rejected an absolute approach to retrospectivity, ruling that even where a law is deemed unconstitutional, a previous conviction based on that law may still stand. An approach that invalidated all actions taken on foot of a law found subsequently to be unconstitutional would in the words of Murray C.J. "... render the Constitution dysfunctional, and ignore that it contains a complete set of rules and principles designed to ensure an ordered society under the rule of law ...". In particular, the Court noted that the State was entitled and was required to observe all laws until such time as they are declared unconstitutional. Neither the State nor individuals are free to disobey a law; officers and institutions of State, moreover, are expected to enforce and uphold the law and can hardly be faulted for so doing.

Thus, if a person was convicted on the basis of an Act which, at the time of trial or on appeal, they did not seek to challenge, the conviction would stand. The Court thus distinguished between a declaration that a law is invalid and the impact of such a declaration on previously concluded cases. As Murray C.J. concluded, final court decisions made on the basis of an Act of the Oireachtas "should not be set aside by reason *solely* of a subsequent decision declaring the Act constitutionally invalid" (emphasis added). The general principle, therefore, is that "in a criminal prosecution where the State relies in good faith on a statute in force at the time and the accused does not seek to impugn the bringing or conduct of the prosecution, on any grounds that may in law be open to him or her, including the constitutionality of the statute, before the case reaches finality, on appeal or otherwise, then the final decision in the case must be deemed to be and to remain lawful notwithstanding any subsequent ruling that the statute, or a provision of it, is unconstitutional."

The only exception arose where "for wholly exceptional reasons related to some fundamental unfairness" the continued detention would amount to a denial of justice. In *A*, the Court agreed that no injustice would result from continued incarceration (see also *Wansboro v D.P.P.* [2017] IEHC 391). A person, however, may still rely on the unconstitutionality of a provision where finality has not been reached in proceedings, where the proceedings are still live. (See *D.P.P. v Cunningham* [2012] IECCA 64, and *D.P.P. v Kavanagh* [2012] IECCA 65.

REMEDIES FOR BREACH OF THE CONSTITUTION

Where a court finds that there is a breach of the Constitution, it will usually make a declaration of invalidity, formally declaring the Act to be unconstitutional. In *NHV v Minister for Justice and Equality* [2017] IESC 35, the Supreme Court found that an absolute ban on asylum seekers working was unconstitutional, but it initially delayed making a declaration to allow the Oireachtas to rectify the problem. (The Court later made a formal declaration). The Court has also awarded damages for breach of constitutional rights as, for instance, in *Meskell v CIÉ* [1973] I.R. 121 and *Kennedy v Ireland* [1987] I.R. 587.

Where there is a finding of unconstitutionality in respect of part of an Act, the courts may sever the offending provisions from the rest of the Act, but only if it is possible to do so without changing the legislative intention. Where such severance would change what the Oireachtas intended, it is not permitted (see *Maher v Attorney General* [1973] I.R. 140).

The courts may also grant an injunction restraining or preventing unconstitutional conduct. Ordinarily, however, the courts will not grant a mandatory injunction requiring the Oireachtas or Executive to act in a particular way. In *TD v Minister for Education* [2001] 4 I.R. 259 the Supreme Court found that such mandatory orders would infringe the separation of powers under the Constitution. The Court could only grant such an order where the Oireachtas or Executive had made a conscious and deliberate decision to breach of the Constitution.

Articles 2 and 3—The Nation and the Position of Northern Ireland

THE IRISH NATION UNDER THE OLD ARTICLES 2 AND 3

The Constitution distinguishes between the Nation and the State. A "nation" is a political concept, an idea of a people united by a common identity or by common traits. Prior to 1999, according to the old Art.2 of the Constitution, the Irish Nation consisted of the "whole island of Ireland, its islands and the territorial seas." This controversial provision effectively amounted to a "claim of legal right" (a legal claim) by Ireland to the disputed six counties of Northern Ireland. (See *McGimpsey v Ireland* [1990] 1 I.R. 110). The former Art.3, however, stated that until the national territory was reunited, the laws of the State would ordinarily apply only to the 26 counties of the State.

THE GOOD FRIDAY AGREEMENT

After decades of violence and political stasis, in 1998, the various political parties in Northern Ireland and the British and Irish governments agreed a compromise that settled how that jurisdiction would be governed. This was called the Good Friday Agreement. Northern Ireland was granted its own Assembly and a "power-sharing" government (executive) consisting of representatives of both traditions in the province. A North-South Ministerial Council was established with representatives from both Northern Ireland and Ireland agreeing on strategies of common interest to both jurisdictions. Article 29.7 of the Constitution expressly allows the State to consent to the British-Irish Agreement between Ireland and the United Kingdom made in tandem with the Good Friday Agreement. Cross-border institutions established by that Agreement may exercise their powers and functions notwithstanding the fact that the Irish Constitution confers similar powers on institutions established by the Constitution.

As part of this settlement, the Government of Ireland promised a referendum on Arts 2 and 3 with a view to removing the legal claim over Northern Ireland.

In the ensuing referendum, the People, by an overwhelming margin, passed the Nineteenth Amendment of the Constitution. This amendment proposed the alteration of Arts 2 and 3 of the Constitution with a view to dropping the legal claim over Northern Ireland. This alteration, however, was conditional upon a government order being made, which occurred on the establishment of a power-sharing Assembly and Executive in Northern Ireland and the parallel establishment of the North-South Ministerial Council. When this body finally first met, in early December 1999, the Government passed a resolution bringing the new Arts 2 and 3 into being.

WHAT DO THE NEW ARTICLES 2 AND 3 SAY?

Under the new Art.2 of the Constitution (as amended in 1999), the following persons may claim to be part of the Irish nation:

- All persons born in the island of Ireland (or on its islands and seas) have an "entitlement and birthright" to be part of the Irish nation; and
- All persons who, though not born on the island, are qualified in accordance with law to be citizens of Ireland are also entitled to be part of the Irish nation.

Article 2 is very carefully worded. Membership of the Irish nation is not forced on those on our island who claim a different nationality.

The new Art.3 contains similarly conciliatory changes. The key element in this context is that the new Articles dropped the territorial claim over Northern Ireland as asserted by the old Arts 2 and 3. In their place there is now a statement in Art.3 of the "firm will of the Irish nation ... to unite all the people who share the territory of the island of Ireland ...". Art.3 also contains:

- An acknowledgement that a united Ireland may only be achieved through peaceful and democratic means;
- An express recognition that there will be no united Ireland until a majority of the people in each jurisdiction (North and South) give their democratically expressed consent to such unification;
- A statement clarifying that until the jurisdictions are reunited, the laws of the State shall ordinarily apply only to the 26 counties of the Republic of Ireland.

While the coming into force of the new Articles was conditional upon the setting up of the institutions envisaged by the Good Friday Agreement, their continuation in force is not conditional upon the survival of those institutions. Thus, now that the new Articles are in force, only the People may remove them, in referendum.

The Irish State

WHAT IS A STATE?

A state is a legal framework of governance by reference to which a particular geographical territory is run. A state, then, effectively comprises a system of government, a set of institutions and functionaries that are responsible for regulating the affairs of a defined jurisdiction.

LANGUAGES AND FLAG

The official languages of the State are Irish and English. Irish is the first official language and national language, while English is "recognised as a second official language" (Art.8). The national flag is the tricolor of green, white and orange (Art.7).

THE NAME OF THE STATE

Article 4 of the Constitution indicates that the official name given to the State is "Ireland" in English or, in Irish, "Éire". Section 2 of the Republic of Ireland Act 1948 states "the description of the State shall be the Republic of Ireland" but this does not alter the name of the State, which remains as outlined in Art.4.

THE STATE HAS SEPARATE LEGAL PERSONALITY

The State is a "juristic person" or "legal person", with legal personality. This means that:

- the State can be sued (see *Byrne v Ireland* [1972] I.R. 241);
- the State can sue other persons (see *Ireland v Mulvey*, *Irish Times*, 11 November 1989);
- the State can enter into contracts for the purchase of items;
- the State can own property in its own right (see *Comyn v Attorney General* [1950] I.R. 142).

THE STATE IS A DEMOCRACY

Article 5 of the Constitution stipulates that Ireland is a "sovereign, independent, democratic State". The State is run in accordance with the Constitution laid down by the People. The President and members of the Dáil are chosen by election. Democratically elected members of the Dáil select the Government. The State, moreover, is run in accordance with the rule of law. This means that the State can only do what it is entitled to do under publicly promulgated laws made in accordance with the Constitution. The democratic nature of the State was emphasized in *McKenna v An Taoiseach (No. 2)* [1995] 2 I.R. 10 where the Supreme Court ruled that State resources must not be spent promoting one side only of a referendum debate, at the expense of the other. Likewise, in *Doherty v Government of Ireland* [2011] 2 I.R. 222, the democratic nature of the State was invoked in support of a conclusion that vacancies in the Dáil must be filled within a reasonable time to ensure constituents are properly represented in Parliament.

THE STATE IS DESCRIBED AS A REPUBLIC

The Republic of Ireland Act 1948 expressly describes the State as a republic. A "republic", in short, is a state where the People generally choose their leaders (and particularly the Head of State) on merit and by election, and where those leaders govern for the public good. Although the State is not described in the Constitution as such, the fact that we elect our head of state, the President, on merit, sets us apart from monarchies, where heads of state owe their position solely to the circumstances of their birth. Another key feature of a republic is that the powers of government are typically divided between various named bodies in what is called the "separation of powers" (see below at Ch.7). That said, the official name of the State does not contain the word "Republic". This use of the latter term in the 1948 Act is said to be a description of the State rather than an alteration of its title.

Despite the lack of an express reference to a republic or republicanism in the Constitution, in *Sinnott v Minister for Education* [2001] 2 I.R. 545 Hardiman J. referred to the separation of powers as being a "vital constituent of the sovereign independent *republican* and democratic State envisaged by the Constitution" (emphasis added). In *Byrne v Ireland* [1972] I.R. 241 Walsh J. speaks of the "new republican form of constitution which was enacted in 1937".

Is the State "independent"?

An important aim of the Constitution of Ireland 1937 was to assert Ireland's full independence from UK control. Article 1 speaks of the right of the Irish nation "to choose its own form of government." Although Art.5 declares that the State is "independent", this is qualified considerably by Ireland's membership of the European Union. Article 29 of the Constitution permits the State to be a full member of this Union. This means that the laws of the European Union and judgments of the courts of the European Union have legal effect within this State, regardless of the will of the Oireachtas. (See Ch.6 below).

Sovereignty

To be sovereign in the widest sense entails being entirely independent from outside control or interference, and not being answerable to external bodies. In respect of a territory, sovereignty involves having the supreme and unqualified power to rule as one pleases. Sovereignty therefore involves the state of being answerable to no higher body.

In Ireland, the ultimate sovereign power is the People. Popular sovereignty entails that the People have the final say on certain important policy matters. In particular, the Constitution and the State owe their origins to a 1937 vote of the People, and the State is subject to that Constitution. Only the People can change the Constitution, albeit at the invitation of the Oireachtas. The courts have consistently emphasised that, in Ireland, it is the People that are ultimately the sovereign power. Article 6 of the Constitution states: "All powers of government ... derive, under God, from the people, whose right it is to designate the rulers of the State and, in final appeal, to decide all questions of national policy, according to the requirements of the common good."

In *Byrne v Ireland* [1972] I.R. 241, Walsh J. observed that the State is the creation of the People and that "in the last analysis the sovereign authority is the People." In *Howard v Commissioners of Public Works* [1994] 1 I.R. 101 Denham J. remarked: "Under the Constitution the People are sovereign. The very word is of interest as it denotes the supreme ruler. Thus, the People are, in the last analysis, the rulers." In *Re Article 26 and the Regulation of Information Bill 1995*, the Supreme Court confirmed that no restraint may be placed on the right of the People to change the Constitution. A constitutional amendment validly enacted by the People cannot be challenged on the basis that it infringes, for instance, the natural law.

However, the State also enjoys a certain type of sovereignty, particularly in the external sphere. In Art.5, Ireland is described as a "sovereign, independent, democratic state." The State is thus externally sovereign. As against all other nation states, the State has the sole power to govern Ireland, to make laws for the State and determine its relations with other nations. With the exception of the European Union, no state or entity other than Ireland may govern Ireland, determine its laws or its relations with other states. This means that as against every other State on the globe, Ireland has the exclusive authority to rule the territory of the State. No other state can make laws for the State. Moreover, only the institutions designated by the Constitution may exercise the powers of the State. (See Art.6). For instance, the Parliament of the United Kingdom cannot make laws for Ireland (the State). Likewise, any attempt to create a rival parliament would be unconstitutional.

This was confirmed in *Crotty v An Taoiseach* [1987] I.R. 713, where the Supreme Court ruled that only the Government of the State could determine Ireland's foreign policy. As *Crotty* illustrates, it is not possible for an organ of State to abdicate its exclusive powers. In that case, the Supreme Court ruled that the Executive had purported to give away its power over foreign relations to an external body, something that was not permitted by the Constitution. This does not mean, however, that the State cannot commit itself to certain international actions. For instance, in *Pringle v Ireland* [2013] 3 I.R. 1 the State's ratification of the European Stability Mechanism was deemed to be an exercise of State sovereignty rather than an abdication thereof. According to O'Donnell J., the Constitution should not be read as confining the State to entering agreements where it retained a veto over future decisions: "[S]uch an interpretation would, in practice, constrain governmental freedom in foreign policy."

State sovereignty is generally external in character. As Budd J. remarked in *Byrne v Ireland* [1971] I.R. 241, within the State "it is the People who are paramount and not the State." Thus, in the latter case, the Supreme Court rejected the proposition that the State was immune from being sued in its own courts. Nonetheless, within the State, it appears that there are aspects of internal sovereignty, as illustrated in *Webb v Ireland* [1988] I.R. 353. In that case, the Supreme Court found that the State, as a necessary ingredient of sovereignty in a modern state, had a right to the ownership of historical objects that had no known owner. (Similarly, state sovereignty also confers a right to regulate and control immigration).

THE ROYAL PREROGATIVE POWERS

In several cases, the Supreme Court has concluded that the State did not inherit a series of royal prerogative powers, residual rights or privileges held by the British monarch. The prerogatives owed their origins (as Finlay C.J. puts it in *Webb v Ireland* [1988] I.R. 353) to the "royal dignity of the King ... [and] ... to his position as sovereign or ruler".

It was once assumed that the State had inherited these prerogative rights. In a series of cases, however, this assumption has been rejected. In *Byrne v Ireland* [1972] I.R. 241, the Supreme Court ruled that the State did not inherit these royal prerogatives. The Court's reasoning was that the British monarch's role in the Irish Free State was radically different from that in the UK, where the King was the personification of the State. By contrast, the King under the Constitution of 1922 had a restricted role, as defined by the Constitution. The King was not, therefore, the personification of the State as he was in the UK, and neither the King in Ireland nor the Irish Free State after 1922 enjoyed prerogative rights. Such rights were inconsistent with the fact that, under Art.2 of the 1922 Constitution and Art.6 of the 1937 Constitution, the powers of the State derived from the People.

Byrne concerned a claim that, by virtue of the royal prerogative of immunity from suit, a woman injured when she fell on a public footpath could not sue the State. The Court ruled that the State was not immune from suit and could be sued. The State had not inherited any royal prerogative right and the Constitution itself did not confer any right of immunity on the State.

Another royal prerogative of the King arose for consideration in *Webb v Ireland* [1988] I.R. 353. In that case the plaintiffs had discovered the famous "Derrynaflan Hoard", consisting of a chalice and paten dating back at least 1,300 years. The State claimed that as part of the royal prerogative of "treasure trove", these items of national heritage that had no known owner belonged to the State. The Supreme Court again noted that the State did not enjoy any royal prerogative powers. The State thus was not the successor to any prerogative of treasure trove. Nevertheless, on the basis of the Constitution alone, and in particular Arts 5 and 10, the Court found that these items did belong to the State, as a necessary ingredient of the State's sovereignty.

A former royal prerogative allowed the State to claim that general statutes did not apply to the State, unless the contrary was expressly stated. In *Howard v Commissioners of Public Works* [1994] 1 I.R. 101, the Supreme Court ruled that the State was subject to its own laws, unless expressly exempted therefrom. Nonetheless, in *Geoghegan v Institute of Chartered Accountants* [1995] 3 I.R. 86 the Supreme Court affirmed that bodies established under royal charter (part of the royal prerogative) were not affected by the demise of the prerogative in Ireland, and continued to exist in law. Likewise, in *Prendergast v HEA* [2008] IEHC 257 Charlton J. concluded that, notwithstanding the demise of the royal prerogative, the State had a "residue of inherited powers".

6 Ireland in the International Order

Article 29 addresses Ireland's position in the international legal order. In Art.29 Ireland broadly commits itself to "the ideal of peace and friendly co-operation amongst nations founded on international justice and morality." It also affirms a preference for resolving international disputes peacefully and by international arbitration or judicial determination. Foreign relations are generally the responsibility of the Government alone, though a declaration of war may not be made without the assent of Dáil Éireann and Dáil assent is required for treaties involving a charge on public funds. Additionally, international agreements may not become part of Irish domestic law without an Act of Parliament.

THE EXCLUSIVE POWERS OF THE GOVERNMENT

Article 29.4 indicates that the executive power "in or in connection with the State's external relations shall in accordance with Art.28 of this constitution be exercised by or on the authority of the Government." Section 3 of the Republic of Ireland Act 1948 states: "The President, on the authority and on the advice of the Government, may exercise the executive power or any executive function of the State in or in connection with its external relations." It is clear, however, that decisions relating to foreign affairs, and the conduct of foreign relations generally lie with the Executive (Government). The President's role is purely ceremonial; he or she acts on the instructions of the Government in this context.

The Courts have confirmed that they will only intervene in the foreign relations functions of the Government in exceptional cases. The conduct of foreign policy is generally left within the exclusive remit of the Government. In *Boland v An Taoiseach* [1974] I.R. 388, Fitzgerald C.J. in the Supreme Court confirmed that "the Courts have no power, either express or implied, to supervise or interfere with the exercise by the Government of its executive functions, unless the circumstances are such as to amount to a clear disregard by the Government of the powers and duties conferred upon it by the Constitution." The Court therefore declined to intervene in relation to a joint communiqué relating to Northern Ireland issued by the Irish and

British governments. The decision suggests that the courts will generally not intervene in foreign policy matters though they reserve judicial power to take action where there is a clear breach of the Constitution. Similarly, in *Horgan v An Taoiseach* [2003] 2 I.L.R.M. 357 Kearns P. noted "the strictly circumspect role which the courts adopt when called upon to exercise jurisdiction in relation to the executive's conduct of international relations generally."

In *Pringle v Ireland* [2013] 3 I.R. 1 the Supreme Court re-emphasised that the role of making foreign policy lies with the Executive alone: "[T]he courts' function in this regard is to enforce those boundaries of, and limitations to, the exercise of the executive power in foreign relations which are either express in, or to be implied from, the constitutional text, and at the same time to reject any attempt to impose limitations on governmental conduct of foreign relations not justified by the Constitution."

Where, however, the Government acts or intends to act in a way that clearly disregards the Constitution, it appears the Courts can intervene. In particular, if there is an actual or threatened breach of constitutional rights, the courts may act. In *Crotty v An Taoiseach* [1987] I.R. 713, the Supreme Court ruled that the Government cannot, in the exercise of foreign policy powers, abdicate or surrender its right to determine the foreign policy of the State, by placing it in the hands of another State or an international or supranational body (without a constitutional referendum permitting this). In this case, a majority of the Supreme Court concluded that Title III of the Single European Act (an EEC Treaty), which required the State to consult with other states with a view to developing a joint European foreign policy, gave away part of the State's sovereignty in respect of foreign policy, such that the State's foreign policy powers might be exercised without regard to the common good of the Irish people. On the other hand, in *Pringle v Ireland* [2013] 3 I.R. 1 the Supreme Court ruled that a Treaty committing Ireland to the European Stability Mechanism was an exercise of foreign policy power and not an abdication thereof. The latter case seems to take a more pragmatic and expansive view than *Crotty*. The majority in *Pringle* recognised, in particular, that an exercise of foreign policy power may require the State to commit itself to a particular joint policy.

DÁIL ÉIREANN AND FOREIGN RELATIONS

Although the Government has an exclusive role in respect of foreign relations, under Art.28 the Government is answerable to the Dáil Éireann. In *Dubsky v Ireland* [2007] 1 I.R. 63 Macken J. noted that "the Dáil possesses ample powers under the Constitution to prevent the government overreaching, should the Dáil consider it to have done so." Presumably, if the Dáil strongly disagreed with the Government's foreign policy, it could vote no confidence in the Taoiseach and compel his or her resignation.

The Constitution in Art.29.5 requires that all international agreements to which Ireland becomes a party (save those of a technical and administrative character) must be laid before Dáil Éireann. Where the agreement is not one of a technical and administrative character and involves a charge on public funds, the agreement is not binding on the State unless approved by the Dáil. For instance, in the *State (Gilliland) v Governor of Mountjoy Prison* [1987] I.R. 201, an extradition treaty with the US was found to create a charge on public funds because the State was required thereunder (amongst other things) to pay for the transport of prisoners. As Dáil Éireann had not approved it, the agreement was thus found not to be binding.

Notably, Dáil approval is required for the State to declare war or participate in a war, though in cases of actual invasion the Government may take necessary steps to protect the State, pending a meeting of the Dáil.

THE IMPACT OF ARTICLE 29

In *Horgan v Ireland* [2003] 2 I.R. 468 an individual citizen claimed that the use of Shannon airport as a "stopover" for US troops and aircraft engaged in the Iraq war infringed the principles of international law. Although it permits such stopovers, Ireland is formally neutral in relation to the specific conflict. The High Court, however, rejected the claim. It agreed that concept of neutrality existed in international law and that customary international law prevented a neutral state from allowing troops or munitions involved in a war from travelling through neutral territory en route to a war. The Court, however, noted that the principles of international customary law entered Irish domestic law only to the extent that the principles did not conflict with domestic law. Kearns P. observed that the Executive enjoyed the power to determine Ireland's foreign relations. This power "can only be depleted or removed by referendum". Thus, it could not be said that the Executive's powers in respect of international relations could be limited by a principle of customary international law. The case again seems to confirm the courts' reluctance to interfere in matters within the Executive's powers.

Articles 29.1–3 affirm (1) the State's "devotion to the ideal of peace and friendly co-operation amongst nations founded on international justice and morality"; (2) the State's adherence to the principle of the peaceful settlement of international disputes by international arbitration or judicial determination; and (3) that "Ireland accepts the generally recognised principles of international law as its rule of conduct in its relations with other states". Nonetheless, in *Horgan,* the High Court concluded that these provisions constituted statements of principle only that were not binding on the Executive. Article 29.1–3, in particular, governed the State's relations with other states and did not confer individual rights that could be invoked against the State. The Supreme Court reached a similar conclusion in *Kavanagh v Governor of Mountjoy Prison* [2002] 3 I.R. 97: Art.29 does not confer on individuals any rights flowing from international law. It concerns the relationship between Ireland and other States as opposed to the relationship between Ireland and its citizens. Article 29, in other words, does not in itself create individual rights that can be relied upon by citizens in the Irish courts.

IRELAND IS A DUALIST STATE

Although the Government has full power to sign and ratify international agreements or treaties, these agreements or treaties do not form part of Irish domestic law unless and to the extent they have been incorporated into Irish law by an Act of the Oireachtas.

In this sense Ireland is said to be a "dualist" rather than a "monist" state. A monist state automatically treats international laws that are binding on the state as enforceable in its national courts. By contrast, a dualist state regards international law (including agreements between nations) as an area of law entirely separate from national or domestic law. It considers international law not to be enforceable in domestic courts unless parliament has expressly "incorporated" it into national law. The State may be bound as a matter of international law by an international agreement to which the Government has agreed. Yet, unless the Oireachtas makes an international agreement part of national law, it is not part of domestic Irish law and cannot be pleaded or relied upon in an Irish court. Article 29.6 stipulates "... no international agreement shall be part of the domestic law of the State save as may be determined by the Oireachtas". The agreement may be binding on the State in its relations with other nations, but it is not binding *in* the State. In *JMcD v PL and BM* [2009] IESC 81 Murray C.J. explained this point:

> "According to the concept of dualism, at national level national law always takes precedence over international law. At international level, as regards a state's obligations, international law takes precedence over its national or internal law, which is why a state cannot generally rely on their own constitutional provisions as an excuse for not fulfilling international obligations which they have undertaken. Coming back to the national level the dualist approach means that international treaties to which a state is a party can only be given effect to in a national law to the extent that national law, rather than the international instrument itself, specifies."

Obligations under an international convention, he continued, "arise under international law and not national law." Therefore, such obligations "reside at international level". The State cannot be made to answer before the Irish courts for a breach of an international agreement unless this is provided for in national law.

In *Re Ó Láighléis* [1960] I.R. 93, for instance, the plaintiff was prevented from pleading the terms of the European Convention on Human Rights to challenge the reasons for his detention without trial. This case was heard at a time before the Oireachtas passed the European Convention on Human Rights Act 2003. The Supreme Court ruled that because the Convention had not been incorporated into Irish law, it could not be taken into account by the court. In particular, domestic law could not be challenged on the basis that it breached the Convention.

In *Kavanagh v Governor of Mountjoy Prison* [2002] 3 I.R. 97, the applicant sought a declaration that his conviction by the Special Criminal Court and part of the Offences against the State Act 1939 were both invalid as being in breach of the International Covenant on Civil and Political Rights. Rejecting this proposition, Fennelly J. remarked that "[t]he Constitution establishes an unmistakable distinction between domestic and international law." The Government, he explained, had exclusive power to enter into international agreements. Nonetheless, the exclusive power to make laws for Ireland resides in the Oireachtas. Where the Government wishes the terms of an international agreement to have effect in domestic law, it may ask the Oireachtas to pass the necessary legislation. If that did not happen, however, the agreement is not part of national law.

A similar approach has, in some cases, been taken to decisions of international courts. In *O'B. v S.* [1984] I.R. 316, Walsh J. in the Supreme Court concluded that a "decision of the European Court of Human Rights could have no bearing on the question of whether any provision of the [Succession Act 1965] is invalid having regard to the provisions of the Constitution." In *Norris v Ireland* (1989) 13 E.H.R.R. 186 the European Court of Human Rights ruled that Irish laws banning consensual sexual conduct between two adult males (even in private) infringed the plaintiff's right to privacy under art.8 of the Convention on Human Rights. Nonetheless, these impugned laws remained in force in Ireland until 1993, when the Oireachtas passed the Criminal Law (Sexual Offences) Act 1993. It was only when the Oireachtas had acted to change Irish law that Irish domestic law was altered to comply with the Convention.

Nonetheless, the Irish courts regularly look to the caselaw of international courts as being "persuasive" in interpreting Irish law: see *Ó Domhnaill v Merrick* [1985] I.R. 151, *Desmond v Glackin (No. 1)* [1993] 3 I.R. 1 and *Doyle v Commissioner of An Garda Síochána* [1999] 1 I.R. 249. Such agreements and court decisions may be used to cast light on the meaning of Irish law.

The Irish courts will, for instance, look to various conventions and decisions of international courts as guidance on their interpretation of the Constitution (see *Murphy v IRTC* [1997] 2 I.L.R.M. 467)

EUROPEAN CONVENTION ON HUMAN RIGHTS

Ireland ratified the European Convention on Human Rights in 1953. The European Convention on Human Rights Act 2003 (the "2003 Act") now allows the Convention to be relied on in specified ways in the Irish courts. In *JMcD v PL and BM* [2009] IESC 81, however, the Supreme Court clarified that the Convention itself is not part of Irish law and can only be invoked in accordance with the specific terms of the 2003 Act. The Convention is not directly applicable. It can only be relied on in an Irish court in compliance with the conditions laid down in the 2003 Act. As McKechnie J. observed in *Foy v An tArd-Chláraitheoir* [2007] IEHC 470, "[i]t is a misleading metaphor to say that the Convention was incorporated into Irish law. It is not. The Rights contained in the Convention are now part of Irish law. They are so by reason of the Act of 2003. That is their source. Not the Convention."

The 2003 Act broadly does three things:

- It requires that, to the extent that it is possible to do so, the courts must interpret and apply Irish legislation or rules of law in such a way as to make them consistent with the Convention (s.2). Section 4 of the Act requires the court, in interpreting the Convention, to take judicial notice of (amongst other things) decision of the European Court of Human Rights.
- Where it is not possible to interpret Irish law in a Convention-compliant manner, and the law is found to infringe the Convention, a declaration of incompatibility may be made (s.5). In *Foy v An tArd-Chláraitheoir* [2007] IEHC 470 McKechnie J. ruled that a law that denied legal recognition of the true gender identity of a person who is transgender infringed the Convention. On that basis, the judge handed down a declaration of incompatibility. In doing so he followed the European Court of Human Rights decision in *Goodwin v United Kingdom* [2002] 35 E.H.R.R. 18 which found that the non-recognition of a transgender person's gender of identity was in breach of art.8 of the Convention. Such a declaration, however, does not invalidate the relevant law, which remains in force until amended or repealed by the Oireachtas (as happened when the Oireachtas passed the Gender Recognition Act 2015).
- Section 3 of the Act requires every organ of State (other than the President, the Oireachtas or a court) to perform its functions in a manner compatible with the State's obligations under the Convention provisions. A person who

has suffered injury, loss or damage as a result of a contravention of this section may, if no other remedy in damages is available, recover damages for such a breach.

EXTRA-TERRITORIALITY

As a general rule, Irish law applies only within the confines of the State. There are, however, some cases in which Irish legislation may be applied to situations that arise outside Ireland. While international law generally requires that sovereign states respect each other's boundaries, it recognises the principle of "extra-territoriality", that is, that one state may in limited circumstances apply its laws to incidents that occur in another state.

Article 29.8 of the Constitution expressly allows Irish legislation to have such "extra-territorial" effects in compliance with international law norms. For instance, the Sexual Offences (Jurisdiction) Act 1996 allows Ireland to prosecute people who are citizens of or ordinarily resident in Ireland who have committed a sexual offence while abroad, provided the act is an offence both in Ireland and in the country where it took place. This is possible notwithstanding the fact that the offence occurred outside Ireland.

It is important to remember, however, that extra-territoriality tends to be the exception rather than the rule. According to the International Court of Justice's decision in the *Lotus Case* (1927) P.C.I.J. Ser. A., No. 10, extra-territorial legislation should only be used where clearly necessary to promote "peace, order and good government" within the state that makes such laws.

THE POSITION OF THE EUROPEAN UNION UNDER THE CONSTITUTION

The European Union is a union of 28 European States (as of 2018) committed to economic, social and political co-operation on matters of mutual interest. In relation to this Union and its rules and principles, two key points need to be made:

- Where there is a conflict between the law of the European Union ("EU law") and Irish law, including the Constitution, EU law always prevails.
- Laws made by the European Union may automatically become part of Irish domestic law.

The supremacy of EU law

In *Meagher v Minister for Agriculture* [1994] 1 I.R. 329, Blayney J. in the Supreme Court remarked "[i]t is well established that Community law takes precedence over our domestic law. When they are in conflict, it is the Community law which prevails." (See also *Campus Oil v Minister for Industry and Energy* [1983] I.R. 82). This is in line with EU law itself, which has consistently held that where a conflict exists between national and European Union law, EU law will always prevail (see *Costa v ENEL* [1964] E.C.R. 585 which confirms the supremacy of EU law over conflicting domestic laws). Thus, in cases of conflict between EU law and Irish law, EU law will always prevail. This is the case even where the Irish law concerned is part of the Irish Constitution. Concerns that this would lead to a breach of human rights led to the adoption of the EU Charter of Fundamental Rights, which applies to the EU and to Member States when implementing or enforcing EU law.

This preference for EU law, even over the terms of the Constitution, is copper-fastened in the Constitution itself by Art.29.4.6°. That provision effectively gives EU law an exemption from having to comply with the Constitution. Thus, an EU provision may become law in Ireland, even where it otherwise offends the terms of the Constitution. Article 29.4.6° covers two types of law: laws made by the EU itself, and laws enacted by the State that are "necessitated by the obligations of membership" of the EU. Such laws need not comply with the requirements of the Constitution.

This exemption, however, only applies to the extent that the State is doing what it is obliged to do by EU law. The State cannot claim such an exemption where it is exercising its own discretion. Where the State is not required to take a particular step in implementing an EU measure, the taking of that step does not attract the constitutional exemption envisaged by Art.29.4.6°. (See, for instance, *Greene v Minister for Agriculture* [1990] 2 I.R. 17 where measures that discriminated against married farmers were found not to have been necessitated by EU membership and thus were not exempt from constitutional scrutiny).

The European Communities Act 1972

The European Communities Act 1972 allows laws made by the EU automatically to become part of Irish law. As amended, s.2 of the European Communities Act 1972 states that the treaties governing the European Union, acts adopted by the European Union and acts previously adopted by the European Communities that are still in force, as well as acts adopted by bodies competent under the EU treaties "shall be binding on the State and shall be part of the domestic law thereof under the conditions laid down in the treaties governing the European Union". This means that the Treaties and Regulations of the European Union are considered part of domestic Irish law and are automatically incorporated into national law by this Act, giving such laws "direct applicability". Other EU measures, such as EU directives, can have "direct effects", allowing ordinary individuals to rely on EU law as giving them rights that may be successfully invoked in Irish courts, notwithstanding the fact that the Oireachtas has not expressly and specifically approved the content of such legislation.

The net effect is that the EU can make law for Ireland. An individual may thus rely on European Union law in an Irish court. But for Art.29.4.6°, this would undoubtedly be an unconstitutional infringement of the Oireachtas' exclusive powers in Art.15.2 to make law for Ireland. Article 29.4.6°, however, states that nothing in the Constitution prevents laws enacted by the EU from having the force of law in Ireland. The European Communities Act 1972 gives the force of law to EU measures, though certain types of EU legislation, namely Directives, while binding as to their outcomes require implementation into national law.

Section 3 of the 1972 Act allows a Government Minister to make regulations (statutory instruments) to give full effect to EU laws, for instance, to implement EU Directives into Irish law. Such regulations may "contain such incidental, supplementary and consequential provisions as appear to the Minister making the regulations to be necessary for the purposes of the regulations". These regulations may include measures repealing, amending or applying other laws, including Acts of Parliament, and may lay down offences and penalties that are proportionate and effective with a view to giving full effect to EU law. Provided the Minister is giving effect to principles and policies contained in EU law, implementing EU law by means of statutory instrument is constitutionally permitted. Likewise, the courts have upheld as constitutional the ministerial power to amend provisions in Acts of Parliament where this is necessary to give effect to EU law. (See *Meagher v Minister for Agriculture* [1994] 1 I.R. 329, and *Maher v Minister for Agriculture* [2001] 2 I.R. 139 and the discussion below in Ch.9).

IS A REFERENDUM REQUIRED EVERY TIME THERE IS A NEW EU TREATY?

In the course of its history the EU has developed considerably. The original scope of the first treaties establishing the European Communities has been significantly extended by a series of amending treaties, the most prominent of which are the Single European Act 1986, the Maastricht Treaty 1992, the Amsterdam Treaty 1997, the Nice Treaty 2001 and the Lisbon Treaty 2007. An "amending" treaty does not come into effect until every Member State that has signed it "ratifies" (i.e. endorses) the treaty in accordance with its own constitutional requirements. In theory, any state (including Ireland) may refuse to ratify a treaty even after it has been signed. In other words, Ireland is never obliged to ratify an amending treaty: it may always choose to do otherwise. As a result, it cannot be said that ratifying these treaties is "necessitated by the obligations of membership of the European Union".

In *Crotty v An Taoiseach* [1987] I.R. 713, Finlay C.J. noted that the European Communities are dynamic in nature and must be expected to change and develop over time. When the Irish people passed the Third Amendment (the original Art.29.4.3°), allowing the State to join the European Communities, such change must have been anticipated. According to Finlay C.J., under the Third Amendment, the State was authorised "not only to join the Communities as they stood in 1973 but also to join in amendments of the Treaties so long as such amendments do not alter the essential scope or objectives of the Communities." To the extent, therefore, that the new reforming EU treaties remained within the broad "purpose and objectives" of the original treaties, the Chief Justice agreed that the changes introduced by the amending treaty would not require a further referendum. If, however, the changes in question altered the essential scope of the original objectives and aims of the Communities, making ground-breaking changes to the earlier treaties, a further referendum may be required if these changes are to enjoy constitutional immunity.

In short, if the proposed amendment to the EU is merely a development of the already approved aims and objectives of the European Union, no referendum will be required. If, however, the proposed changes significantly alter the purpose or powers of the European Union, a new referendum will be required if the new provisions would otherwise conflict with the Constitution.

7 The Separation of Powers

The principle of the separation of powers requires that the various powers of the State be divided on a pre-arranged basis between the different institutions established by the Constitution. Each institution is said to have exclusive powers that only it can exercise. (See Art.6 of the Constitution). Any attempt by one institution of State (or for that matter by a body that is not an institution of State) to invoke or use powers exclusively reserved to another institution would constitute an unconstitutional "invasion" of the powers of that body. The reason for such separation lies in the perceived danger of placing all State power in one person or body alone, with the attendant likelihood of corruption and abuse of power by that person or body. The institutions of State are said to exercise their powers in a manner that provides a system of checks and balances, with various powers to supervise and oversee the activities of the others institutions.

Each institution of State and its powers are examined below in Chs 9–13. Nonetheless, this chapter endeavours to set out a general overview of the rules around the separation of powers.

TYPICALLY THE POWERS OF THE STATE ARE DIVIDED BETWEEN:

1. A "legislature" that performs the law-making power. In Ireland this power is exercised by Parliament, or, as it is better known, the Oireachtas;
2. An "executive", or Government that administers and oversees on a day-to-day basis the operation and implementation of laws made the legislature; and
3. A "judiciary", that is, judges administering justice in courts of law. This involves, in particular, adjudicating in disputes as to the meaning and application of the law.

THE LEGISLATIVE ROLE—MAKING LAW

The national Parliament (the Oireachtas) has certain exclusive powers that only it may exercise. Indeed, Art.15.2 of the Constitution states that only the Oireachtas can make laws in respect of the State. No other legislative body (except those of the European Union) may create laws applicable within the

State. In particular, restrictions apply in relation to the delegation of legislative powers by the Oireachtas to other bodies, such as the Government. Under the Constitution itself, furthermore, Parliament and its members enjoy certain privileges that, for instance, prevent the courts from intervening in the internal workings of the Houses of the Oireachtas. Members are privileged (i.e. not answerable to a court), moreover, in respect of their utterances before either House. (For more detail see Ch.9 below). The courts are generally deferential to the Oireachtas in respect of its law-making role.

THE EXECUTIVE ROLE—GOVERNING THE STATE, ADMINISTERING THE OPERATION OF LAWS

The Government too enjoys certain powers that are not extended to other functionaries. For instance, the sole and exclusive power to determine the State's foreign policy is reserved to the Government (see *Crotty v An Taoiseach* [1987] I.R. 713). The courts have repeatedly stressed their reluctance to intervene in respect of the State's executive power in the area of foreign relations. (See *Boland v An Taoiseach* [1974] I.R. 388, *Horgan v Ireland* [2003] 2 I.R. 468 and *Dubsky v Ireland* [2005] IEHC 442). The courts will only interfere where there is a clear and serious disregard of the Constitution. Arguably, the principle of Cabinet confidentiality reflects also the reluctance of judges to interfere in the functioning of the Government, by protecting the right of the Government to preserve the secrecy of its deliberations (Art.28.4.3°). (For more detail see Ch.11 below).

THE JUDICIAL ROLE—INTERPRETING AND ENFORCING LAW

By the same token, the judicial role (as we will see in Ch.13) is deemed to be the sole preserve of the courts. Article 34.1 ascribes the sole and exclusive power to "administer justice" to the judiciary (judges) in courts of law. Thus, subject to the provisions of Art.37, only a court may determine the results of legal disputes or impose legal liabilities or penalties on litigants or accused persons. Article 35.2 moreover asserts that in the performance of their role judges are independent of all, though they remain subject to the "Constitution and the law". Thus, for instance, in *Buckley v Attorney General* [1950] I.R. 67, an Act of the Oireachtas purporting to suspend a case before the High Court and to impose a legislative result in that case was declared unconstitutional. Once a case is pending before a court, the Supreme Court held, it can only be decided by a judge, and not by Act of Parliament. The courts have also been quite assertive in confirming that the imposition of a sentence on conviction of a particular offender is a matter exclusively for the courts. (For more detail see Ch.13 below).

CHECKS AND BALANCES

The separation of powers in Ireland, however, is not applied quite as rigidly as might first appear. The relationship between the various arms of the State is in fact quite complex, involving a delicate series of checks and balances. Not least among these is the power of judicial review explicitly afforded to the courts by the Constitution (see Ch.3). The courts have a right, after all, to review the constitutionality of measures taken by both the Oireachtas and Executive, and to make declarations of unconstitutionality. Similarly:

- The Government is not in fact fully independent of the other institutions of State. The Taoiseach is effectively chosen by Dáil Éireann, which may also dismiss him or her from office (see Arts 13.1.1°–2° and Arts 28.10–11). The Government, moreover, is answerable to the Dáil for its decisions (Art.28.4). Thus, the Government depends on the Dáil not only for its initial creation but also for its continued survival. In addition, the Taoiseach (being the Head of Government) requires, for his or her appointment, the support of a majority of Dáil members. He or she can, furthermore, be forced to resign if he or she loses that support during his or her time in office (see below in Ch.11).
- The Taoiseach, in turn, has some role in the selection of Members of Parliament. The Taoiseach first elected after a general election appoints eleven members of the Seanad. This usually secures for the Government of the day a majority in that House (see below pp.78–79).
- Although judges are independent in the performance of their functions (Art.35.2), the President appoints all judges, on the advice of the Government (see Art.35.1 and Art.13.9). This means that the appointment of judges is effectively an executive function.
- The Oireachtas is also empowered to impeach (remove from office) a judge or the President for stated incapacity or misbehaviour.

MANDATORY ORDERS

In *T.D. v Minister for Education* [2001] 4 I.R. 259 the Supreme Court overturned a High Court order mandating the Minister for Education to provide secure care facilities for young people with behavioural difficulties. At that time, the State had no such facility. In the High Court, Kelly J. had ordered the

State to establish a secure unit to contain and support these young persons. The Supreme Court, however, reversed this order, noting that the decision to establish, operate, and fund such units was a matter for the Legislature and the Executive, and not for the courts. The Supreme Court thus ruled that Kelly J. had infringed the separation of powers doctrine, as the courts could not dictate how the Legislature and Executive exercised their exclusive powers. In particular, the Supreme Court disapproved of the use of mandatory orders to require the Executive to establish such units. Such an order, the majority concluded, could only be deployed in exceptional cases to prevent the Executive from acting in clear disregard of its constitutional duties, in particular where there was a conscious and deliberate decision to breach the Constitution. (See also the similar reasoning applied in *Sinnott v Minister for Education* [2001] 2 I.R. 545).

Money matters

The Dáil and the Executive (Government) have an interconnected role in relation to public spending. Art.17.2 states that Dáil Éireann shall not pass any vote or resolution, and no law shall be enacted, for the appropriation (allocation) of revenue or other public moneys unless, in a message signed by the Taoiseach, the Government recommends the purpose of the appropriation. What this means is that money cannot be set aside for a particular purpose without the approval of both the Government and the Dáil.

The courts generally take the view that the fair distribution of the State's financial resources lies within the exclusive remit of the elected legislature and the Government and not that of the courts. The power to determine how State revenue will be collected, and how it will be spent is reserved to the Oireachtas, and more specifically the Dáil acting in tandem with the Government. While it is possible for the courts to order payment of compensation to restore parties' legal entitlements and to redress losses (the process of "commutative justice"), decisions involving the redistribution of existing wealth patterns (achieving "distributive justice") are left to the Dáil and Government. This is sometimes termed the "deferential" approach, noting the deference that the courts accord to the other institutions of State in the performance of their functions.

For instance, in *O'Reilly v Limerick Corporation* [1989] I.L.R.M. 181, Costello J. refused to order the State to provide basic amenities (such as running water to members of the Traveller Community). To do so, the judge reasoned, would involve the court ordering the State to spend finite resources in a particular way, a matter peculiarly within the province of elected representatives. While the courts concern themselves with specific instances of alleged injustice, the Oireachtas has to consider the overall distribution of wealth, in situations where there are many competing demands for limited State resources. (In other words, if a court were to rule that State resources be distributed in a particular way, how would it decide from where that money would come? Who would in turn be deprived of those resources?).

The courts have also generally proved reluctant to identity and enforce socio-economic rights that may affect the distribution of resources. See for instance, *T.D. v Minister for Education* [2001] 4 I.R. 259 and *In Re Article 26 and the Health (Amendment) (No. 2) Bill 2004* [2005] IESC 7).

The President

Although not described as such in the Constitution, the President is the Head of State in Ireland. Since 1938, there have been nine Presidents, the latest being President Michael D. Higgins (2011–). The first President was President Douglas Hyde (1938–1945).

While the President is deemed by Art.12 to "take precedence over all other persons in the State", the role of the President is effectively quite limited. The functions of the President are largely ceremonial and are generally exercised on the advice of the Government. In practice, the President is typically expected to avoid getting involved in political disputes and matters of policy. This gives the role of President a "unifying" character.

How long does a President serve?

The normal term of office of a President lasts seven years. A sitting or former President may be re-elected to that office, but only once. No person may serve as President for longer than 14 years in total. Four Presidents (Séan T. Ó Ceallaigh, Éamon de Valera, Patrick Hillery, and Mary McAleese) have each served for 14 years.

The President may lose office if he or she dies or resigns. For instance, President Erskine Childers died one year into his term of office, while President Cearbhall Ó Dálaigh resigned after two years as President. The Oireachtas may remove the President from office for stated misbehaviour. (See Art.12.10). If permanently incapacitated, the President may also be removed, such incapacity being confirmed by a Supreme Court consisting of no fewer than five judges. (See Art.12.3).

Electing the President

The People of Ireland elect the President. This is a hallmark of republican democracy: the people choose their leaders by democratic means and on merit, rather than by accident of birth.

Any citizen of Ireland aged 35 or over is eligible to be elected President (Art.12.4). A referendum seeking to reduce the minimum age for the

Presidency to 21 was defeated in 2015. There is no restriction on a person born outside the State or a naturalised citizen serving as President, provided he or she is a citizen at the time of election.

In order to run for election, however, a person must be nominated in the manner set out in Art.12.4. This provides three options for nomination:

- a person may be nominated by no fewer than 20 sitting members of the Oireachtas;
- alternatively, a person may be nominated by no fewer than four county or borough councils (e.g. Donegal County Council, Cork City Council);
- an outgoing (retiring) President may nominate himself or herself (subject to the requirement that a President may serve no more than two terms in office).

If only one candidate's name is put forward, no election is required. Otherwise, the election of a President proceeds by direct vote of those citizens of Ireland who are ordinarily resident in Ireland and registered to vote. The method of election is the single-transferable-vote system of proportional representation.

THE LIMITED POWERS OF THE PRESIDENT

The Constitution significantly limits the powers of the President. He or she usually acts on the "advice" (effectively the instructions) of other organs of State, typically the Government but also the Dáil and the Taoiseach, although there are several exceptions to this rule. Articles 13.9 and 13.11 in most cases prevent the President from acting otherwise than under the instructions of the Government. As the High Court pointed out in *State (Walshe) v Murphy* [1981] I.R. 275: "The President has a very great number of powers and functions which he performs on the advice of the Government, without any discretion on his part. In respect of these matters, apparently, he cannot refuse to accede to that advice within the Constitution." Indeed, even if the President were to refuse to perform a particular task, a Commission established under Art.14 could effectively perform this task in his or her place. Notably, the President may not leave the State while in office, without government approval.

In a small number of specified cases, however, the President may act at his or her own discretion, in other words, free of any obligation to obey another person or organ of State (though, usually, having sought the advice of the Council of State). The most important of these is Art.26, which allows the President to refer a Bill to the Supreme Court to determine whether it or any part thereof is repugnant to the Constitution. (This is discussed earlier, at pp.16–19). The President may also refuse to dissolve the Dáil where the Taoiseach no longer has majority support in that House. In exercising this specific power, the President need not consult with the Council of State. The key point, however, is that these discretionary powers are the exception rather than the rule.

CASES WHERE THE PRESIDENT ACTS ON THE NOMINATION OF THE DÁIL

- The President appoints each new Taoiseach on the nomination of the Dáil. Effectively, the President must comply with the choice of Dáil Éireann (Art.13.1.1°).

CASES WHERE THE PRESIDENT ACTS ON THE ADVICE/INSTRUCTIONS OF THE TAOISEACH

- The President summons and dissolves Dáil Éireann on the instructions of the Taoiseach. The President may, however, refuse to follow the Taoiseach's advice where that Taoiseach has lost the support of a majority in the Dáil (Art.13.2.1–2°).
- The President appoints the members of the Government on the instructions of the Taoiseach, though subject to the approval of Dáil Éireann (Art.13.1.2°).
- The President appoints the Attorney General on the instructions of the Taoiseach (Art.30.2).
- The President must terminate the office of a Minister or of the Attorney General if requested to do so by the Taoiseach (Art.28.9.4° and Art.30.5).

CASES WHERE THE PRESIDENT ACTS ON THE ADVICE/INSTRUCTIONS OF THE GOVERNMENT

- The President is Supreme Commander of the Defence Forces. All commissioned officers of the armed forces are appointed in his or her name (Art.13.4). Nonetheless, the exercise of the supreme command is regulated by law.
- The President appoints all judges, on the instructions of the Government (Art.35.1).
- Where the President is given any powers under legislation, these powers may only be exercised on the instructions of the Government (Art.13.11).

The President also plays a formal role in the law-making process by signing all Bills passed by the Houses of the Oireachtas into law, though his role in this context is largely ceremonial.

Cases where the President may exercise discretion

In the following cases, the President may act alone, i.e. entirely at his or her own discretion. In all but the first and last of these cases, the President must first seek the advice of the Council of State, although in every such case he or she is free to ignore the advice that it gives (Arts 31–32).

- The President may, at his or her absolute discretion, refuse a Taoiseach's request to dissolve the Dáil, where that Taoiseach has lost the support of a majority of Dáil members (Art.13.2.2°). (The Council of State need not be consulted in relation to this matter). The Constitution does not define what is meant by a loss of majority support in this context, though one might speculate that it would probably be indicated by the loss by the Taoiseach of a vote of confidence, or a defeat of a budget vote. (This power has yet to be exercised by a President).
- The President may refer a Bill (or part thereof) passed by the Dáil and Seanad to the Supreme Court in order to test its constitutionality (Art.26).
- The President may establish a Committee of Privileges to determine whether a Bill is a "Money Bill" for the purposes of Arts 21–22.
- The President may, in times of emergency, agree to the shortening of the time available for the consideration of a Bill by Seanad Éireann (Art.24).
- The President may address the Houses of the Oireachtas, or the Nation, on a matter of national or public importance. (The content of the address, however, must be pre-approved by the Government.) (Art.13.7). The President is also generally entitled to convene a meeting of either or both Houses of the Oireachtas (Art.13.2).
- Under Art.27, the President may accept a request that he or she should refuse to sign an ordinary Bill passed under the provisions of Art.23 of the Constitution unless the Bill is approved by the People in a referendum or approved by the Dáil following a general election. A Bill passed under Art.23 is a Bill which the Dáil, by resolution, has deemed to have been passed by both Houses, notwithstanding the opposition of the Seanad. In response, a majority of the Seanad and at least one-third of the members of the Dáil may jointly petition the President. If, having been petitioned, the President decides that the Bill raises a matter of sufficient national importance, the President, having consulted with the Council of State, has a discretion to refuse to sign the Bill unless the Bill is either approved by the People in a referendum or approved by the Dáil after an election. Rather unusually, a Bill that is the subject of an Article 27 referendum will be deemed to have passed unless the people by a majority representing at least one-third of those entitled to vote veto (vote against) the Bill. In other words, unless the required number of votes is cast against the Bill, it will be regarded as having passed. For example, if 50 per cent of the electorate votes, and 51

per cent of those voting vote against, the Bill would nonetheless pass as the number of "no" votes is lower than one-third of the entire electorate. (To date, Art.27 has never been used.)
- The President may, at his or her own discretion, appoint up to seven members of the Council of State (Art.31.3). (The other members of the Council need not be consulted in relation to such appointments).

ACCOUNTABILITY AND IMPEACHMENT

In respect of the performance of his or her powers and functions, the President is not answerable to the Oireachtas or to the courts (Art.13.8). In *O'Malley v An Taoiseach* [1990] I.L.R.M. 461, Hamilton P., while agreeing that the distribution of TDs between electoral constituency boundaries breached the terms of the Constitution, declined to prevent the President from dissolving the Dáil on the advice of the Taoiseach, on the basis that the courts could not interfere in the President's functions.

This does not mean, however, that every decision formally made by the President is exempt from judicial review. In *State (Walshe) v Murphy* [1981] I.R. 275 a question arose as to whether a judge had been validly appointed to his role. Judges are formally appointed by the President, but on the advice of the Government. The High Court noted that Art.13.8 prevented the President from being "made or forced to answer or give account of his conduct" to the Oireachtas or the courts. This challenge, however, did not involve making the President account for or explain his role in appointing the judge. The issue was whether the judge met the requirements for appointment. The Court also pointed out that the President formally performs many functions on the advice of the Government. While the law formally requires the President's intervention, in fact it is the Government that decides. In such cases, the President has no discretion to act otherwise. If all such decisions were immune from challenge, the Court noted, the Government would be free to act in breach of the Constitution in a multiplicity of areas, without the prospect of court review, a proposition that the court rejected. The Court thus concluded that it was possible to review the judicial appointment.

The President may be impeached and removed from office for stated misbehaviour. For this purpose, one House of the Oireachtas (acting on the basis of at least a two-thirds majority) must lay a charge before the other House, which that latter House will then investigate. The President may only be removed by a vote of two-thirds or more of the members of the latter House. (See Art.12.10).

The President's salary cannot be diminished while he or she is in office, the purpose being to protect the President from being driven out of office by salary cuts.

THE COUNCIL OF STATE

The Council of State is a body that advises the President on matters relating to the performance of his or her discretionary powers (Art.31). In certain cases, the President is obliged to seek the Council's advice before acting. In every such case, however, the President is entitled to accept or reject this advice as she he or sees fit. While obliged to seek the advice of the Council, he or she is not required to follow such advice.

The Council of State consists of the following persons:

- The current Taoiseach, Tánaiste, Chief Justice of the Supreme Court, the Presidents of the Court of Appeal and High Court, the Attorney General, and the Chairpersons (the Ceann Comhairle and Cathaoirleach respectively) of Dáil and Seanad Éireann.
- Every past President, Taoiseach, Chief Justice and Prime Minister of the Irish Free State ("President of the Executive Council") still willing and able to sit on the Council.
- Up to seven persons nominated by the President at his or her sole discretion.

While the President is generally required to consult with the Council on most matters that are within his or her discretion, he or she is not obliged to consult with the Council regarding a decision not to dissolve the Dáil where the Taoiseach has lost the support of a majority in that House or in relation to the President's nomination of seven members of the Council of State.

ARTICLE 14

In a case where the President is either unable or unwilling to perform his or her functions, such functions and powers may be exercised by a Commission established under Art.14 of the Constitution. This Commission consists of the Chief Justice of the Supreme Court and the Chairpersons of the Dáil and Seanad respectively. The Commission may act, for instance, where the President is deceased, permanently or temporarily incapacitated, absent from the State, or otherwise simply unable or unwilling to perform his or her functions.

The Oireachtas

The Oireachtas is the National Parliament, the body charged with creating laws for the State. It consists of the President and two Houses, Dáil Éireann (the Lower House, described in the Constitution as the "House of Representatives") and Seanad Éireann (the Upper House, also called the "Senate"). Generally, the role of the President is confined to signing and promulgating (putting forward as law) legislation passed by the two Houses. The respective powers of each House are considered below in Ch.10.

THE EXCLUSIVE POWERS OF THE OIREACHTAS: ONLY THE OIREACHTAS MAY MAKE LAWS

Article 15.2 states that only the Oireachtas may create laws: "The sole and exclusive power of making laws for the State is hereby vested in the Oireachtas; no other legislative authority has power to make laws for the State." Article 29.6, furthermore, prevents an international agreement from changing Ireland's domestic laws without the consent of the Oireachtas. In other words, an international convention will only become part of Irish law where an Act of Parliament has been enacted incorporating that agreement into national law (see above at pp.39–42).

There is one important exception to this principle. Article 29.4.6° and the European Communities Act 1972 effectively allow the European Union to make laws that apply directly in this State, notwithstanding the provisions of Art.15.2. (See above at pp.42–45).

The rule that only the Oireachtas may make laws has important ramifications. It means that neither the Government nor the courts can "usurp" (take over) this role by making laws themselves.

JUDGES' RELUCTANCE TO ENGAGE IN LAW-MAKING

Much of the case law on this point addresses the reluctance of the courts to make policy or law for the State. Indeed, the Supreme Court has regularly observed that it is not the courts' job to make new laws. In practice, it must be acknowledged that the courts' role in interpreting laws, in reviewing their constitutionality and, in particular, in developing the common law and equity significantly shape the content of the law. According to the "declaratory theory", however, the courts in so doing are simply discovering or declaring what the law is, and are not "making" new law.

The Supreme Court noted in *Norris v Attorney General* [1984] I.R. 36 that it does not engage in law reform. In other words, the courts consider that in performing their functions, they are limited to stating what the law is, rather than what it ought to be. Thus, in *McGrath v McDermott* [1988] I.L.R.M. 647, the Supreme Court refused to accept that it could "add to or delete from" legislative provisions with a view to closing off loopholes in the tax code. To do so, it said, would involve altering the law of the State, a function that is reserved solely to the Oireachtas.

In *Maher v Attorney General* [1973] I.R. 140, the Supreme Court considered the constitutionality of Oireachtas legislation stipulating that the results of a blood sample taken from a person alleged to be driving having taken more than the permitted level of alcohol would be "conclusive evidence" of the driver's guilt. This meant that such evidence simply had to be accepted by the judge and could not be tested in a court of law. The Supreme Court considered that this was unconstitutional, as it obstructed the courts' role in determining the facts of a case as well as in determining the guilt or innocence of specific defendants in criminal cases.

The Court furthermore rejected the suggestion that it should read the legislation as if the term "conclusive" was absent therefrom. While this might have cured the legislation of its unconstitutionality, it would have amounted to an invasion of the Oireachtas' role in making (and changing) legislation. While the courts may interpret (determine the meaning) of legislation, they are not entitled to change its meaning outright. The courts may only sever an unconstitutional provision from legislation where what is left behind represents the will of the Oireachtas. In this case, it could not be said that the operation of the clause with the offending words removed from the text would represent the will of parliament.

State (Murphy) v Johnston [1983] I.R. 235 clearly establishes that a court cannot change legislation so as to rectify even an obvious error in such measures. In this case, the High Court refused to amend legislation so as to alter a mistake in cross-referencing between sections, ruling that only the Oireachtas had the power to alter legislation in this manner.

This reluctance on the part of the courts to fix legislation is mirrored in *C.C. v Ireland* [2006] IESC 33. There the Supreme Court struck down a law banning sexual intercourse with a girl under the age of 15, on the grounds that the law did not afford a defence of mistake as to the age of the girl. Having so ruled, the Court declined to issue an order in terms that would have upheld the relevant section subject to the inclusion of such a defence. This, Hardiman J. ruled, would have involved the Court in "a process akin to legislation", which was the job not of the courts but of the legislature. Given also that there were a variety of ways in which such a defence might be framed, the Court felt it was inappropriate for them to choose how the defence would be introduced.

Behind this reluctance lies a democratic imperative. The People of Ireland elect TDs (and indirectly elect Senators) to make laws and policy for the State. If they do not approve of the policy made by those legislators, the People are free to remove the latter at subsequent elections. By contrast, judges are not elected and remain, moreover, independent in the performance of their roles. They, quite rightly, cannot be removed for making a decision of which the People disapprove. Many commentators thus argue that judges should leave policy-making to the elected Parliament. The courts have regularly remarked that it is the Oireachtas' role to make law and have criticised it for failing to make law on socially controversial and complex matters such as abortion and surrogacy (see for instance, *Attorney General v X* [1992] 1 I.R. 1, *OR v An tArd Chláraitheoir* [2014] IESC 60.)

THE GOVERNMENT'S ROLE IN DELEGATED LEGISLATION

Every year the Government ("Executive") passes hundreds of "statutory instruments", ministerial orders that supplement rules laid down in Acts of Parliament. Acts of Parliament regularly give Government Ministers and others the power to make such "secondary legislation". Such instruments are generally technical in nature, containing considerable detail on matters that the Oireachtas might not have sufficient time to consider.

The question that arises in this context is whether the making of such instruments involves engaging in making laws, something that only the Oireachtas may do under Art.15.2. It has been held in the courts that the Government may continue to make statutory instruments provided that two conditions are met:

- The statutory instrument must follow the law as set out in the Act of Parliament, seeking to implement the principles and policies set out by the Oireachtas. This is called the "principles and policies" test.
- The statutory instrument must not attempt to "change, amend or repeal" the law as set out in an Act of Parliament.

THE "PRINCIPLES AND POLICIES" TEST

In *Cityview Press v An Comhairle Oiliúna (AnCO)* [1980] I.R. 381, the question arose as to whether the Oireachtas could delegate certain powers to the defendant body, AnCO, which was at that time responsible for training people for work in various industries. The legislation in question, the Industrial Training Act 1967, had allowed AnCO to set and impose certain levies on industry to help pay for this training. The plaintiff complained that only the Oireachtas could set and impose such levies.

In the Supreme Court, O'Higgins C.J. outlined the appropriate test as being "whether that which is challenged as an unauthorised delegation of parliamentary power is more than a mere giving effect to principles and policies which are contained in the statute itself." Casey has described this rule as requiring that the Oireachtas "may delegate a power to put flesh on the bones of an Act; but anything going beyond this will be constitutionally suspect." (James Casey, *Constitutional Law in Ireland*, 3rd edn (Dublin: Round Hall, 2000) at p.225.)

A power may therefore be delegated by the legislature where it involves no more than the mere "giving effect" to principles and policies already contained in primary legislation made by the Oireachtas. In other words, the Government and other agencies are empowered only to fill in the fine details of legislation based on and following clearly prescribed pre-existing principles and policies laid down by the Oireachtas.

In *Cityview Press* itself, the Supreme Court ruled that the powers conferred on AnCO by the Act were in keeping with the Constitution. Applying the principles and policies test, the Supreme Court concluded that, in setting and collecting these levies, AnCO was merely following the policy of Parliament and not setting policy on its own. The policy of the State was that employers should pay for the training of workers. AnCO was merely giving effect to this policy.

In *Re Article 26 and the Health (Amendment) (No. 2) Bill 2004* [2005] IESC 7, the Supreme Court (while striking down the Bill for other reasons) upheld the delegation of power to the Minister for Health to make regulations for the future imposition of charges for nursing home care. The Bill allowed the Minister, subject to certain exceptions, to set charges for such care, effectively affording her discretion as to the level of fees to be set. The Supreme Court concluded that this constituted "no more than the implementation of the principles and policies contained in the Act" and was thus permissible. A power given to the CEO of a Health Board to waive or reduce charges in cases of hardship was also upheld.

In *Bederev v Ireland* [2016] IESC 34 the Supreme Court considered a law that allowed the Government, by order, to deem certain substances to be controlled drugs for the purpose of the Misuse of Drugs Act 1977. This meant that it would be an offence to possess such drugs with intent to sell them. The Court of Appeal found that the law infringed the principles and policies test, as it considered that there was insufficient guidance in the Act to constrain the Government. The Act had given the Government law-making powers in the absence of appropriate principles and policies and thus had given the Government too much latitude to ban new drugs.

The Supreme Court, however, overturned the Court of Appeal verdict, ruling that it was possible, reading the whole Act (including the Schedule to the Act) to determine sufficient principles and policies for the Government's guidance. In particular, the Schedule to the Act listed various controlled drugs that were banned. Charlton J. suggested that, in seeking to determine the principles on which a new drug might be banned, the Government should look to the entire enactment "to find the boundaries to the power to add new substances." Specifically, individual sections and the Schedule "describe[d] and delimit[ed] the kind of drugs needing control." The overall import of the Act was that only drugs dangerous to human health and subject to abuse could be added to the list of controlled drugs. The Court also took into account the fact that all orders under the Act had to be laid before each House of the Oireachtas. Either House could annul such regulations. This meant that the measures were subject to democratic oversight and scrutiny. Therefore, according to the Supreme Court, the relevant provision was not unconstitutional, as it was possible to identify sufficient principles and policies in the Act to guide and constrain the Government's actions.

On the other side of this line stands *Laurentiu v Minister for Justice, Equality and Law Reform* [1999] 4 I.R. 26. In this case the Supreme Court ruled that in determining the criteria upon which non-EU nationals could be deported from the State, the Minister for Justice was in fact making policy, rather than merely giving effect to principles and policies contained in the Aliens Act 1935. The legislature, in passing the Act, conferred on the Minister a general power to make provision for the exclusion and deportation of foreign nationals. In this case there were simply no principles or policies in the legislation for the Minister to follow. The Minister was effectively given the bare power to create these policies himself. This, the Court concluded, was unconstitutional. (See also the High Court decision in *McDaid v Sheehy* [1991] 1 I.R. 1)

In *John Grace Fried Chicken Ltd. v. Catering J.L.C.* [2011] IEHC 277, the High Court considered legislation that permitted the Labour Court to make Employment Regulation Orders (EROs) applicable to various employment sectors. This legislation set out minimum terms and conditions, and minimum wage levels for workers in those sectors. The High Court (Feeney J.) found that the relevant Acts contained no principles or policies to provide guidance in the creation approval of the EROs. In particular, the Acts were silent on the factors to be taken into account in making the EROs.

Similarly, in *McGowan v Labour Court* [2013] IESC 21, the Supreme Court found that the provisions of Pt III of the Industrial Relations Act 1946 were unconstitutional. Part III had provided for the registration and enforcement of registered employment agreements. Once registered, these apply to all businesses in a sector, even if they had not all been party to the original agreement. The Supreme Court found that Pt III granted unlimited law-making power in the absence of direct statutory guidance on how such power should be exercised. The Act, moreover, did not provide sufficient principles or policies to guide the exercise of the power of registration or to limit or direct the exercise of power.

The overall impression emerges that the Oireachtas enjoys relatively wide latitude in delegating its powers. Provided it has set out some overarching policies or principles that the delegate has to follow, the delegation will be upheld. It is clear, nonetheless, that where an Act contains minimal or no principles or policies, leaving a Minister to his or her own devices, the measure will more than likely be unconstitutional.

CHANGING, AMENDING OR REPEALING LEGISLATION

In making statutory instruments, the Government is generally prohibited from changing, amending or repealing (reversing outright) any law set down by the Oireachtas in an Act of Parliament. Its responsibility is to administer and implement the law as set out by Parliament. Because the Oireachtas has the sole power to make laws, a Minister cannot in a statutory instrument alter or repeal parts of an Act of Parliament. This principle is subject to the exception noted below in respect of statutory instruments implementing EU law.

On the basis of this general principle, the courts have read Acts of Parliament granting delegated powers to Ministers in a manner that prevents the Ministers from altering the original Act or removing rights conferred by the Act. In two cases, the Supreme Court held that the relevant Acts were constitutionally valid, but that the relevant Ministers had acted outside of their powers ("ultra vires") in attempting to remove rights conferred by Acts of Parliament.

In *Cooke v Walsh* [1984] I.R. 710, the Supreme Court ruled that an Act of Parliament that allowed a Minister to make statutory instruments did not entitle the Minister to take away a right that a citizen enjoyed under the Act. In that case, the Minister for Health attempted to deprive the plaintiff of free medical care to which he was entitled under the Health Act 1970. The Supreme Court held that, by so acting, the Minister had attempted to alter a right conferred by Act of Parliament, something that he was not entitled to do. Likewise, in *Harvey v Minister for Social Welfare* [1990] 2 I.R. 232, the Supreme Court ruled that the Minister for Social Welfare could not by statutory instrument reverse the plaintiff's entitlement to certain social welfare payments. As that right was guaranteed by a law created by the Oireachtas, the Minister could not alter the plaintiff's right to such payments.

A positive decision by the Government never to enforce an Act of Parliament that has not yet been terminated by Parliament itself would, according to McCarthy J. in *Norris v Attorney General* [1984] I.R. 36, be unconstitutional. The Government is, after all, not entitled to "repeal" a law, that is, to suspend or terminate its operation, this being within the exclusive powers of the Oireachtas. For instance, in *Hoey v Minister for Justice* [1994] 3 I.R. 329, Lynch J. concluded that it was not possible for a Minister to exempt a local authority from a duty expressly conferred on it by an Act of Parliament.

In *Duggan v An Taoiseach* [1989] I.L.R.M. 710, a Government decision not to collect any taxes imposed under the Farm Tax Act 1985 was found to be in breach of Art.15.2. As the Act was still in force, the unilateral decision of the Government not to collect these taxes amounted to an unconstitutional attempt to alter the legislative will of the Oireachtas. It could not be repealed by Government action or, for that matter inaction.

DELEGATED LEGISLATION AND THE IMPLEMENTATION OF EU LAW

Special considerations apply to domestic measures implementing EU law. In many cases, measures passed by the European Union (such as EU Regulations) are directly applicable and automatically become part of Irish law on enactment by the EU. Nonetheless, some EU legislation (such as Directives) requires Ireland to take steps to implement the measures and make them part of Irish domestic law. In many cases, this is done by means of a statutory instrument made by a Minister. Section 3 of the European Communities Act 1972 allows a Minister to implement an EU measure by means of statutory instruments. In doing so the Minister is permitted to vary, alter or repeal any inconsistent piece of legislation, as he or she sees fit (see s.3(2)). Such measures have "statutory effect" (the same force as an Act of Parliament). Likewise, the European Communities Act 2007 allows powers to create statutory instruments contained in Acts of Parliament other than the 1972 Act to be used to give effect to EU law in a manner similar to s.3 of the 1972 Act. This can be done where the Act in question deals with substantially the same topic covered in the relevant EU measure. Does this approach offend the doctrine of the separation of powers?

Because EU law prevails over Irish law, the State has no choice but to give effect to EU law in preference to conflicting domestic measures. (See the discussion of EU law and Art.29.4 above in Ch.6). It appears, therefore, that the implementation of EU law may be achieved by statutory instrument provided that the Minister is merely giving effect to principles and policies contained in the parent EU legislation. In *Meagher v Minister for Agriculture* [1994] 1 I.R. 329, the Supreme Court concluded that this method of implementing EU law in Ireland, including the power to amend Acts of Parliament to give effect to EU law, was constitutionally permitted. In most cases, Directives and certainly EC Regulations are clear as to the principles and policies involved. The State usually is involved only in giving effect to these principles, for which purpose a statutory instrument is perfectly sufficient. Given the volume of EU legislation that is passed each year, it would be impractical to require the Oireachtas to pass Acts of Parliament to give statutory effect to all of these EU provisions, particularly given that EU law might leave no policy matters for further decision. Where, however, the EU legislation itself leaves to the Member States a discretion to create certain new principles and policies that go beyond the scope of what EU law requires, an Act of Parliament may be required for the State to exercise such a discretion. Otherwise, a Minister would be making principles and policies, in breach of the principles and policies test.

The Supreme Court further clarified this verdict in *Maher v Minister for Agriculture* [2001] 2 I.R. 139, observing that statutory instruments were not always sufficient for the implementation of EU law. *Maher* concerned the manner of implementation into Irish law of an EC milk quota Regulation. The State decided to implement the EU Regulation by means of a statutory instrument. The plaintiff argued that the method of implementation contravened Art.15.2. The Supreme Court ruled, however, that in passing this statutory instrument, the Minister was in fact doing no more than giving effect to the principles already contained in the EU measure. "The choices as to policy", Keane C.J. observed, "... have in truth been reduced to vanishing point".

The Court clarified, however, that Art.29.4.6° did not of itself justify the use of statutory instruments for the purpose of giving effect to EU law. In sum, a statutory instrument may be used only when the instrument is implementing policies fully contained in the EU measure, and not where the EU measure leaves certain important policy decisions to the Member State. In the latter case, an Act of Parliament would be necessary in order to create new policy not contained in the EU legislation.

LAW-MAKING BY REFERENCE

In *Leontjava and Chang v DPP* [2004] 1 I.R. 591 the Supreme Court considered s.2 of the Immigration Act 1999, which purported to give certain statutory instruments made by the Government on foot of the Aliens Act 1935 the same effect as an Act of Parliament. The Supreme Court upheld this approach, and concluded that the Oireachtas is entitled to make legislation by reference to material not contained in the body of the Act itself, giving the force of law to documents external to the Act. The Court observed that the sole power of making legislation for the State lies, by virtue of Art.15.2 of the Constitution, with the Oireachtas. The Constitution grants the Oireachtas a wide latitude in adopting whatever legislation it deems appropriate in the circumstances. Where the Oireachtas has clearly and unequivocally stated that a particular instrument should have the force of law in the State, it is entitled to have such an effect. Thus the decision to incorporate the provisions of statutory instruments by reference to them rather than by verbatim reproduction of their contents in the Act was a decision that the Oireachtas was entitled to make.

THE *SHEEHAN* PRINCIPLE: DELAYING THE COMING INTO FORCE OF LEGISLATION

When a piece of legislation is passed by the Oireachtas, and signed by the President, it is quite common to make the coming into force of that legislation conditional upon an Order made by a Government Minister. This is called commencement of the legislation, the idea being that the Act does not have the force of law until the relevant provision is commenced by a Government Minister. This is designed to allow the Government time to prepare for the full impact of the Act in question. So, what happens if the Minister refuses to bring the relevant Order into force, or if he or she otherwise unreasonably delays in putting the Act into operation?

This issue was considered in *State (Sheehan) v Government of Ireland* [1987] I.R. 550. In this case the Oireachtas had enacted s.60 of the Civil Liability Act 1961, in order to change an old anomaly in the common law of negligence. The Government was empowered by the Act to bring the measure into force as and when it saw fit. Up to the date of the judgment, it had not brought the relevant legislation into force. In 1987, Sheehan unsuccessfully attempted to get the Supreme Court to force the Government to pass the necessary Order. The Supreme Court ruled, based on the wording of the Act, that the Government was entitled to delay the Order indefinitely, even though this arguably involved the effective reversal of legislative policy. Nonetheless, the Court concluded that the Government had a full, unfettered discretion as to when the measure would become operative.

PARLIAMENTARY PRIVILEGE

Articles 15.10, 15.12 and 15.13 afford certain rights and freedoms to the Houses of Parliament and their members. These provisions are broadly based on measures found in the Bill of Rights 1689, which reflected an agreement between, on the one hand, King William III and Queen Mary, and on the other hand, the British Parliament. The purpose of these measures was to confirm the rights of Parliament, and to prevent the monarchy from abridging those rights by, for instance, penalising members in respect of their utterances, or preventing them from attending Parliament, as previous monarchs had done.

POWER OF THE HOUSES TO REGULATE THEIR INTERNAL OPERATION

Article 15.10 allows each House of Parliament to make and administer its own rules. Where these rules are broken, each House may impose penalties on its members. This gives each House a power to control its internal operation. Nonetheless, the courts may supervise the exercise of these internal powers in certain circumstances, in particular to ensure that fair procedures are being followed. In *Callely v Moylan* [2014] IESC 26 a majority of the Supreme Court ruled that a senator could challenge a penalty imposed on him by a Seanad Committee for alleged wrongdoing. In doing so, the Supreme Court rejected the State's claim that the workings of the Seanad's disciplinary proceedings were not subject to court review. The majority pointed out that, in the absence of an express exemption, the courts had the power to ensure that disciplinary proceedings were carried out in compliance with principles of constitutional justice. It seems, therefore, that where the constitutional rights of an individual, including a member of a House of the Oireachtas, are at stake, the court has power to ensure the Constitution is being observed. In particular, where the operations of the House potentially impinge on the rights of those who are not members of either House, the courts are not so reticent to intervene. In both *Re Haughey* [1971] I.R. 217 and *Maguire v Ardagh* [2002] 2 I.R. 385, the procedures of Oireachtas committees were scrutinised to ensure that the personal rights of non-members were observed, the Supreme Court concluding in each case that fair procedures had not been observed.

On the other hand, where a House of the Oireachtas is directly exercising its law-making power, the courts will be more reluctant to intervene in that process. For instance, in *O'Malley v Ceann Comhairle of the Dáil* [1997] 1 I.R. 427, the High Court declined to hear a challenge to a decision of the Ceann Comhairle (Speaker of the Dáil) to alter a question posed by a TD. Because of the constitutional separation of powers, the Court was unwilling to intervene in the Dáil's internal machinery of debate. It appears, therefore, that the courts draw a distinction between a House's internal operation as it relates to the process of making law (where the courts are reluctant to intervene) and other functions and powers conferred on the House (where the courts will more readily intervene to uphold constitutional rights).

Article 15.10 also affords to each House a "power" to "protect its official documents and the private papers of its members, and to protect itself and its members against any person or persons interfering with, molesting or attempting to corrupt its members in the exercise of their duties." The nature and extent of this power was considered in *Howlin v Morris* [2004] 2 I.L.R.M. 53, [2006] I.L.R.M. 440 where the Supreme Court noted that Art.15.10 confers a power on each House of the Oireachtas to pass resolutions protecting the private papers of its members. This right, however, was the right of the House, rather than that of individual members. This right, moreover, was not self-executing: it required a formal enactment of rules by the relevant House, expressly invoking the power and setting out the conditions for the protection of the papers. Neither the Dáil nor the Seanad had enacted such express rules in order to assert this power. The Houses of the Oireachtas would only be entitled to withhold their members' papers from a tribunal or court where the relevant House had clearly and expressly invoked the power to do so.

Parliamentary privilege in respect of utterances

Articles 15.12 and 15.13 protect every TD and Senator in respect of utterances made in either House. Such utterances are privileged. They also privilege the Official Reports and publications of the Oireachtas or of either House. This means that a Member of Parliament cannot be sued, prosecuted, or otherwise brought before a court of law in respect of such comments on the grounds, for instance, that they were defamatory (i.e. libelled or slandered a person), breached confidentiality, or incited to hatred contrary to hate speech legislation. The TD or Senator may be made to answer to the House for such comments, but not to any external body such as a court or tribunal. This privilege applies to the statement "wherever published", which means that the verbatim republication of the statement by parties outside the House (e.g. in a newspaper or on radio) is also privileged provided, of course, that the statement was first made in the Dáil or the Seanad. According to Budd J. in *An Blascaod Mór Teo v Commissioners for Public Works (No. 4)* [2000] 3 I.R. 565, this privilege is designed to safeguard freedom of speech in the Oireachtas, and to ensure free debate in each House. In that case, Budd J. concluded that a Minister could not be faulted in a court of law for allegedly misleading the Dáil.

In *Ahern v Mahon* [2008] 4 I.R. 704 the High Court concluded that Art.15.13 meant that TD and Senators could not be made to answer to a tribunal of inquiry in relation to statements made in either House. It was thus not possible to interrogate a TD or Senator about inconsistences between statements made inside and outside the House, with a view to demonstrating that the statement made inside the House was misleading. While the tribunal could reproduce the statement made in parliament, it could not inquire into whether such statements were true or suggest that such statements were false or misleading.

The privilege is restricted to statements made in either House, though the privilege also applies where such a statement (first made in either house) is repeated or published outside the Oireachtas. If a member of either House voluntarily, consciously, and deliberately repeats the same comments outside the House in circumstances where it was clear he or she was consciously abandoning the privilege, this would amount to a waiver of their right to immunity, thus removing privilege in respect of those comments. However, in *Attorney General v Hamilton (No. 2)* [1993] 3 I.R. 227 a majority of the Supreme Court concluded that an elaboration on Dáil statements before the Tribunal (before which the TDs were compelled to testify) did not constitute a waiver of the privilege in respect of the TDs' sources. The TDs, indeed, had expressly stated that they did not wish to waive their privilege. The Tribunal could thus not compel the TDs to reveal the sources of information upon which the TDs made statements in the Dáil. By the same token, however, a member of either House cannot confer privilege on himself in respect of a comment first made outside the House, simply by subsequently repeating it in the House.

In *Kerins v McGuinness* [2017] IEHC 34 the High Court rejected a claim for damages brought by a person who appeared before and was questioned by the Public Accounts Committee (a Dáil committee) relating to the operation of a charity. Kerins claimed she had been subjected to unfair treatment before the committee, including lengthy, derogatory questioning. The High Court concluded that Art.15.12 and 15.13 meant that the committee members' questions to and comments about the plaintiff could not be the subject of court proceedings. This was necessary to ensure freedom of speech within Parliament. The responsibility for ensuring that the questioning was fair lay with the Oireachtas, not the courts. Notably, Kerins had not been compelled to attend the Committee, and no findings were made in respect of her work.

Likewise, in *O'Brien v Clerk of Dáil Éireann* [2017] IEHC 179 the plaintiff unsuccessfully sought to challenge certain comments made by members of the Dáil on the floor of the House. The plaintiff claimed that these statements injured his good name and breached the *sub judice* rule as they concerned matters then before the courts. In the High Court, Ó Raifeartaigh J. ruled that she could not interfere as Art.15 put parliamentary utterances beyond judicial scrutiny. The question as to whether the TDs had acted inappropriately was one for the Dáil, not the courts. (Both *O'Brien* and *Kerins* have been appealed to the Supreme Court).

Protecting sources

No TD or Senator can be forced in either a court of law or tribunal to reveal the sources of information used by him or her in parliamentary debates. Nor can the Deputy or Senator be penalised in any way for invoking the privilege. In *Attorney General v Hamilton (No. 2)* [1993] 3 I.R. 227, the Supreme

Court ruled that Dáil Deputies who had made allegations in the Dáil based on information from external sources could not be forced to disclose those confidential sources to the Beef Tribunal. O'Flaherty J. observed that, were they to be forced to reveal their sources, or penalised for not doing so, this would effectively be in breach of Art.15.13.

Privilege from arrest

Article 15.13 prevents the arrest or detention (otherwise than for treason, a felony (an indictable offence), or breach of the peace) of a Member of Parliament in certain circumstances. These circumstances are where the member is going to, is returning from, or is within the precincts of either House of the Oireachtas, the purpose again being to ensure that Oireachtas members' right of free speech and right to vote are not curtailed through arrest. On a strict interpretation, however, this does not necessarily prevent a member from being charged with an offence, provided he or she is not arrested in or on the way to or from the Oireachtas.

The powers of Oireachtas committees

In *Maguire v Ardagh* [2002] 1 I.R. 385, the Oireachtas had set up a special sub-committee to inquire into and make findings of fact in relation to the tragic circumstances surrounding the shooting dead of John Carthy by Gardaí in Abbeylara in April 2000. While the sub-committee's findings would have no direct legal effect, there was nonetheless the possibility that a finding of unlawful killing might be made, which might reflect adversely on the Gardaí. Certain members of the Gardaí, having been compelled to attend as witnesses, challenged the constitutional standing of the Committee, arguing that the Oireachtas did not have the inherent power to establish such a committee.

The Supreme Court, by a majority, agreed, concluding that the Oireachtas did not have any inherent general power to set up an investigative committee of this nature. There was neither an express nor an implied power within the Constitution permitting the Oireachtas to do so. While the UK Parliament and US Congress have inherent powers to investigate a range of matters, by 1922 such powers were largely discredited, and had led to legislation allowing independent tribunals of inquiry to investigate such matters. Considering the historical context, a majority of the Supreme Court was satisfied that the Oireachtas had not inherited any inherent power of investigation into events or matters of public interest.

Some of the judges acknowledged that the Oireachtas had limited powers to inquire into certain matters with a view to assisting in the constitutional functions of the House. In particular, the power of the Oireachtas to inform itself with a view to assisting in the process of making legislation is broadly accepted. The sole purpose of the Abbeylara inquiry, however, was to establish the facts surrounding an admittedly very serious incident. This was beyond the inherent powers of the Oireachtas.

The Court noted, in particular, that the powers of the Oireachtas did not encompass the power to make findings of fact that could potentially damage the good name of persons who were not members of either House. Although the sub-committee could not penalise a person in respect of any wrongdoing, the findings of the sub-committee as to culpability were nonetheless capable of damaging the good name of a person. (This is protected by Art.40.3.2° of the Constitution). The Oireachtas did not have such a general investigative power. In a similar vein, some of the judges expressed concern about the potential for politicisation of such inquiries, given that elected politicians presided over such inquiries, and that such politicians may have a vested interest in discrediting the Government or, alternatively, shielding it from blame.

A referendum proposing to enact a Thirtieth Amendment to the Constitution was defeated in 2011. It had proposed giving each House the power to conduct inquiries into matters of general public importance, in the course of which the conduct of any person might be investigated and findings made in respect of that conduct. In this context, the Amendment had proposed to allow the Oireachtas to determine the appropriate balance between personal rights and the public interest. Although this referendum was defeated, the Oireachtas later passed the Houses of the Oireachtas (Inquiries, Privileges and Procedures) Act 2013 which gives the Oireachtas limited powers to inquire into certain matters, including wrongdoing on the part of a member of the Oireachtas.

The Dáil and the Seanad: Making Legislation

The Oireachtas consists of the President and two Houses, Dáil Éireann and Seanad Éireann. Of the two Houses of the Oireachtas, the Dáil is clearly the more powerful institution, particularly in relation to finance, legislation, and the oversight of Government.

THE DÁIL

The Dáil is the lower House of the Oireachtas. In almost all matters, it is more powerful than the Seanad. It currently has 158 members elected from 40 constituencies. There are several important constitutional principles concerning the conduct of a Dáil election (see generally Art.16).

VOTING

- Any citizen of Ireland, not otherwise disqualified from voting and aged 18 or over, may vote in a Dáil election. A person must be ordinarily resident in Ireland and registered in order to vote. Most voters must vote in person at a polling station, but legislation allows some categories of person (including people with a disability) to vote by post. That said, there is no *constitutional* right to vote by post (see *Draper v Attorney General* [1984] I.R. 277, *Breathnach v Ireland* [2001] 3 I.R. 230).
- The Electoral (Amendment) Act 2006 allows prisoners to exercise the right to vote by postal ballot. Prior to 2006, while prisoners had a right to vote, in practice they had no way of doing so as they were not released to vote, and could not vote by post. (See decision of the European Court of Human Rights in *Hirst v United Kingdom* (No. 2) (2006) 42 E.H.R.R. 41).
- The Constitution (under the Ninth Amendment to the Constitution 1984) also allows legislation to confer a right to vote on non-Irish citizens resident in Ireland. Under this provision, the right to vote in Dáil elections has been extended to British citizens living in Ireland (on the basis of reciprocal rights being granted to Irish citizens living in the UK).
- There may be no more than one TD for every 20,000 of the population but no fewer than one TD for every 30,000.

- While absolute equality is not required, representation must be as equal as practicable throughout the State. In *O'Donovan v Attorney General* [1961] I.R. 114, the High Court ruled that Art.16.2 had been breached because the number of TDs per head of population in rural constituencies was significantly greater than that in urban constituencies.
- Constituency boundaries generally must be reconsidered after each census, to ensure equal Dáil representation throughout the State. Failing that, the constituencies must be revised at least once every 12 years. Where the census demonstrates a significant change in the distribution of population, the Oireachtas is obliged to revise the constituencies. In *Murphy and McGrath v Minister for the Environment* [2007] IEHC 185, Clarke J. observed that where census results revealed a clear disparity in the representation of constituencies, there is a duty on the Oireachtas to act urgently to cure the inequality in representation. In that case, however, the judge ruled that it would not have been practically possible for the Oireachtas to act in the very short time between the publication of the 2006 census results and the calling of the 2007 general election.
- Constituencies must consist of no fewer than three seats.
- Voting must proceed by proportional representation. Voters rank the candidates in order of preference. Two attempts to remove this requirement, in 1959 and 1968 respectively, were defeated in referendums.
- Voting must proceed by secret ballot. In *McMahon v Attorney General* [1972] I.R. 69, a system whereby fraudulent votes could be traced and identified was declared unconstitutional on the grounds that it infringed the secrecy of the ballot box. (On the right of visually impaired people to vote by secret ballot, see *Sinnott v Minister for the Environment, Community and Local Government* [2017] IEHC 214.)

FAIRNESS IN THE CONDUCT OF ELECTIONS

While the Oireachtas is entitled, under Art.16.7, to regulate the conduct of elections, the courts retain a right to strike down conditions that infringe constitutional rights. In particular, the Constitution leans against measures that disproportionately or unfairly undermine or restrict the right to run for election.

- In *Redmond v Minister for the Environment* [2001] 4 I.R. 61, Herbert J. struck down a requirement that any person wishing to run for election had to put down a deposit of IR£300 (€381), only refundable where the candidate received a minimum number of votes. This, the court reasoned, was unconstitutional, as it struck unreasonably at the right of citizens to run for election, placing a particularly discriminatory burden on economically disadvantaged candidates.

- In *Cooney, King, Riordan and the Minister for the Environment* [2006] IESC 61, the Supreme Court struck down as disproportionate measures that required non-party candidates to be formally nominated in person by 30 electors. The Court concluded that the measures adopted were unconstitutional as they were excessively onerous on non-party candidates, and posed a real risk that a candidate might be unfairly barred from election.
- Candidates, parties and groups campaigning in elections and referendums are entitled to be treated equally by the State. It is unconstitutional for the State to favour one candidate, party or campaign over another. See *Kelly v Minister for the Environment* [2002] 4 I.R. 191, *McKenna v An Taoiseach (No. 2)* [1995] 2 I.R. 10, and *Coughlan v Broadcasting Complaints Commission* [2000] 3 I.R. 1, discussed below at pp.165–166.

Nonetheless, the Oireachtas may regulate elections, provided the relevant measures are proportionate and can be justified in the public interest. For instance, in *Ring v Attorney General* [2004] I.R. 185, Laffoy J. upheld as constitutional legislation prohibiting one person holding a dual mandate—a county councillor elected to the Dáil was thus required to give up his council seat. The judge reasoned that the objective behind this measure—to strengthen governance at local and national level—supported any restriction on the plaintiff's rights. In particular, she noted that nothing in the proposal prevented county councillors from running for the Dáil. It simply required them, if elected, to choose between one job and the other.

BY-ELECTIONS

In *Doherty v Government of Ireland* [2011] 2 I.R. 222 the High Court held that there had been an unreasonable delay in holding a by-election to fill a vacant Dáil seat in breach of the applicant's constitutional rights. The seat had been vacant for 16 months. In light of the constitutional requirement of equal representation, the Court interpreted the Electoral Act 1992 as requiring that by-elections be held within a reasonable timeframe after the vacancy arose. To do otherwise, Kearns P. reasoned, would infringe Art.16 of the Constitution, which broadly requires equal representation across Dáil constituencies. The High Court therefore read the Act, which did not contain a time limit, as necessarily requiring that a by-election be called within a reasonable time period after the vacancy arose.

MEMBERSHIP OF THE DÁIL

Article 16.2 permits only Irish citizens aged 21 or over to run for the Dáil. Certain office holders and persons, moreover, may not be members of the

Dáil. These include the President, sitting judges, Gardaí, members of the defence forces and persons serving a prison sentence of longer than six months. A county or city councillor or member of the Seanad, moreover, cannot simultaneously hold a Dáil seat (though they could resign their prior position on election to the Dáil).

THE SEANAD

The Seanad (Senate) is the upper House of the Oireachtas. In almost all matters, it is less powerful than the Dáil. In 2013, a referendum proposing the abolition of the Seanad and the creation of a unicameral (one chamber) Parliament was defeated by popular vote. The Seanad has 60 members, elected as follows.

- Forty-three members are drawn from five panels representing various vocational strands of national life. Under legislation, county and city councillors, incoming Dáil members and outgoing Senators elect these members. The Constitution itself, however, does not preclude these members from being elected in some other way, for instance, directly by citizens.
- The Taoiseach first elected after a General Election appoints 11 members. As a result, it is rare (though still possible) that the Government elected by the Dáil will not also have majority support in the Seanad.
- The graduates of the National University of Ireland and of the University of Dublin (Trinity College Dublin) elect three members each. While the Seventh Amendment 1979 allowed for the extension of voting rights to graduates of other educational institutions, this extension has yet to occur.

MAKING LEGISLATION

In making legislation, the Dáil is more powerful than the Seanad. Although a Bill (other than a "Money Bill" or Bill proposing to amend the Constitution) may be introduced in either House, no provision of a Bill may become law without Dáil assent. By contrast, a Bill or part of a Bill that is rejected by the Seanad can become a law, even in the face of such opposition.

In relation to the making of laws, the Dáil is clearly the more powerful House. It can veto outright any legislative proposal (or amendments to legislation) put forward by the Seanad. Proposals made by the Dáil, by contrast, may only be delayed by the Seanad and cannot be vetoed.

Article 23 permits the Seanad to delay a Bill that it opposes for only 90 days from the date on which it was first sent by the Dáil to the Seanad. Once this period expires, the Dáil may pass a resolution deeming the Bill to have been passed by both Houses of the Oireachtas. Thus, despite Seanad opposition, the Bill may become law.

Even where the Seanad rejects a Bill proposed by the Dáil, it can nonetheless be passed into law by a resolution of the Dáil. Article 23 allows the Dáil to override the Seanad's rejection of a Bill after a 90-day delay. Article 23 operates as follows:

- A Bill is introduced in the Dáil and passed by that House.
- The Bill is then sent to the Seanad, which:
  - rejects the Bill;
  - proposes amendments of which the Dáil does not approve; or
  - neither rejects nor accepts the Bill (i.e. does nothing).
- In such cases, the Bill will be delayed for 90 days, starting on the date that the Bill was first sent to the Seanad.
- After that 90-day period has expired, the Dáil may, within 180 days of that expiry, pass a resolution deeming the Bill to have been passed by both Houses (even in the face of Seanad opposition).

Thus, the Seanad is limited in its powers to reject a Bill that has been passed by Dáil Éireann. The most it can do is delay the Bill for 90 days.

"Money Bills"

In financial matters the Seanad has next to no power. The Constitution clearly considers that the directly elected Members of Parliament alone should be allowed to determine the financial policy of the State. It is worth noting that the person holding the office of Minister for Finance can only be drawn from the Dáil and not from the Seanad (Art.28.7).

A Bill that is defined as a "Money Bill", furthermore, may only be introduced in the Dáil. (See Art.21). The Seanad may only make recommendations regarding a Money Bill, which recommendations may, furthermore, be ignored by the Dáil.

Article 22 defines a "Money Bill" as any Bill dealing *only* with one or more of the following matters:

- the imposition and collection of taxes;
- the approval of public expenditure;
- the creation of a charge on public monies;
- the creation and management of public debts;
- the supply of public monies.

A good example would be the annual Finance Bill and the Appropriation Bill of each year.

A "Money Bill" may only be initiated in Dáil Éireann. The Seanad, furthermore, is entitled only to make "recommendations" regarding such a Bill, which recommendations the Dáil may safely ignore (Art.21). In addition, if the Seanad does not make recommendations within 21 days, the Bill will be deemed to have passed both Houses at the expiry of that 21-day period. The apparent reason behind these restrictions is that the Dáil, as the directly elected chamber, is considered to be the most appropriate decision-maker in relation to the public finances.

In normal circumstances, the Chairperson of Dáil Éireann decides whether a Bill is or is not a "Money Bill". The Seanad, however, if aggrieved by such a decision, may pass a resolution calling on the President to refer the issue to a "Committee of Privileges". The President may, at his or her own discretion, decide to do so, but the President is not obliged to accede to their request. If he or she does decide to establish such a committee, it will consist of an equal number of members from each House, with a Supreme Court judge as Chair. This Committee then decides, by majority vote, whether or not the Bill is a "Money Bill". Either way, the Committee's decision is final and conclusive and cannot be challenged in a court of law (Art.22).

GOVERNMENT IS RESPONSIBLE TO THE DÁIL

The Dáil has certain exclusive powers in relation to the operation of the Government. While the President officially appoints each Taoiseach, this is always on the nomination of the Dáil. In practice, then, it is the Dáil that selects each new Taoiseach (Art.13.1.1°) and that must approve his or her proposed new Government before it may take office. Most of the members of the Government must also be members of the Dáil. While the Taoiseach may appoint Senators to the Government, no more than two Senators may hold ministerial office at any one time. In addition, Senators are not eligible to be appointed as Taoiseach, Tánaiste or Minister for Finance. Each of these roles is reserved for members of the Dáil (see Art.28.7).

The Government, moreover, is responsible to the Dáil at all times in respect of its decisions and actions (Art.28.4). The Government, indeed, depends on the Dáil alone for its continued survival. If the Taoiseach loses the support of a majority of Dáil members, he or she must resign unless the President can be persuaded to dissolve the Dáil (Art.28.10). Where a Taoiseach resigns, the Government as a whole is deemed to have resigned with him or her (Art.28.11). By contrast, a Government may survive for years without the support of a majority of Senators. After all, even if the Seanad rejects a

Bill, the Dáil may override its rejection under Art.23. The Seanad, moreover, cannot remove a sitting Taoiseach under any circumstances.

THE ROLE OF DÁIL ÉIREANN IN DECLARATIONS OF WAR

It is worth noting that the Oireachtas has the exclusive right to raise an army; Art.15.6 bans the establishment and operation of any army not permitted by the Oireachtas. The Constitution does not, however, require the State to be neutral; Irish neutrality is simply a matter of Government policy. The Constitution does not prevent the State from participating in a war or siding with particular allies in a combat situation. Notably, however, Art.29.4.9° prevents the State from adopting a decision of the European Council to establish a common EU defence where that defence would include Ireland. In other words, such a decision would require a referendum.

Article 28.3.1° stipulates a specific role for the Dáil alone in relation to situations of international conflict, stating that "war shall not be declared and the State shall not participate in a war save with the assent of Dáil Éireann". In both *Horgan v Ireland* [2003] 2 I.R. 468 and *Dubsky v Government of Ireland* [2005] IEHC 442, the plaintiffs challenged the right of the Government to permit stopovers in Shannon airport by US army planes and personnel involved in respectively, the war in Iraq and the war in Afghanistan. Both litigants essentially claimed that this action amounted to a participation in wars without the consent of the Dáil. In *Horgan*, the Dáil had in fact passed a resolution indicating that while the State was not participating in the Iraq conflict, it approved of the provision to the US military of Shannon airport facilities. Noting that the decision of the Government and of the Dáil attracted the presumption of constitutionality, Kearns J. appeared to defer heavily to both bodies in refusing to intervene. The conduct of foreign policy was a matter exclusively reserved to the Government, and the declaration of war a matter solely within the remit of the Dáil. These were matters in which the courts could only interfere where there was an "egregious [outrageously reprehensible] disregard of constitutional rights and duties."

A similar conclusion prevailed in *Dubsky*, Macken J. concluding that the plaintiff had failed to discharge the burden on him of proving that the State was participating in a conflict in Afghanistan. Reflecting the decision in *Horgan*, the judge again noted that the courts would only intervene in the workings of the Dáil and the Government where the plaintiff could clearly establish a serious breach of the Constitution. For this purpose, the Court ruled that the term "war" did not include an armed conflict outside the State in which the State was not a participant.

11 The Government

The Government (or "Executive") comprises the "executive branch" of the State. The Government of the State consists of An Taoiseach (the Prime Minister), An Tánaiste (the Deputy Prime Minister), and a number of other Government Ministers. Article 28.1 allows the Government to have no fewer than seven members and no more than 15 (including the Taoiseach and Tánaiste). At present, the Government ordinarily consists of 15 members.

The nature of the executive function is vague but it broadly confers "executive responsibility" for the day-to-day governance and running of the State. The Government is, in particular, responsible for the implementation of laws passed by the Oireachtas, and is also responsible broadly for conducting Ireland's foreign relations. The Government also plays an active role in proposing new laws to the Oireachtas.

As noted above in Ch.10, the Government is responsible to Dáil Éireann. In particular, the Taoiseach is chosen by the Dáil and may ultimately be removed by the Dáil should he or she no longer command majority support in that chamber. As discussed previously, however, the courts cannot generally intervene to require the Government to perform its executive functions in a particular way. In particular, unless the Government is in clear disregard of the Constitution (in the sense of a conscious and deliberation decision to ignore the Constitution), the courts may not issue a mandatory injunction forcing the Government to exercise its functions in a particular manner or to implement a particularly policy (see *TD v Minister for Education* [2001] 4 I.R. 259).

AN TAOISEACH

The head of the Government is called the Taoiseach, also described in the Constitution as "Prime Minister". The President, on the nomination of Dáil Éireann, appoints each new Taoiseach (Art.13.1.1°). In appointing the Taoiseach, however, the President must effectively act on the instructions of the Dáil, which may only choose a Taoiseach from among its own ranks.

The Taoiseach has overall responsibility for the running of the Government. Beyond this, however, his or her precise role tends to be somewhat vague. In addition to his or her overall brief, the Taoiseach has the following specific duties and powers:

- The nomination of Government Ministers (Art.13.1.2°), including the Tánaiste (Art.28.6.1°);
- The power to ask the President to summon and dissolve the Dáil (the President may only refuse a request to dissolve the Dáil when the Taoiseach has lost the support of a majority of Dáil members; Art.13.2.2°);
- A Taoiseach first appointed after a general election must appoint 11 members of the Seanad (Art.18.3);
- The responsibility to inform the President generally concerning matters of national and international policy (Art.28.5.2°);
- The power to ask a Minister to resign and, if the request is refused, to demand that resignation (Art.28.9.4°);
- The power to nominate the Attorney General (Art.30.2);
- The Taoiseach is automatically deemed a member of the Council of State, as are all former holders of that office (Art.31); and
- The Taoiseach represents Ireland in the European Council, the body responsible for the overall policy direction of the European Union, and at intergovernmental conferences of the EU.

RESIGNATION OF THE TAOISEACH

Subject to certain conditions, a Taoiseach must resign if he or she loses the support of the majority of Dáil Éireann (Art.28.10). The Taoiseach may, however, remain in office if the President, on the Taoiseach's advice, decides to dissolve Dáil Éireann. On such dissolution the Taoiseach and his or her ministers are entitled to remain in office until such time as the Dáil has reassembled after a general election. If at that point the Taoiseach can secure the support of a majority in the Dáil, he or she need not resign at all. If, however, he or she fails to secure such a majority when the Dáil first convenes after the election, the Taoiseach must resign (Art.28.10).

The Taoiseach's resignation has the knock-on effect of terminating the appointments of all the other Government Ministers (Art.28.11). In other words, every Minister depends for his or her continued appointment on the survival of the Taoiseach. That said, the members of the Government (including the Taoiseach) may continue their duties in a care-taking capacity until such time as a new Government is appointed. Similar provisions apply to Ministers in office immediately prior to the dissolution of the Dáil. They continue to hold office until their successors are appointed.

THE APPOINTMENT OF MINISTERS

Once a new Taoiseach is appointed, he or she will ask the President to appoint Ministers to the Government (Art.13.1.2°). The Dáil must first approve such

Ministers. Only members of the Dáil may hold the positions of Taoiseach, Tánaiste and Minister for Finance (Art.28.7.1°). All other ministers must be members of the Oireachtas, either the Dáil or the Seanad, though no more than two Senators may hold ministerial office at any one time (Art.28.7.2°).

Nonetheless, it is at least theoretically possible for an unelected person to be made a Minister. The Taoiseach would first have to appoint such person as one of his or her 11 nominees to the Seanad. Once that happens, the relevant person could be given a ministerial position, as happened, for instance, to Professor James Dooge, Minister for Foreign Affairs from 1981 to 1982.

The Taoiseach may assign Ministers "portfolios", making them responsible for certain tasks or issues, and for Departments of State. The exact confines of each Department and Ministerial position can and do change from time to time, with new Taoisigh often altering the distribution of Ministerial responsibilities.

THE REMOVAL OF MINISTERS

A Minister may voluntarily resign by handing his resignation to the Taoiseach. This is then delivered to the President who, with the consent of the Taoiseach, terminates the Minister's term of office (Art.28.9.3°). The Taoiseach is also entitled to ask a Minister to resign for any reason that, to the Taoiseach, appears sufficient. If the Minister fails to accede to this request, the Taoiseach is empowered to order that the President terminate the appointment of that Minister (Art.28.9.4°). This happened in 1990, when the then Taoiseach Charles Haughey, under pressure from his Cabinet colleagues, sacked Minister Brian Lenihan Sr. following unproven allegations that the latter had sought to persuade the President not to dissolve the Dáil in 1982.

FOREIGN AFFAIRS

The Government has exclusive powers in respect of determining and implementing Irish foreign policy and in making treaties on behalf of the State. The courts have proved very reluctant to interfere in or supervise these functions, unless there is a clear disregard of the terms of the Constitution. In *Boland v An Taoiseach* [1974] I.R. 388, Fitzgerald C.J. remarked that "... the Courts have no power, either express or implied, to supervise or interfere with the exercise by the Government of its executive functions, unless the circumstances are such as to amount to a clear disregard by the Government of the powers and duties conferred upon it by the Constitution."

In exercising these powers, however, the Government cannot give away or abdicate its right to determine Irish foreign policy to an external body. In

Crotty v An Taoiseach [1987] 1 I.R. 713, the Supreme Court concluded by a majority that the State's ratification of Title III of the Single European Act, an EEC treaty, infringed the Constitution in that the Government was agreeing to give away its powers to determine foreign policy based on the common good of the Irish people, and therefore had sought to concede part of the State's sovereignty. As Henchy J. remarked, "any attempt by the Government to make a binding commitment to alienate in whole or in part to other states the conduct of foreign relations would be inconsistent with the Government's duty to conduct those relations in accordance with the Constitution." The courts were entitled to intervene to prevent this from happening.

On the other hand, in *Pringle v Government of Ireland* [2013] 3 I.R. 1 the Supreme Court ruled that the Government had not ceded its executive powers in agreeing to the European Stability Mechanism, the purpose of which is to create a rescue fund for Eurozone states in financial difficulty. The State was exercising rather than abdicating its sovereignty. As Denham C.J. remarked: "The State has not ceded policy making for the future. The State has not ceded power to another institution to enable the creation of policy in the future." There had been no transfer of sovereignty or abdication of freedom of action or to give up powers to conduct foreign relations. "Rather, it is an election by the Government of a policy in union with other States in pursuit of an identical policy."

CABINET CONFIDENTIALITY

Discussions between Government members around the Cabinet table are privileged, which is to say they must generally be kept confidential. The Government has "collective responsibility" for its actions (Art.28.4.2°). This means that it must think and act as one body. Each Minister, thus, takes personal responsibility for the decisions of the Government as a whole. If Ministers, thus, were able to reveal disagreements or conflicts in the Cabinet, it is thought that the collective responsibility of Government might thereby be undermined.

The principle of Cabinet confidentiality was confirmed in *Attorney General v Hamilton (No. 1)* [1993] 2 I.R. 250). In this case, the Beef Tribunal (inquiring into certain irregularities in the beef industry) had been questioning a Minister regarding his recollections of a Cabinet meeting. In the course of this line of questioning, the Attorney General interjected, alleging that the rule regarding Cabinet confidentiality prevented the Minister from divulging such information.

While the High Court (O'Hanlon J.) rejected this proposition, the Supreme Court on appeal ultimately affirmed that discussions at the Cabinet table between members of Government could not be divulged, even before a tribunal of inquiry. The majority's reasoning was that to allow disagreements and differences of opinion to be exposed outside the Cabinet room would undermine the collective responsibility and authority of the Government. The Court also reasoned that by rendering Cabinet discussions confidential, Government Ministers would be encouraged to give frank opinions on matters that were sensitive or controversial.

This case initially had a number of important consequences, some of which have been tempered by the enactment of the Seventeenth Amendment:

- Government Ministers could not be questioned regarding the details of Cabinet discussions, even before a court or tribunal (though see the exceptions discussed below).
- Government Ministers were precluded from revealing the substance of such discussions, even if they wanted to do so.
- Courts and tribunals were precluded from obtaining pertinent evidence where such evidence comprised of discussions at the Cabinet table, or where it related to documents prepared for or discussed at such meetings.

It is important to note that Cabinet confidentiality is a collective right of the Government rather than any individual Minister's right. An individual Minister cannot, even after he or she leaves office, waive such confidentiality. In other words, Cabinet confidentiality imposes a duty on ministers, not a right.

THE SEVENTEENTH AMENDMENT

To remedy the rigidity of this rule, the People amended the Constitution in 1997, adding the Seventeenth Amendment. This inserted a new Art.28.4.3°. While reaffirming the principle of Cabinet confidentiality, it introduces two important exceptions to its operation. Although the principle of Cabinet confidentiality remains largely intact, the High Court may lift the requirement of Cabinet confidentiality in two cases:

- On application by a tribunal of inquiry seeking information concerning Cabinet discussions. Such an application may be granted only if it is established that there is "an overriding public interest" in such disclosure. This provision applies only to a tribunal established by the Government under authorisation from the Oireachtas.
- On application by any court of law, where such disclosure is shown to be in the "interests of the administration of justice".

The Attorney General — 12

The Attorney General is the chief legal adviser to the Government on matters of law and legal opinion. Officially, the President appoints the Attorney General, but this is done on the nomination of the Taoiseach. In effect, therefore, it is the Taoiseach who chooses the occupant of the post. While the Attorney General cannot be a member of the Government (Art.30.4), his or her continued occupancy of this role depends on the continued approval of the Taoiseach. Just as the Taoiseach chooses the Attorney General, so too can the former demand the Attorney General's resignation. If the Attorney General should refuse this request, the President shall terminate the Attorney General's appointment if the Taoiseach so advises. The Attorney General also shall retire from office on the resignation of the Taoiseach, though he or she may continue to carry on the duties of the role until a successor is appointed.

In addition to his or her role advising the Government, the Attorney General may also take a case seeking to have the law (including, in particular, the Constitution) enforced. (See for instance, *Attorney General v X.* [1992] 1 I.R. 1, and the *Attorney General v Hamilton (No. 1)* [1993] 2 I.R. 250).

INDEPENDENCE

Despite his or her dependency on the Taoiseach's continued favour, the courts have clearly asserted that the Attorney General is independent of Government. In *McLoughlin v Minister for Social Welfare* [1958] I.R. 1 the Supreme Court concluded that an employee of the Chief State Solicitor's Office, a constituent part of the Attorney General's Office, was not a "government" employee for the purposes of social welfare law. In the course of his judgment, Kingsmill Moore J. observed that the Attorney General was not a servant of the Government but rather an independent Constitutional Officer. This was underlined by the fact that the Constitution provided for the forced or voluntary resignation of the Attorney, acknowledging that the Attorney may be required in certain circumstances to pursue proceedings in the face of Government opposition.

Prosecution of Offences

Article 30.3 states that all non-summary crimes and offences should be prosecuted in the name of the People. The Article applies to prosecutions other than those taken in a court responsible for trying only minor offences (generally the District Court). It was originally envisaged that the Attorney General would be primarily responsible for the taking of non-summary prosecutions. Article 30, however, provides that "some other person authorised in accordance with law" may act instead of the Attorney General. Owing to the heavy workload of the Attorney General, the Prosecution of Offences Act 1974 created the office of Director of Public Prosecutions (DPP) with responsibility for taking prosecutions against alleged offenders. Nowadays, as a result, most non-summary prosecutions are taken by the DPP, although the Attorney General retains the sole power to instigate certain types of prosecution, for instance for genocide. The DPP retains the independence enjoyed by the Attorney General in respect of such offences.

The Courts

The Constitution provides for a system of courts presided over by judges. These courts have the sole and exclusive power (subject to Art.37) to administer justice, that is, broadly speaking, to determine legal disputes. Although all courts must comply with the Constitution, constitutional challenges to legislation are heard in the High Court and, on appeal, in the Court of Appeal and Supreme Court.

THE SUPREME COURT

The Supreme Court is the highest court in the land. It operates almost exclusively as an appeal court. In fact, it only has "original jurisdiction", i.e. the exclusive right to hear a case not previously considered by another court, in two specified situations. These exceptions are laid out in Art.12.3 (the power to determine the incapacity of the President) and Art.26 (the power to review the constitutionality of Bills before they become law).

The Supreme Court consists of the Chief Justice and nine ordinary judges. Additionally, the Presidents of the Court of Appeal and High Court are members of the Supreme Court and may hear cases before that court. The court sits in chambers of three, five, or (very occasionally) seven judges. In cases concerning the constitutionality of a Bill under Art.26, at least five judges must be present.

Since the 33rd Amendment to the Constitution, the Supreme Court may select the appeals it hears. In particular, it may hear appeals from decisions of the Court of Appeal, but only where the Supreme Court is satisfied that the decision involves a matter of general public importance, or that in the interests of justice it is necessary that there be an appeal to the Supreme Court. Ordinarily, High Court appeals go to the Court of Appeal, though a case may be appealed from the High Court directly to the Supreme Court (a "leap-frog" appeal) if the Supreme Court is satisfied that there are exceptional circumstances warranting a direct appeal to it. For this to happen, the Supreme Court must be satisfied that the case involves a matter of general public importance or that it is in the interests of justice that the appeal proceed directly to the Supreme Court. No law may be enacted removing the power of the Supreme Court or Court of Appeal to hear appeals in cases involving the constitutional validity of a law.

The Court of Appeal

The Thirty-third Amendment to the Constitution in 2013 introduced a new Court of Appeal. The purpose of the Court of Appeal broadly is to reduce the workload of the Supreme Court, allowing the latter to focus on significant matters of public importance. The Court of Appeal replaces the former Court of Criminal Appeal. The Court of Appeal hears appeals from the High Court in civil matters and, in criminal matters, from the Circuit Criminal Court and Central Criminal Court (the latter being the title of the High Court when exercising its criminal jurisdiction). It consists of 10 judges (including the President) who sit in groups of three to hear cases.

The High Court

The High Court is the main court of first instance. It has full original jurisdiction to determine all judicial matters, whether of law or fact, civil or criminal (Art.34.3). In particular, the constitutionality of a law may be challenged only in the High Court and not in any other court, subject to the prospect of an appeal to the Court of Appeal or the Supreme Court. (See *People (DPP) v M.S.* [2003] 1 I.R. 606.)

Other courts

Article 34.3.4° allows for the creation of courts of local and limited jurisdiction. The two main courts in this category are the Circuit Court and the District Court.

Article 38.3 of the Constitution allows for the establishment of special courts for the trial of offences. This has occurred on three occasions since the founding of the State, with the current Special Criminal Court having been established in 1972. The key feature of the Special Criminal Court is that, instead of a jury, the accused is tried before a court which generally consists of a High Court judge, a Circuit Court judge, and a District Court judge sitting together. This means that an accused is effectively deprived, in such cases, of his or her usual right to a trial by jury. This may only be done where "the ordinary courts are deemed inadequate to secure the effective administration of justice, and the preservation of public peace and order".

JUDGES

Officially, the President formally appoints all judges under Art.35.1. In fact, all of these appointments are made on the advice of the Government, which in turn receives recommendations from the independent Judicial Appointments Advisory Board. (There are proposals to replace this with a Judicial Appointments Commission). To be eligible to serve as a judge, one must usually have served as a practising solicitor or barrister for a minimum period of time.

Article 35.5 stipulates that, during the course of his or her office, the State cannot ordinarily reduce a judge's salary. This is designed to protect the independence of the judiciary. Nonetheless, the Twenty-ninth Amendment to the Constitution allows for reductions in specific cases. In particular, where cuts are made to public sector salaries, and such cuts are stated to be in the public interest, proportionate reductions may also be made to judges' salaries. In addition, the imposition of ordinary taxes or levies on a judge's salary does not constitute a reduction for these purposes. (See *O'Byrne v Minister for Finance* [1959] I.R. 1 and Art.35.5.2°.)

When being invested as a judge, the person in question must take the oath of office laid out in Art.34.6, promising in particular to perform his or her duties "without fear or favour, affection or ill-will" towards any person. Judges, moreover, cannot simultaneously hold down any other office or paid position, including membership of either House of the Oireachtas. In *Dublin Wellwoman Centre v Ireland* [1995] 1 I.L.R.M. 408, the late Carroll J. was prevented from hearing a case relating to the right to distribute information on abortion. This was because Carroll J., as Chairperson of the Commission on the Status of Women, had made certain public representations concerning this very issue. While the Supreme Court agreed that there was no doubt that the judge herself would act completely impartially in this case, it pointed out there was a reasonable perception of objective bias that precluded her from hearing the case.

THE INDEPENDENCE OF THE JUDICIARY

Article 35.2 guarantees the independence of the judiciary, subject only to the Constitution and the law.

Buckley v Attorney General [1950] I.R. 67 concerned the ownership of funds held in the name of "Sinn Féin". The ownership of the money being in dispute, proceedings were taken in the High Court to decide which of a number of parties was entitled to the money. While these proceedings were pending, the Oireachtas passed the Sinn Féin Funds Act 1947. This Act purported to end the case and redistribute the money involved as determined by that Act. The Supreme Court ruled that this approach was unconstitutional; once a case has been initiated in the courts, only the courts may decide the outcome of the case. The intervention of the Oireachtas in this case amounted to a breach of the separation of powers and an interference with the independence of the judiciary.

In *Murphy v British Broadcasting Corporation* [2005] 3 I.R. 336, McKechnie J. concluded (despite the right to a jury conferred by Art.38.5) that contempt of court, even where non-minor, does not ordinarily require a trial by jury (though, according to other case law, some limited exceptions may apply where the matter is criminal, non-minor and the facts are in contention). He stressed that the conduct of court cases was a matter exclusively reserved to the judiciary, who were deemed independent in the performance of this function. This independence could not be maintained, he observed, if the courts "could not master their own destiny". The courts are therefore entitled to protect their integrity and dignity against unjust comment, a power that would have been undermined if they had to "cede any part of [this] self-protecting obligation to a jury".

The courts have stressed their right to determine what evidence should be heard in a case and the weight to be attached to it. In particular, legislation that deprives the courts of their role in the determination of the guilt or innocence of a person may be deemed unconstitutional. In *Murphy v Dublin Corporation* [1972] I.R. 215, the Government claimed it had an inherent right or privilege to withhold certain documents from the court. This, the court held, infringed the court's right and duty to consider all relevant evidence in a case before it, and potentially undermined its ability to achieve justice in a particular case; the courts have power to compel the production of such documents. Where a claim is made that the production of the document would be contrary to the public interest, the decision as to whether the document should be kept confidential was for the court alone to make. There was, furthermore, no class of documents that could generally be excluded from court scrutiny; judges have to decide on a case-by-case basis whether or not certain documents should be withheld on public interest grounds.

Likewise, in *Maher v Attorney General* [1973] I.R. 140 legislation that deemed a certificate to be "conclusive evidence" that a person was over the legal alcohol limit for driving was deemed unconstitutional on the basis that it deprived the court of its right to test that evidence. The legislation sought to give the certificate the final say on essential ingredients of the offence that should have been for the court to determine. As Fitzgerald C.J. concluded, "[i]n so far as the statutory provision in question here purports to remove such determination from the judges or the courts appointed and established under the Constitution, it is an invalid infringement of the judicial power".

(See, also, *Oates v Browne* [2016] IESC 7.) In the *State (McEldowney) v Kelleher* [1983] I.R. 289 a provision of an Act required the District Court to refuse an application for a permit to collect money from the public if a Garda Inspector or higher ranked officer stated on oath that he or she believed that the money would be used for unlawful purposes. This deprived the court of its power to decide on the matter, and was thus unconstitutional.

REMOVAL OF JUDGES FROM OFFICE

As a consequence of the independence of the judiciary, a judge once appointed cannot normally be removed from office until he or she retires. (Compulsory retirement ages are set by law). In particular, a judge cannot be removed for issuing a judgment considered unfavourable to the Government or Oireachtas. Article 35.4.1°, however, confers on the Oireachtas a power to remove him or her from office; this may be done only "for stated misbehaviour or incapacity, and then only upon resolutions passed by Dáil Éireann and by Seanad Éireann calling for his removal".

By contrast with Art.12.10, which lays down a relatively detailed process for the impeachment of the President, Art.35.4 is vague on the precise procedures to be applied in removing a judge. Nor is any guidance offered on the meaning of "misbehaviour" for this purpose, the point presumably being for the Oireachtas to determine in each case. In *Curtin v Dáil Éireann* [2006] 2 I.R. 556, the Supreme Court approved a process adopted by the Oireachtas for the proposed removal of a judge for alleged misbehaviour. The process required a joint committee to gather evidence, which would be presented to each House of the Oireachtas, following which each House would then separately consider a resolution to remove the judge from office. The Supreme Court concluded that it was open to the Oireachtas to adopt this particular procedure for removal. Noting the doctrine of the separation of powers, the courts would interfere only where there was a clear disregard of constitutional principles, which had not occurred in this case. The Supreme Court also rejected the proposition that the sub-committee's power to compel a judge to give evidence infringed the independence of the judiciary. While judges normally are not answerable to the Oireachtas, Art.35.4 necessarily required that, in order to carry out its function, the Oireachtas needed to be able to ask the judge relevant questions.

Nonetheless, considerations of fairness, as well as a close reading of the Article, required that, before the Houses decided whether or not to remove the judge, "[he] should be entitled to a distinct hearing and decision on the facts". The Court observed that the wording of Art.35.4 required first that there be a determination of "stated misbehaviour" and only then separate resolutions for removal.

JUSTICE TO BE ADMINISTERED IN PUBLIC

Article 34.1 requires that, subject to limited exceptions, justice shall be administered in public. An aspect of this right of publicity necessarily involves permitting the media to access and report from the courts. (See, e.g. *Irish Times v Ireland* [1998] 1 I.R. 359 and *Sutter v Switzerland* (1984) 6 E.H.R.R. 272).The courts (per Walsh J. in *Re R. Ltd.* [1989] I.R. 126) administer justice "on behalf of all the inhabitants of the State". Members of the public generally have a right to attend court, to know what the courts are doing on their behalf, and to see that the Constitution and the law are being observed. This ensures that there can be confidence in the administration of justice. More urgently, the prospect that an accused person might be unfairly treated is heightened if he or she is tried behind closed doors, but less likely where justice is administered in the glaring light of publicity. It is important that the public perceives judges to be fair and impartial, that justice not only is done but is seen to be done. Where decisions are made in secret, it is easy for the perception of unfairness, whether justified or not, to flourish.

The rule regarding publicity is not absolute but may be limited "in such special and limited cases as may be prescribed by law". For instance, specific legislation restricts public access to the courts in family law and child protection cases, though in recent years researchers, court reporters, and members of the press have been granted access to such cases subject to the requirement to preserve the anonymity of litigants. The public may also be excluded from cases involving allegations of rape and other sexual offences (the purpose being to protect the alleged victim) and for the protection of trade and business secrets. In the main, such restrictions are permitted where necessary to uphold other constitutional rights or legitimate interests.

As a general rule, such restrictions must be set out in legislation. The courts, however, have an inherent jurisdiction, in the absence of legislation, to restrict publicity in order to preserve the constitutional rights of others, most notably the right of an accused to a fair trial. This power must, however, be exercised sparingly. In *Irish Times v Ireland* [1998] 1 I.R. 359 the Supreme Court agreed that the right to a fair trial took precedence over the requirement of publicity in Art.34.1. However, in that case the court concluded that a ban on contemporaneous reporting of a specific trial was disproportionate and therefore not justified. Restrictions could be applied only where there was a real risk of an unfair trial that could not be alleviated by directions to the jury. In this case, there was insufficient evidence of a risk significant enough to justify restrictions on what the courts assumed would be accurate reporting of the trial. (See also *Foley v Sunday Newspapers* [2005] 1 I.R. 88 and *Independent Newspapers v Anderson* [2006] IEHC 62.)

DEFINING THE JUDICIAL ROLE

Subject to Art.37, only judges may administer justice. Various bodies other than courts are given powers to make decisions, but this does not necessarily mean they are engaging in the administration of justice. An administration of justice or the judicial role basically presupposes a power to determine (decide) in an authoritative and binding manner a dispute concerning the existence of legal rights and liabilities or the imposition of legal penalties.

In *McDonald v Bord na gCon (No. 2)* [1965] I.R. 217, Kenny J. identified five characteristic features of a judicial function:

- it involves a dispute or controversy as to the existence of legal rights or as to a violation of the law;
- it results in a determination or decision as to the existence of legal rights or obligations, the imposition of legal liability, or the infliction of a legal penalty;
- the determination of the court is final (though in most cases subject to appeal) as regards the presence of legal rights or liabilities or as regards the imposition of a penalty;
- the State is obliged to enforce those rights, liabilities and penalties; and
- the function is one that has traditionally been performed by courts in this country.

On a number of occasions, the courts have been called on to determine whether a body other than a court is performing a function reserved to judges alone. In *Re Solicitors Act 1954* [1960] I.R. 239, the Supreme Court ruled that a decision to strike practitioners from the roll of solicitors was a judicial function (a function that could ordinarily be performed only by a court or judge). The crucial factor in this decision was that the function was traditionally one carried out by the Chief Justice, the solicitor being an officer of the court. It involved also the "imposition of a penalty", which one judge likened to a severe prison sentence.

On the other hand, in *Keady v Garda Commissioner* [1992] 2 I.R. 197, the Supreme Court concluded that a disciplinary tribunal investigating alleged indiscipline on the part of a Garda that ultimately led to his dismissal from the force was not performing a judicial function. The act of disciplining of a Garda was not a function historically reserved to the courts, and did not involve a contest between parties. Likewise, in *McDonald v Bord na gCon (No. 2)* [1965] I.R. 217 the Greyhound Board's power to discipline greyhound owners was found not to be a judicial function.

Even though it may be presided over by a judge, a tribunal of inquiry (to which the provisions of the Tribunals of Inquiry (Evidence) Acts 1921 to 2004 apply) is not a court. The sole function of a tribunal, according to the Supreme Court in *Goodman International v Hamilton (No. 1)* [1992] 2 I.R. 542, is to determine certain facts and to report those facts to the Oireachtas. This does not, the Court concluded, impinge upon any judicial function. It is no part of the tribunal's role to resolve legal disputes, determine legal liability or impose penalties on errant parties on the basis of its findings of fact or otherwise. As a result, the Supreme Court held that the Beef Tribunal, as a body merely charged with the finding of facts and no more, was not performing a judicial function. Similarly, the courts have ruled that issuing search warrants is not an inherently judicial function, and may be performed by persons other than judges, provided they are sufficiently independent of the criminal investigation.

THE DETERMINATION OF THE GUILT OR INNOCENCE OF A PERSON IN A CRIMINAL TRIAL

Only a court (either a judge or jury) may decide that a person is guilty or not guilty of a crime. In *Re Haughey* [1971] I.R. 217, the Supreme Court determined that an Oireachtas Committee could not "try and convict" a person (not being a member of the Oireachtas itself) who had refused to give evidence before the Committee. Although the Committee could refer the matter to the High Court, the Committee itself was not empowered to determine the guilt of the accused.

THE IMPOSITION OF A SENTENCE UPON CONVICTION

Where a person has been convicted of a crime, only a court may decide that person's punishment. In *Deaton v Attorney General* [1963] I.R. 170, the Supreme Court ruled that a law that gave the Revenue Commissioners the power to decide the penalties to be imposed on those convicted of customs offences was unconstitutional. Only a judge, it said, could impose such a penalty. In *State (Sheerin) v Kennedy* [1966] I.R. 379, a power given to the Minister for Justice to add "hard labour" to a juvenile convict's sentence was deemed to amount to a breach of the judiciary's exclusive powers to determine the punishment of offenders. (See also *State (O.) v O'Brien* [1973] I.R. 50.)

In *Re Gallagher* [1991] 1 I.R. 31, however, the Supreme Court ruled that an accused person could be detained at the pleasure of the Government where he had been found "guilty but insane". Such a verdict technically amounts to an acquittal; indeed, nowadays the appropriate verdict would be "not guilty by reason of insanity". As such there is no "punishment" to be handed down. Instead, the acquitted party is placed in the care of the Executive, which must decide when he or she is cured sufficiently of his or her mental illness.

Neither the Government nor the legislature may impose a penalty on a particular offender or increase the harshness of an already existing criminal penalty. Nonetheless, it is open to the Minister for Justice, under s.23 of the Criminal Justice Act 1951, to set aside ("remit") a punishment or to replace it with a lesser punishment (to "commute" such punishment). These powers are formally vested in the President under Art.13.6; the Article, however, permits these powers to be transferred by law to other officials.

MAXIMUM AND MANDATORY PENALTIES

In *Deaton*, the Supreme Court clarified that it is within the powers of the Oireachtas to prescribe minimum and maximum penalties for certain offences. (See also *Osmanovic v DPP* [2006] 3 I.R. 504.) While the power to impose a penalty in a specific case is reserved to the judge alone, the Oireachtas is entitled to set out in legislation the range of penalties that will be open to the courts where a particular type of crime has been committed. In short, the Oireachtas decides what penalties should, as a principle of general application, be available to the court; the court, in a specific case, decides what penalty will in fact be imposed on a specific offender.

The Oireachtas may prescribe a mandatory penalty, where one set penalty is fixed by legislation and has to be applied in all cases where a person is convicted of that crime. (For instance, murder attracts a mandatory life sentence.) In *State (O'Rourke) v Kelly* [1983] I.R. 58 the Supreme Court indicated that setting a mandatory penalty for an offence is "within the competence of the Oireachtas". Likewise, in *Deaton*, Ó Dálaigh C.J. distinguished between setting a fixed penalty for an offence, which the Oireachtas may do, and selecting a penalty in a particular case, which only a judge may do. Where a range of penalties is available, only a court may select the particular penalty. This, however, does not prevent the Oireachtas from mandating a single, fixed penalty for all cases where a person is convicted of a particular crime. The Supreme Court confirmed this view in *Whelan and Lynch v Minister for Justice, Equality and Law Reform* [2012] 1 I.R. 1, rejecting the contention that the mandatory life sentence for murder infringed the constitutional separation of powers. The legislature is entitled to set a mandatory penalty, provided the penalty is proportionate to the crime.

ARTICLE 37

Article 37 operates to allow certain limited types of judicial function to be performed by bodies other than courts. There are two basic requirements in Art.37:

- the function must not relate to "criminal matters", and
- the function must be limited in terms of its impact.

By "limited" it is meant that the effects of the exercise of such a function should not be unduly serious in their impact on those against whom it is exercised. By necessity, therefore, a non-limited power is one that (according to the Supreme Court in *Re Solicitors Act 1954* [1960] I.R. 239) "is calculated ordinarily to affect in the most profound and far-reaching way the lives, liberties, fortunes or reputations of those against whom [it is] exercised".

In *Re Solicitors Act*, the Supreme Court concluded that striking a person off the roll of solicitors was a judicial function and could not therefore be performed by the Law Society of Ireland. The Article 37 exception could not apply to the relevant provision of the Act, moreover, because of the serious and far-reaching effects of such a decision, namely, depriving a person of his or her livelihood and profession. By contrast, in *Central Dublin Development Association v Attorney General* (1975) 108 I.L.T.R. 69 a Minister was empowered to determine whether properties were exempted from planning permission. Although this involved an administration of justice, it was considered "limited" in its impact and thus permitted by Art.37. A person aggrieved by such a decision could appeal to the High Court and could still apply for planning permission in the normal manner.

Similarly, in *Melton Enterprises v Censorship of Publications Board* [2004] 1 I.L.R.M. 260 the Supreme Court concluded that, while the functions of the Censorship Board may be judicial in nature, they are limited in scope. A ban on the distribution of a specific publication is neither as profound nor as far-reaching as losing one's right to a carry on a profession. The Board's powers to censor publications were therefore upheld as constitutional.

The Court noted, moreover, that while the allegations of indecency and obscenity might also have provided the basis for a separate criminal prosecution this did not mean that the Board was considering criminal matters within the meaning of Art.37. A "criminal matter", according to *State (Murray) v McRann* [1979] I.R. 133, necessarily involves "a procedure associated with the prosecution of a person for a crime". The ultimate question in such matters is whether a crime has been committed. The censorship of a publication does not constitute a decision that anyone has committed a crime; simply that the general moral wellbeing of the citizens of the State demands that certain publications should not be publicly available.

Matters of internal prison discipline, it seems, may also be dealt with without recourse to the courts. This is so even where the breach of discipline, if proved, would also amount to a crime. In *State (Murray) v McRann* [1979] I.R. 133, a prisoner was alleged to have assaulted a prison officer. The governor of the prison, having investigated the matter, ruled that she should forfeit certain privileges normally extended to prisoners. The High Court concluded that even if this was the exercise of a judicial function, the power was of limited scope. Nor did the imposition of a punishment for breach of prison discipline make this a criminal matter for the purposes of Art.37.

In summary, one must ask:

(a) Is the function a judicial function?
- If not—it can be performed by a body other than a court.
- If so—proceed to (b).
(b) If it is a judicial function, does it relate to a prosecution for a crime?
- If so—it can only be performed by a court.
- If not—proceed to (c).
(c) Is this judicial function limited in its effects?
- If so—it can be performed by a body other than a court.
- If not—it can only be performed by a court.

14 Liberty and the Right to a Fair Trial

As a general principle, a person has the right to liberty under Art.40.4.1°. A person cannot be detained by the State unless certain formal procedures have been followed. Indeed, even where a person has been lawfully detained or imprisoned, that person continues to enjoy certain rights, the infringement of which may render the detention illegal.

In particular, under Art.40.4.1°, no citizen shall be deprived of his or her personal liberty save in accordance with law. Where it is alleged that a person has been detained unlawfully, any person may apply to the High Court for habeas corpus. This requires the person who is detaining another person to bring the detainee to the High Court with a view to justifying the detention. If the detention cannot be justified, the court will order the release of the detainee.

Rights on arrest

Generally, a person may be arrested only for the purpose of that person being charged with a crime and being brought before the courts at the earliest reasonable opportunity. In particular, ordinarily, arrest and detention cannot be used where it is only intended to question a suspect. Under the Criminal Justice Act 1951, such person must, as soon as practicable after arrest, be brought before a District Court judge. In some cases, however, certain legislative provisions qualify this requirement by allowing for extended detention following arrest for the purpose of the investigation of the offence without obstruction or interference. For instance, extended powers of detention following arrest are permitted in respect of certain offences: under s.30 of the Offences Against the State Act 1939, s.4 of the Criminal Justice Act 1984, s.2 of the Criminal Justice (Drug Trafficking) Act 1996, and the Criminal Procedure Act 2010.

Where a person has been arrested, that person enjoys certain rights:

- the right to be informed of the charges against him or her (*People (DPP) v Walsh* [1980] I.R. 294);

- the right to be brought before the District Court at the earliest reasonable opportunity;
- the right to have access to and to consult with a lawyer (*People (DPP) v Healy* [1990] I.L.R.M. 313);
- the right to free legal aid, if required (*State (Healy) v Donoghue* [1976] I.R. 325);
- the right to medical treatment, if required;
- the right to remain silent (subject to certain exceptions) and the right to be told of that right;
- the right to be given food and time to sleep; and
- the right not to be oppressively interrogated.

Although a person has a right to reasonable access to a lawyer following arrest, and to consult with that lawyer, there is no constitutional right to have a lawyer present during questioning by police. In *Lavery v Member in Charge, Carrickmacross Garda Station* [1999] 2 I.R. 390, the Supreme Court observed that the right of access to a lawyer does not entitle a suspect to have a lawyer present during questioning. This was confirmed by a majority of the Supreme Court in *DPP v Doyle* [2017] IESC 1, with Denham C.J. remarking that "[t]he right is one of access to a lawyer, not of the presence of a lawyer during an interview".

Where a person is questioned by Gardaí while detained, such questioning cannot be oppressive. (See *People (DPP) v McNally* (1981) 2 Frewen 43, and *People (DPP) v Lynch* [1982] I.R. 64.) Nor will confessions be admitted as evidence where made while the accused is under the influence of alcohol, hypnosis or a controlled drug. (See the judgment of Griffin J. in *People (DPP) v Shaw* [1982] I.R. 1.)

THE INVIOLABILITY OF THE DWELLING

Art.40.5 declares that "[t]he dwelling of every citizen is inviolable and shall not be forcibly entered save in accordance with law". This means, in particular, that the entry to a person's home without the householder's consent is prohibited unless it is permitted by law and complies with fundamental constitutional norms. This protection applies only to dwellings, i.e. places in which people live, and not businesses (though the common law offers some protection to the latter). It can be invoked only by the person whose home the dwelling is, although the person need not be the owner of the property. Where no consent is forthcoming, the law will usually require a search warrant to be obtained from an independent decision-maker, though in some cases a statute may permit entry without a warrant, if justified by the exigencies of the situation.

Forcible entry to a dwelling may also be permitted where required to vindicate constitutional rights, such as to protect the life and safety of the inhabitants. (See *DPP v Michael Delaney* [1997] 3 I.R. 453.)

Where a search warrant is required to search a dwelling, it is possible for it to be issued by a person other than a judge, but certain constitutional safeguards apply. In *Damache v DPP* [2012] 2 I.R. 266, the Supreme Court declared s.29(1) of the Offences Against the State Act 1939 to be unconstitutional. It allowed senior ranked Gardaí to issue search warrants in order to collect evidence of certain specific offences, even where they were connected with the relevant investigation. The Supreme Court held that the provision infringed the inviolability of the dwelling, as warrants should only be issued by an independent decision-maker, unconnected with the investigation, who is able to act impartially and judicially.

FAIRNESS IN THE TRIAL OF OFFENCES

Article 38.1 of the Constitution requires that no person be tried in relation to an alleged offence except "in due course of law". This means that a criminal trial may only proceed in accordance with the law and, in particular, with reference to certain rules of fairness. The trial, in other words, must be a fair trial. As Costello J. remarked in *Heaney v Ireland* [1994] 3 I.R. 593, Art.38.1 "implies a great deal more than a simple assertion that trials are to be held in accordance with laws enacted by parliament. It ... has been construed as a constitutional guarantee that criminal trials will be conducted in accordance with basic concepts of justice." The following are some of the main principles of a fair trial.

THE CRIME MUST BE ONE KNOWN TO THE LAW AND MUST BE SUFFICIENTLY CERTAIN AND CLEAR

In *Attorney General v Cunningham* [1932] I.R. 28 O'Byrne J. identified "the fundamental doctrine recognised in these Courts that the criminal law must be certain and specific, and that no person is to be punished unless and until he has been convicted of an offence recognised by law as a crime and punishable as such". In *People (Attorney General) v Edge* [1943] I.R. 115, the Supreme Court held that the defendant could not be convicted of "kidnapping" a minor with the minor's consent but against the will of his parents. This was because the alleged offence (in the words of O'Byrne J.) was "not an indictable offence at common law" [1943] I.R. 146. There was, in short, no such offence known to the law at that time.

In *King v Attorney General* [1981] I.R. 233 the Supreme Court declared a law unconstitutional on the basis that it was too vague, arbitrary and subjective in nature. The offence in question involved the frequenting by "every suspected person or reputed thief" of certain specific places with the intention of committing a felony. As Kenny J. remarked, "[i]t is a fundamental feature of our system of government by law (and not by decree or diktat) that citizens may be convicted only of offences which have been specified with precision by the judges who made the common law, or of offences which, created by statute, are expressed without ambiguity." The phrases "suspected person" and "reputed thief" however, "are so uncertain that they cannot form the foundation for a criminal offence". The arbitrary nature of these concepts, and the possibility of their unequal application, meant that the law in question infringed the right to due process under Art.38.1, the right to liberty (Art.40.4) and the equality guarantee in Art.40.1.

A person is entitled to know with reasonable certainty whether certain conduct is or is not unlawful. Vague laws may be found unconstitutional on this basis. In *Douglas v DPP* [2014] 1 I.R. 510 the High Court concluded that a law that made it an offence to "cause scandal or injure the morals of the community" was, according to Hogan J., "hopelessly vague and subjective in character", lacked "any clear principles and policies in relation to the scope of what conduct is prohibited" and risked being applied arbitrarily and inconsistently. The law in question was thus found to be unconstitutional on the basis that it infringed the principle of legal certainty under Art.38.1 and the right to personal liberty under Art.40.4.1°. The law also risked unequal application in breach of Art.40.1. (See also the similar outcome in *McInerney v DPP* [2014] IEHC 101 concerning the former crime of "offending modesty".)

A CRIMINAL OFFENCE CANNOT BE CREATED RETROSPECTIVELY

Article 15.5 of the Constitution states that the Oireachtas cannot make something an infringement of the law with retrospective effect, that is, to render something unlawful that was not unlawful at the time of its commission. Thus, if the Oireachtas were to ban gambling on Friday, it would not be permissible to backdate the new law to cover a bet that was legally made the previous Tuesday.

THE PRESUMPTION OF INNOCENCE

It is always the case that, until found guilty by a court of law, a person is assumed innocent of all wrongdoing. There is, moreover, no requirement on the accused to prove his innocence. In other words, the onus or burden of proving his guilt beyond reasonable doubt is on the prosecution. In *O'Leary v Attorney General* [1993] 1 I.R. 102 and *Hardy v Ireland* [1994] 2 I.R. 550 alike, the Supreme Court acknowledged that this common law right was also a right protected by Art.38.1 of the Constitution.

In *O'Leary v Attorney General* [1993] 1 I.R. 102, the accused had been convicted of membership of an illegal organisation. When arrested, Mr O'Leary had been found in possession of 37 posters depicting a man brandishing a rifle and the words "IRA call the shots". The law under which he was convicted stated that the possession of such "incriminating documents" would constitute "evidence until the contrary is proved" that the person belonged to an illegal organisation. The Supreme Court rejected a claim that this measure infringed the presumption of innocence. It observed that throughout the plaintiff's trial, the overall onus of proving membership of an illegal organisation was on the prosecution. The provision in question simply provided evidence (and not proof) of such membership. While this evidence may have made it substantially easier to convict the accused, it did not shift the overall burden of proving the guilt of the accused.

Similar provisions were also unsuccessfully challenged in *Hardy v Ireland* [1994] 2 I.R. 550. The legislation in question in that case stated that a person found in possession of an explosive substance would be guilty of an offence, unless that person could show that the explosives were to be used for a lawful purpose. This "reverse-onus" provision was again upheld. The Supreme Court noted that it simply moved the evidential burden (and not the overall burden of proof) onto the accused. It rendered such possession evidence but not proof of the accused's guilt, evidence that could be contradicted by evidence of a lawful purpose.

THE RIGHT TO BAIL

As a corollary to the presumption of innocence, a person who had been arrested or charged with an offence may seek to be released on bail pending trial. When bail is granted, a suspect may be released on the condition that he or she returns to court to face trial. To ensure that this happens, the suspect or another person acting as surety may be asked to deposit a sum of money that will be forfeited if the suspect does not turn up for trial.

Prior to 1997, bail could be denied only in two specific cases, namely where the court had a well-founded fear either:

- that it was likely that the suspect would "skip bail" and not face trial; or
- that the suspect would use his or her time on bail to intimidate witnesses to the alleged crime or otherwise interfere with evidence.

It was formerly not possible, in particular, to refuse bail on the grounds that the court believed that the accused would "reoffend" while on bail (see *People (Attorney General) v O'Callaghan* [1966] I.R. 501 and *Ryan v DPP* [1989] I.R. 399). To assume this, the courts believed, would presuppose that the suspect was guilty of the crimes of which he or she was accused, an assumption that infringed the right to be presumed innocent until proven guilty. Such "preventative detention" was not permitted.

In 1996, however, the Constitution was amended to expand the circumstances in which bail might be refused. Under the terms of the Sixteenth Amendment to the Constitution (Art.40.4.6°), it is now possible to deny bail to a suspect "where it is reasonably considered necessary to prevent the commission of a serious offence by that person". On foot of this Amendment, the Bail Act 1997 was enacted. Under the Act, bail may be denied where the suspect is accused of specified "serious offences" as listed in the Schedule to the Act (they include murder, manslaughter, rape, various other sexual offences, assault, robbery, burglary, and certain offences involving firearms and/or explosives). A serious offence is further defined as an offence attracting a maximum penalty of not less than five years' imprisonment.

In deciding whether to deny bail, the court must have regard to the following:

- the degree of seriousness of the offence;
- the strength of the evidence against the accused;
- the likely sentence that the accused may be given, if convicted;
- any previous convictions that the accused has attracted (especially for crimes committed while on bail);
- the likelihood of absconding from justice, or interfering with witnesses or evidence;
- the fact that the accused has a drug addiction (if this is the case); and
- the likelihood that the accused will commit a serious offence while on bail.

THE RIGHT TO A REASONABLY EXPEDITIOUS TRIAL

Although the wheels of law typically move at a slow pace, an accused cannot be indefinitely denied the right to clear his or her name. Although there is no statute of limitations on criminal prosecutions, it is clear that an unreasonable and excessive delay in proceeding to trial may prevent prosecution where the delay would likely result in prejudice to the accused.

In *State (O'Connell) v Fawsitt* [1986] I.L.R.M. 639, the accused, who had first been charged in 1981, was not tried until 1985. There having been no good reason for this inordinate delay, the Supreme Court ruled that the trial could not proceed. Of particular note was the fact that, by the time the case came up for trial, an important defence witness was no longer available to testify. In these circumstances, the court concluded, the accused could not be guaranteed a fair trial.

In *N.C. v DPP* [1991] 1 I.R. 471, a nine-year delay in raising a complaint of sexual abuse was deemed to have diminished the accused's right to a fair trial. A key point in the case was the unexplained nature of the delay. There was evidence, moreover, that the delay might have prejudiced the accused's right to a fair trial.

That said, much longer periods of delay may nonetheless result in a successful prosecution. There is no fixed period of time after which a criminal trial cannot proceed, and the fact of delay in itself is not enough to halt a trial in the absence of the likelihood of an unfair trial. The question that arises here is whether the delay has been extensive to the point of being "excessive and prejudicial", undermining the right to a fair trial (See *H. v DPP* [2006] IESC 55.) This is a matter to be considered in each individual case by reference to the facts of that case. The length of time between the alleged offence and the prosecution thereof may affect the accused's ability to defend himself. Witnesses may, in the meantime, have forgotten crucial facts, or may, indeed, have died. On the other hand, if the court believes that a fair trial is still possible, the case may proceed, despite the delay. Thus, in *B. v DPP* [1997] 2 I.L.R.M. 118, for instance, a trial was allowed to proceed even after a 20–30-year gap since the alleged offences had been committed, the Supreme Court ruling that there was no real risk that the accused would not obtain a fair trial. Nonetheless, Denham J. noted that the trial judge in this case would have to give "appropriate directions" where it was felt that the passage of time might have diminished the reliability of evidence or other matters.

THE RIGHT TO BE PRESENT AT ONE'S TRIAL

A suspect has the right to be present at his or her trial. In *Lawlor v Hogan* [1993] I.L.R.M. 607 the High Court observed that "[t]he right of an accused to be present and to follow the proceedings against him is a fundamental constitutional right of the accused which every court would be bound to protect and vindicate". In that case, Murphy J. noted that where the law "expressly requires matters to be dealt with by or in relation to the individual accused, clearly he must be present to enable those functions to be performed". On the other hand, if the accused has consciously decided to absent himself from the trial, and his presence at that time is not essential to require a particular procedure to be carried out, the trial judge is entitled to continue the trial in the accused's absence. In *Lawlor* itself, the High Court concluded that the District Court judge had properly exercised his discretion in allowing a trial to proceed notwithstanding the absence of the accused.

In the *People (Attorney General) v Messitt* [1972] I.R. 204, after a trial that proceeded after the accused had been forcibly removed from the court for misbehaviour, the Court of Criminal Appeal quashed the verdict, as highly prejudicial evidence against the accused had been heard in his absence. Likewise, in *O'Callaghan v Clifford* [1993] 3 I.R. 603, the Supreme Court found that there was "an absence of due process" in allowing a trial to proceed in the accused's absence. Where, however, the accused's absence is voluntary or self-imposed (as, for instance, in *People (Attorney General) v Kelly* [1982] I.L.R.M. 1, where the suspect had absconded during his trial), the accused might be considered to have waived this right.

THE ABILITY TO UNDERSTAND THE PROCEEDINGS

An accused person has the right to an interpreter in cases where he or she does not sufficiently understand the language in which the proceedings are being heard. Similar considerations apply in the case of persons who are deaf or hard of hearing (i.e. such persons would have the right to a sign language interpreter). This right flows from the principle that an accused must be able to understand the proceedings of the trial. For example, in *State (Buchan) v Coyne* (1936) 70 I.L.T.R. 185, a conviction was quashed on the grounds that the accused, a Scotsman, and his solicitor were unable to understand Irish, the language in which the trial had been heard. As he had not been afforded an interpreter, his conviction was deemed unsafe and was quashed.

THE RIGHT TO AN IMPARTIAL JUDGE AND JURY

An accused person is entitled to a fair trial in front of a judge (and, where relevant, a jury), who is (or are) impartial and independent. The principle that is said to apply in this context is *nemo iudex in causa sua*, that is, that one cannot be a judge in one's own case. Thus, where a judge or juror has a vested interest in the result of a case, that person will not be permitted to hear that case. In the *People (Attorney General) v Singer* [1975] I.R. 408, a jury verdict was quashed on the ground that the foreman of the jury had a vested interest in the result. He was in fact a victim of the specific crime that was being tried by that very jury. The test in such cases is whether "a reasonable person [would] have a reasonable apprehension that the appellant would not, in the circumstances receive a fair and impartial trial". (*Bula v Tara Mines (No. 6)* [2000] 4 I.R. 412, *People v Tobin* [2001] 3 I.R. 469). In *Tobin*, the Court of Criminal Appeal quashed a conviction and ordered a retrial of a rape and sexual assault case in circumstances where a member of the jury had a prior experience of sexual abuse. The Court concluded that "in the special circumstances of this case a reasonable and fair-minded observer would consider that there was a danger, in the sense of a possibility, that the juror might have been unconsciously influenced by his or her personal experience and, for that reason the appellant might not receive a fair trial".

A trial may also be suspended where pre-trial publicity, for instance in the media, might threaten the accused's prospects of getting a fair trial before a jury. Thus in *Magee v O'Dea* [1994] 1 I.R. 500, Flood J. refused to allow the extradition of the plaintiff, on the grounds that his right to a fair trial had been prejudiced by unfavourable comments in the UK media.

THE RIGHT TO A PROPORTIONATE SENTENCE

Any sentence handed down on conviction and any consequences flowing from the conviction must be proportionate ("the punishment must fit the crime"). This means that there must be a rational relationship between the serious of the crime and the punishment imposed. (See *Cox v Ireland* [1992] 2 I.R. 503 and *Lovett v Minister for Education* [1997] I.L.R.M. 89.)

THE RIGHT TO SILENCE

Generally, a person who is arrested on suspicion of a crime cannot be forced to answer questions, either in police custody or in court. This is called the right to silence, or the "privilege against self-incrimination". An important aspect of this right is that a court cannot ordinarily assume that a person's silence in the face of an accusation implies guilt. An inference of guilt cannot usually be drawn from such silence. In *People (DPP) v Finnerty* [1999] 4 I.R. 364, the Supreme Court ruled that a rape conviction was unsound as the prosecution had been allowed to question the defendant on his refusal to answer Garda questions during detention. A trial judge, moreover, cannot ordinarily draw attention to the fact that the defendant refused to answer questions while in police custody, or in court. Nor can the fact that an accused does not testify in his or her defence during a trial be taken as implying guilt. Legislation may, however, restrict the right to silence in certain contexts.

In *Heaney v Ireland* [1994] 3 I.R. 593, the Supreme Court ruled that the right to silence is a constitutional right protected by Art.40.6 of the Constitution as a corollary to the right to free expression. The right to silence, however, is not absolute. It has to be balanced against the public's right to be protected against crime. Thus, in *Heaney* itself, the Supreme Court ruled that an Act of Parliament was constitutional even though it made it an offence to refuse, when arrested, to answer questions concerning the suspect's whereabouts at a particular time. In this case, the Court concluded that the Act struck an appropriate and proportionate balance between respecting the rights of the prisoner and protecting the public generally. (Although, in *Heaney v Ireland* (2001) 33 E.H.R.R. 264, the European Court of Human Rights determined that the same measure infringed art.6 of the European Convention on Human Rights).

In *Rock v Ireland* [1997] 3 I.R. 484, a suspect was arrested in possession of what turned out to be counterfeit US dollars. His failure to answer questions regarding his possession of these items led to certain inferences being drawn under ss.18 and 19 of the Criminal Justice Act 1984 (as amended by the Criminal Justice Act 2007). These provisions allow the Gardaí to question persons in relation to any object, substance or mark that is found in his possession, on his person, on his clothing or footwear or in the place of arrest. The person may also be asked to account for his or her presence in that place. Failure to answer questions concerning these matters may lead to the court drawing conclusions or inferences from such silence. (At the time of questioning, the accused must be informed of these possible consequences.) Such inferences, however, may be drawn only if supported by "corroborating" evidence that endorses such conclusions.

The Supreme Court concluded that these provisions had not breached the suspect's right to silence. The court considered that the legislation, as in *Heaney*, represented an appropriate balance between the rights of the accused and the interests of the public at large.

(See also s.30 of the Criminal Justice Act 2007, which allows inferences to be drawn where a person, who is arrested for certain serious offences, fails, prior to or at the time of being charged, to raise a point that is later used in his defence, if the circumstances of arrest clearly demand an explanation from the accused.)

THE RIGHT TO PREPARE AND PRESENT A DEFENCE

A person has the right to defend himself or herself in court. As a corollary, an accused party has the right to adequate time, facilities and expertise to prepare and present an adequate defence. An accused generally has the right, also, to hear and test the evidence against him or her and in particular to cross-examine witnesses for the prosecution so that the accuracy of their evidence may be tested. (See *Re Haughey* [1971] I.R. 217).

There is, however, no constitutional right to physically confront one's accuser. In *Donnelly v Ireland* [1998] 1 I.R. 325, an accused person challenged the provisions of the Criminal Evidence Act 1992. The Act allows the evidence of a child alleged to have been a victim of sexual abuse to be given in a separate room and broadcast into open court via a live video link. This, Mr Donnelly alleged, denied him the right to confront his accuser. The Supreme Court, however, ruled that the Act did not breach the accused's rights. The right to a fair trial, the Court concluded, did not include a right to physically confront the alleged victim or other witness. The Act still permitted the cross-examination of the alleged victim by the defendant's legal team, during which time the judge and jury could observe the reactions and demeanour of the witness. The Court did not accept that the manner in which evidence was to be given was unfair to the accused.

ACCESS TO A LAWYER AND LEGAL REPRESENTATION

As another aspect of the right to defend oneself, an accused person has the right to reasonable access to a lawyer, both following arrest and during trial.

This is an essential safeguard of the accused's rights, designed to ensure that the accused has access to a skilled advocate who will assist him or her in his or her defence. Where a person cannot afford a lawyer, according to *State (Healy) v Donoghue* [1976] I.R. 325, the State is obliged to grant legal aid for the provision of such a lawyer. This is not to say, however, that an accused cannot be tried where he or she refuses (for reasons other than lack of funds) the assistance of a lawyer. An accused is perfectly entitled to choose to mount his or her own defence, unassisted by legal representatives.

The right to legal advice was confirmed by the Supreme Court in the *DPP v Gormley and White* [2014] IESC 17. The Court noted that the right to fair procedures and due process applied not just at trial, but also during the pre-trial process. A suspect can waive his or her right to legal advice, but only if he or she is acting freely and knowingly. In *Gormley*, the Gardaí failed to postpone an interview pending the arrival of the accused's solicitor. Statements made by the accused before his solicitor arrived were relied upon in evidence. On that basis, the Supreme Court quashed his conviction. As noted above, however, while a person has a right to consult a lawyer following arrest, there is no constitutional right to the presence of a lawyer during police questioning (*DPP v Doyle* [2017] IESC 1).

UNCONSTITUTIONALLY OBTAINED EVIDENCE

An important question arises as to whether evidence obtained in breach of a person's constitutional rights can be used in evidence against that person. Over the years, different approaches have been taken to this problem. From 1990 to 2015, a strong exclusionary rule applied, ruling out the introduction of unconstitutionally obtained evidence, save for in exceptional circumstances. In the *People (DPP) v Kenny* [1990] 2 I.R. 110 the Supreme Court had ruled that evidence gathered in breach of constitutional rights "must be excluded unless a court is satisfied that either the act constituting the breach of constitutional rights was committed unintentionally or accidentally, or is satisfied that there are extraordinary excusing circumstances which justify the admission of the evidence in its (the court's) discretion". In applying this test, it was no defence for Gardaí to claim that they did not know an action was in breach of constitutional rights if they had intended to act as they did. It was the knowledge of their acts rather than the knowledge of unconstitutionality that rendered the breach knowing and deliberate. In this context there was, Finlay C.J. concluded, "an obligation to choose the principle which is likely to provide a stronger and more effective defence and vindication of the right concerned".

In the *DPP v JC* [2015] IESC 31, however, the Supreme Court, by a 4:3 majority, adopted a different, less demanding test. The decision in *JC* represents a departure from the strict exclusionary rule in *Kenny*, the philosophy being that a better balance needed to be struck between the protection of rights and the right of the public to the effective prosecution of crime. The test laid down by the majority was one that broadly excuses breaches that are due to inadvertence, where the Gardaí did not know they were acting unconstitutionally. If, on the other hand, the constitutional breach is made knowingly, recklessly or in a grossly negligent manner, the evidence will be excluded unless there are exceptional circumstances. The onus is on the prosecution to show that the evidence was gathered constitutionally or that, if it was gathered unconstitutionally, the evidence should still be heard.

Where evidence is obtained in deliberate and conscious breach of the Constitution, it should be excluded unless there are exceptional circumstances. Notably, "deliberate and conscious" means that those who collected the evidence *were aware that they were acting unconstitutionally* and not simply that they intended or were aware of the acts they were carrying out. Where the breach is not deliberate and conscious (i.e. the Gardaí did not know they were acting unconstitutionally) there is still a presumption against admission of the evidence, though the evidence could be admitted if the prosecution can show that the breach was inadvertent. (See *People (AG) v O'Brien* [1965] I.R. 142.)

CRIMINAL INTENT AND THE CONSTITUTION

While ignorance of the law is no defence, the law generally requires that a person should not be convicted of a serious crime if he or she lacks mens rea, that is, if he or she is not aware that he or she is carrying out the criminal act (whether or not he knows it is an offence.) Subject to some exceptions, the Constitution generally prohibits the criminalisation of persons who are mentally innocent of wrongdoing.

In *Re Article 26 and the Employment Equality Bill 1996* [1997] 2 I.R. 321, the Supreme Court ruled that an attempt to criminalise a person in respect of an act of which they had no knowledge infringed Arts 38.1 and 40.1 of the Constitution. A provision of the Bill stipulated that an employer could be held vicariously liable for the actions of its employees, even if the employer itself had no knowledge of those actions, and had not approved such actions. The penalty for breach was a maximum fine of €19,050 and/or a term of imprisonment of up to two years. This, the Court reasoned, constituted a breach of Art.38.1 of the Constitution in that it purported to impose very severe criminal sanctions which "in circumstances which are so unjust, irrational and inappropriate would make any purported trial of such a person not one held in due course of law".

Similarly, in *C.C. v Ireland* [2006] IESC 33, the Supreme Court declared a law criminalising sexual intercourse with a girl under the age of 15 unconstitutional, on the basis that the relevant measure did not excuse a genuine mistake as to age. The law effectively meant that the accused could be convicted despite the fact that he was not aware that the girl was under the age of 15. The section, Hardiman J. concluded, "contains no balance: it wholly removes the mental element and expressly criminalises the mentally innocent". As a result, the Court ruled that the measure unfairly denied the plaintiff his right to liberty and to his good name under that Art.40. The Court noted in particular the heavy penalty for the crime in question (life imprisonment), and the significant social stigma attaching to a conviction under the Act.

TRIAL BY JURY

Every person who is tried on foot of a criminal charge must be tried before a jury, except in three specified cases:

- where the offence is a "minor" offence;
- where the offender is being tried before the Special Criminal Court; or
- where the offender is being tried before a court martial (i.e. in a military court in accordance with military law). (See the Defence Acts 1954–2015.)

Unless the offence falls within one of the exceptions listed in Arts 38.2–38.4, "no person shall be tried on any criminal charge without a jury". This seems to suggest that, even if an accused preferred no jury, he would still have to be tried before a jury of his peers (i.e. he would not be able to waive that right). (See *Re Haughey* [1971] I.R. 217 and *Holohan v Donohue* [1986] I.R. 45.)

WHAT IS A "MINOR" OFFENCE?

A "minor" offence is an offence that may be tried without a jury, before what is called a court of "summary" jurisdiction (with a judge and no jury). The Constitution does not expressly define what is "minor" for these purposes. In *Melling v Ó Mathghamhna* [1962] I.R. 1, the Supreme Court observed that while one must look to the moral quality of the act and the state of the law and public opinion at the time that the Constitution was enacted, the primary consideration in determining whether an offence is or is not minor is the severity of the maximum penalty available on conviction of that offence. Based on these principles, the courts have ruled that the offence of drink driving attracting a maximum six-month prison sentence is a minor offence (*Conroy v Attorney General* [1965] I.R. 411), while a single offence attracting a maximum two-year prison sentence is not a minor offence (*Mallon v Minister of Agriculture* [1996] 1 I.R. 517). An offence attracting an unlimited fine or term of imprisonment is not a minor offence (*Re Haughey* [1971] 1 I.R. 217) and thus requires a jury trial. Likewise, in *Kostan v Ireland* [1978] I.L.R.M. 12, a fishing offence that resulted in the confiscation of a boat worth €128,570 was deemed to be a non-minor offence, owing to the size of the penalty.

Currently, an offence attracting a maximum penalty of more than one year in prison and/or a fine of €5,000 or more would constitute a non-minor offence. The Fines Act 2010 allows fines of up to €5,000 to be imposed for certain "class A" summary offences.

Primary v secondary punishment

In determining whether an offence is non-minor, the court may only look to the sentence that might be handed down (the primary punishment) and not to any secondary consequences that also flow from a guilty verdict. The court is not entitled to have regard to any consequential side-effects of a finding of guilt, such as the loss of a statutory licence. For instance, in *State (Pheasantry) v Donnelly* [1982] I.L.R.M. 512, a publican asserted that because he stood to lose his licence to sell alcohol as a result of several successive licensing offences, the third such offence should not have been treated as a minor offence. The High Court rejected this argument: in considering the severity of a penalty the court need only look to the primary punishment and not to any secondary consequential injury that the convict would suffer as a side-effect of the verdict. (See also *Charlton v Ireland* [1984] I.L.R.M. 39, where the loss of a bookmaker's licence subsequent to conviction was deemed to be secondary only, and not relevant to the issue of whether the offence was non-minor.) Likewise, in *Conroy v Attorney General* [1965] I.R. 411, the Supreme Court held that the fact that the law also required that the loss of a driving licence for one year following a conviction for drink driving was a "secondary consequence" that could not on its own lift the offence into the category of non-minor offences.

The Special Criminal Court

Article 38.3 allows for the establishment of Special Courts for the trial of offences. The key feature of these courts is that, instead of a jury, the accused is tried before three judges drawn from the ordinary courts of the State. This means that an accused is effectively deprived, in such cases, of his or her right to a trial by jury. These courts are established where the State fears that a jury would be intimidated, corrupted, or threatened by persons connected to the accused. Thus trials before the Special Criminal Court tend to involve accused persons alleged to be associated with known terrorist organisations and criminal gangs. In *Kavanagh v Ireland* [1996] 1 I.R. 321 the Supreme Court confirmed that the Special Criminal Court can be used for crimes other than political or subversive crimes.

Provision is made for the establishment of a Special Criminal Court in the Offences Against the State Act 1939. Part V of that Act allows the Government to set up such a court whenever it considers that "the ordinary courts are inadequate to secure the effective administration of justice and the preservation of public peace and order". The decision to establish the court is essentially a political one entrusted to the Government and Oireachtas. As illustrated by *Kavanagh v Ireland* [1996] 1 I.R. 321 and *Gilligan v Ireland* [2001] 1 I.L.R.M. 473 the courts are very reluctant to intervene in such a decision. In *Kavanagh*, Keane J. remarked "judicial restraint of an unusual order is called for before the courts intervene" in this context, though such a decision "cannot be regarded as forever beyond the reach of judicial control".

TRIAL FOR CONTEMPT OF COURT

Where a person is charged with contempt involving scandalising the court, prejudicing a fair trial or otherwise interfering with the process of the courts, the right to trial by jury may be limited in order to protect the courts' independence. (See the discussion of *Murphy v British Broadcasting Corporation* [2004] IEHC 440 above at p.88).

THE GENERAL PRINCIPLES OF A JURY TRIAL

The primary function of a jury in a criminal trial is to determine the guilt or innocence of accused persons. In this context, it stands as an important defence against State tyranny, requiring that a person may only be tried before a jury of his peers. A person tried before a jury is entitled to certain safeguards. First, the jury must be independent and impartial (see above). Secondly, the panel from which the jury is selected must be as representative as practicable of society at large. In *de Búrca v Attorney General* [1976] I.R. 38, the Supreme Court declared the Juries Act 1927 unconstitutional as it automatically exempted all women and excluded those who were not rate-payers (the owners or occupiers of land) from serving on juries. Besides infringing the requirement of equality in Art.40.1, the Supreme Court found that this legislation deprived the accused of her right to be tried before a "fair cross-section of society".

Equality

Article 40.1 guarantees that all citizens, as human persons, will be treated as equal before the law. This does not mean, however, that all persons will in all cases be treated alike. The terms of what is sometimes called the "proviso" to Art.40.1 permit the State to have regard to relevant differences, physical, moral and social, between different people. As Walsh J. remarked in *de Búrca v Attorney General* [1976] I.R. 38 at 68: "Article 40 does not require identical treatment of all persons without recognition of differences in relevant circumstances but it forbids invidious [unjust] or arbitrary discrimination." In short, like situations are to be treated in like manner, but relevant differences may be taken into account in formulating the laws and policies of the State (dissimilar situations may be treated differently). (See, for instance, *Dillane v Ireland* [1980] I.L.R.M. 167, where different treatment of Gardaí as compared with how members of the public were treated was justified by the different social function performed by them.) Such differences of treatment, however, must serve a legitimate legislative purpose and must not be arbitrary or unjust.

The Supreme Court has suggested that certain forms of discrimination may require stronger justification to escape a finding of unconstitutionality. In *Re Article 26 and the Employment Equality Bill 1995* [1997] 2 I.R. 321 the Supreme Court noted: "The forms of discrimination which are, presumptively at least, proscribed by Article 40.1 are not particularised [but] manifestly, they would extend to classifications based on sex, race, language, religious or political opinions."

Nonetheless, the guarantee of equality has generally proved to be relatively weak. At its most robust it has been used to strike down inequality on grounds of gender and in ensuring fairness in relation to elections and referendums. In other contexts, however, it has proved too susceptible to justification on the basis that different treatment serves other constitutional interests, or on speculative hypothetical bases that do not always bear up to scrutiny. The courts have also often restricted the application of the equality guarantee by reference to a "human personality" doctrine, ruling that only inequality based on human characteristics or some integral aspect of the human personality (such as sex, race or religion) can be the subject of a finding of unconstitutionality. In *Quinn's Supermarket v Attorney General* [1972] I.R. 1, Walsh J. noted that Art.40.1 "is a guarantee of equality *as human persons* and ... is a guarantee related to their dignity as human beings and a guarantee against any inequalities grounded upon an assumption, or indeed a belief, that some individual or individuals, by reason of their human attributes or their ethnic or racial, social or religious background, are to be treated as the inferior or superior of other individuals in the community".

GENDER EQUALITY

It is generally (though not always) unconstitutional to treat one gender more favourably than (or indeed just differently from) the other, unless there is an objectively sound reason for such different treatment. For instance, in *de Búrca v Attorney General* [1976] I.R. 38, the Supreme Court declared unconstitutional the Juries Act 1927 partly on the ground (per Walsh J.) that it breached the guarantee of equality. This was because the Act required only men, and not women, to serve on juries. Women could serve on juries, but were generally exempted and could serve only if they expressly applied to be made a juror. Men, on the other hand, did not enjoy this general exemption. As a result, before 1976 juries almost invariably consisted solely of men. (An added ground of unconstitutionality in this case was the fact that the Juries Act 1927 required that all jurors be rate payers.)

Similarly discriminatory provisions were declared unconstitutional in *T.O'G. v Attorney General* [1985] I.L.R.M. 61. In that case, a child had been placed for adoption with a married couple. Sadly, before the adoption was finalised, the plaintiff's wife died. In these circumstances the law said that a widower (a bereaved husband) could not adopt a child placed with him unless he already had other children in his care. This requirement, however, did not apply to widows. The High Court concluded that the difference in treatment, based on gender, was unconstitutional.

In *McKinley v Minister for Defence* [1992] 2 I.R. 333, the Supreme Court went so far as to extend a common law right to women so as to cure an incident of inequality. The law formerly allowed a husband, but not a wife, of an injured party to claim damages for loss of consortium (the loss of a spouse's company and care, including the ability to engage in sexual intercourse) from the person who caused this injury. In *McKinley*, however, the Supreme Court agreed to extend the common law right to sue to a wife, on the ground that the tort would otherwise be in breach of the constitutional guarantee of equality. Similarly, common law rules that treated wives as inferior to or subordinate to their husbands have been declared unconstitutional. (See *State (DPP) v Walsh* [1981] I.R. 412 and *W v W* [1993] 2 I.R. 476.)

In *S.M. v Ireland* [2007] IEHC 280, Laffoy J. declared that s.62 of the Offences Against the Person Act 1861 was unconstitutional and had thus not survived the passage of the Constitution. The measure in question imposed a maximum 10-year sentence in respect of indecent assault on a male. The corresponding legislation applicable at the relevant time to indecent assault on a female imposed a much lesser maximum sentence of two years' imprisonment. (The alleged offences had been committed between 1966 and 1976. The law has since been changed prospectively.) Thus, at the relevant time, different maximum sentences applied depending on whether the offence was committed against a male or a female. Ruling that there was no rational basis for such differentiation, Laffoy J. declared s.62 an unconstitutional breach of the right to equal treatment. There was no legitimate legislative purpose, she concluded, in protecting men more vigorously than women.

It is important to note, however, that not every instance of gender inequality is unconstitutional. If a difference of treatment is found to have a rational basis, it may be upheld as constitutional. In *MD (A Minor) v Ireland* [2012] IESC 10 a young man accused of engaging in sexual acts with a girl under 15 claimed that a provision that exempted girls under 17 from criminal liability in respect of an act of sexual intercourse with a boy under 17 was unconstitutional as no similar exemption was available to underage boys. (Criminal Law (Sexual Offences) Act 2006, s.5.) The Supreme Court concluded, however, that the Oireachtas was entitled to confine this exemption to girls on the basis that it took into account the risk of pregnancy for women, a risk that does not arise for males. Notably, the exemption applies only in respect of sexual intercourse. Likewise in *Lowth v Minister for Social Welfare* [1998] 4 I.R. 321, the Supreme Court reasoned that more favourable social welfare supports for deserted wives (and less favourable supports for deserted husbands) could be justified by the fact that deserted wives were, on average, more financially vulnerable than their male counterparts.

In *Norris v Attorney General* [1984] I.R. 36, the plaintiff complained that laws that penalised male but not female homosexual sexual activity were in breach of the guarantee of equality between the sexes. The Supreme Court reasoned (though not entirely convincingly) that parliament was entitled to consider that homosexual behaviour between males posed a greater "threat" to the social order than like female activity, and that the distinction was therefore constitutional. Likewise, in *Somjee v Minister for Justice* [1981] I.L.R.M. 324, Keane J. upheld laws that (at that time) made it easier for a woman to acquire citizenship through marriage than a similarly placed male. The court seemed to suggest that the State was entitled to take the view that women did not pose much threat to the security of the State, and could thus be treated with less caution than men. The court also noted that if the relevant privilege for women was declared unconstitutional, it would be of no benefit to Mr Somjee, as it would result in an "equalizing downwards" (women would be subject to the same rules as men). The court could not change the legislation to extend the privilege to Mr Somjee.

EQUALITY IN THE POLITICAL PROCESS

Given the importance of maintaining the integrity of the democratic process, equality is very much at a premium in the context of elections and referendums. The courts have thus frequently intervened to combat examples of unequal treatment favouring one candidate or side of a referendum or election campaign over another.

In *McKenna v An Taoiseach (No. 2)* [1995] 2 I.R. 10, the Supreme Court ruled that State funding to promote a "Yes" vote in the divorce referendum of 1995 infringed (amongst other things) the constitutional guarantee of equality. The Court suggested that extending public funds to one side of the campaign, but not the other, breached the equality rights of the citizen by "putting the voting rights of one class of citizen (those in favour of the change) above those of another class of citizen (those against)". Similarly, an unfair imbalance in the time given by public broadcasters to one side of a referendum debate over another is an unconstitutional breach of the guarantee of equality (see *Coughlan v Broadcasting Complaints Commission* [2000] 3 I.R. 1). Similar principles would apply to the coverage of election campaigns.

In *Kelly v Minister for the Environment* [2002] 4 I.R. 191 the plaintiff, an aspiring election candidate, challenged the validity of rules relating to a cap on election spending imposed on all candidates. While the court agreed that such a cap on spending would normally be legitimate, it noted that the rules exempted from consideration the value of Oireachtas facilities such as free postage, telephone calls and equipment available to existing Members of Parliament who were defending their seats. This, the court concluded, unjustifiably favoured sitting Members over aspiring candidates, an outcome that breached the constitutional guarantee of equality.

OTHER EXAMPLES

In *McMahon v Leahy* [1984] I.R. 525, the Supreme Court ruled that a prisoner who had escaped from a prison in Northern Ireland in 1975 was entitled to be treated in the same manner as the four other prisoners with whom he had escaped. These four other prisoners had been caught in the Republic some time previously but had not been extradited back to Northern Ireland because their offences were considered (at that time) to be "political offences". In the intervening period, however, the political offence doctrine had changed such that the accused was no longer able to take advantage of it. Nonetheless, the Supreme Court ruled that as the accused could not be treated any differently from similarly placed persons, it could not allow his extradition. (On the application of the equality guarantee in the criminal law context, see also *King v Attorney General* [1981] I.R. 233, and *Moore v D.P.P.* [2016] IEHC 244).

In *An Blascaod Mór Teo. v Commissioners of Public Works* [2000] 1 I.L.R.M. 401, the Supreme Court declared unconstitutional legislation that discriminated between relatives of those born on the Blasket Islands and persons who were not so related. The legislation in question purported to exempt from a compulsory purchase order in respect of the islands any person who was related to a former resident of the islands. This, the court found, breached the requirement that persons be treated equally before the law.

Equality also formed part of the reasoning in *NHV v Minister for Justice and Equality* [2017] IESC 35, where O'Donnell J. noted "a right to work at least in the sense of a freedom to work or seek employment is a part of the human personality and accordingly the Art.40.1 requirement that individuals as human persons are required be held equal before the law, means that those aspects of the right which are part of human personality cannot be withheld absolutely from non-citizens". (See, further, p.123).

WHERE THE INEQUALITY MAY BE JUSTIFIED ON OTHER GROUNDS

In some cases the courts have found that, although legal measures discriminate between similarly placed individuals, there may be a good reason for such a distinction. In such cases the equality guarantee will not have been breached.

In *O'B. v S.* [1984] I.R. 316, for instance, the Supreme Court ruled that measures that discriminated between children born inside and outside marriage respectively were justified (though not mandated) by the constitutional preference for marriage contained in Art.41.3.1°. Thus a law that excluded a child born outside marriage from claiming from the estate of her father (who died without making a will) was not unconstitutional, despite the fact that she would have succeeded in her claim had she been a child born inside marriage. (The law has since been changed by the Status of Children Act 1987.)

In *Murphy v Attorney General* [1982] I.R. 241 the Supreme Court accepted that tax provisions that discriminated against married couples in favour of unmarried couples were offset by corresponding privileges enjoyed exclusively by married couples. The Court thus reasoned that there had been no breach of Art.40.1 (although it proceeded to find the legislation unconstitutional on foot of the provisions in Art.41).

The Supreme Court also rejected an argument based on equality in *Fleming v Ireland* [2013] IESC 19, dismissing the proposition that a ban on assisted suicide discriminated against people who could not, due to a disability, take their own lives without assistance. The law in question applied to all, and was neutral on its face. As Denham C.J. remarked, "[t]he Court does not consider that the constitutional principle of equal treatment before the law ... extends to categorise as unequal the differential indirect effects on a person of an objectively neutral law addressed to persons other than that person." This appears to be a rather limited view of equality, excluding the unconstitutionality of indirect discrimination (where a law is neutral on its face but, in practice, impacts more severely on certain categories of people).

Personal Rights

16

The Constitution acknowledges various personal rights which are guaranteed by Art.40.3. There are some "enumerated rights" that are explicitly and expressly mentioned in the text of the Constitution. They include the right to liberty (Art.40.4), freedom of expression (Art.40.6.1°) and the right to practise and profess one's religion (Art.44). Article 40.3.2° also expressly enumerates (sets out) a number of important personal rights, including the right to life discussed below in Ch.17. The right to one's good name and individual property rights are also expressly protected by Art.40.3.2°.

Article 40.3.2° requires the State to protect the personal rights of the individual, four specific rights being expressly listed. The Constitution, however, also protects certain rights that are not expressly mentioned in the text of the document. For instance, although the Constitution does not explicitly create a right to privacy, it is nonetheless recognised as a protected constitutional right. Such rights, not explicitly mentioned in the constitutional text, are known as "unenumerated" rights.

In theory, most of the personal rights protected by the Constitution are not rights created by the Constitution itself, but are recognised by the Constitution as already existing. Indeed, the courts have often interpreted some of these rights as applying to both citizens and non-citizens alike, on the basis that these are universal human rights.

SOME IMPORTANT EXAMPLES OF ENUMERATED RIGHTS

GOOD NAME

The right to one's good name (Art.40.3.2°) and the right to liberty (Art.40.4) were both relied upon in *C.C. v Ireland* [2006] IESC 33. In that case, the Supreme Court declared unconstitutional a law criminalising sexual intercourse with a person under the age of 15, with no defence as to genuine mistake as to age. This effectively meant that the accused could be convicted despite the fact that he was not aware that the girl was under 15. Thus, Hardiman J. concluded, "the Section contains no balance: it wholly removes the mental element and expressly criminalises the mentally innocent". As a result, the court ruled that the measure infringed Art.40 of the Constitution, in that it unfairly denied the plaintiff his right to liberty and to his good name under that Article.

The right to one's good name also featured prominently in *Maguire v Ardagh* [2002] 1 I.R. 385. The Oireachtas had set up a special sub-committee to determine the facts surrounding the unfortunate shooting dead of John Carthy in Abbeylara in April 2000. While the sub-committee's findings would have no direct legal effect, there was nonetheless the possibility that a finding might be made that would reflect adversely on certain members of the Gardaí. The Supreme Court concluded that the Oireachtas did not have the inherent power to set up an investigative committee of this nature. While the sub-committee could not penalise a person, the sub-committee's findings as to culpability were nonetheless capable of damaging the good name of a person, contrary to Art.40.3, and required fair procedures in order to protect that right. (See also *Re Haughey* [1971] 1 I.R. 217.)

Evidently the right to one's good name is vindicated by the tort of defamation (i.e. libel and slander), which allows a person to sue for untrue statements that damage the reputation and standing of the individual. (See the Defamation Act 2009.)

Protection of the person

In *Kinsella v Governor of Mountjoy Prison* [2012] 1 I.R. 467 Hogan J. invoked the right to the protection of the person, expressly mentioned in Art.40.3.2°. A shortage of single cells and concerns around safety led to a prisoner being detained in a small padded cell with no access to recreational or sanitation facilities. Hogan J. noted that "the State was obliged ... not merely to protect the integrity of the human body of a citizen, but also the integrity of their mind and personality". While acknowledging the challenges involved in managing a prison, these conditions constituted a breach of the plaintiff's right to the protection of the person. This right may also be applied as between citizens (horizontally). In *Sullivan v Boylan (No. 2)* [2013] IEHC 104 constant harassment, intimidation and threats from a debt collector (causing acute mental distress) led to a finding that the latter had breached the right to inviolability of dwelling (Art.40.5) and right to protection of the person, resulting in an award of damages.

Unenumerated rights

On what basis do the courts recognise a right that is not expressly mentioned in the Constitution?

In *Ryan v Attorney General* [1965] I.R. 294, Kenny J. had to consider whether there was a constitutional right to bodily integrity. Although there is no express mention of such a right in the text of the Constitution, Kenny J. agreed that citizens did enjoy such an "unenumerated" right, and that it was, moreover, protected by the Constitution. Kenny J. looked at the provisions of Art.40.3, which require that the State defend and vindicate certain rights "in particular ... the life, person, good name and property rights of every citizen". The judge pointed out that by using the phrase "in particular", the Article necessarily implied that these express rights were not the only rights that warranted protection. Other rights, he concluded, were within the contemplation of the Article, unenumerated rights that, he said, flowed from the "Christian and Democratic nature of the State".

How does one determine the content of these unenumerated rights?

The courts have taken a number of different approaches to identify these unwritten rights. It is clear, however, that in recent years the courts have proved more reticent about identifying such rights unless they are reasonably implicit in the text of the Constitution.

1. Implied rights

Perhaps the most concrete of the tests for determining the existence of unlisted rights is that of "implication" from enumerated rights. The presence of certain express rights in the Constitution is said necessarily to imply that certain other implicit rights enjoy constitutional protection. For instance, one could say that the right to practise one's religion (in Art.44) necessarily implies a corollary right not to practise a religion. Similarly, the courts have implied from the constitutional right to associate, to form unions and associations, a right not to associate, that is to "dissociate" (see *Educational Company v Fitzpatrick (No. 2)* [1961] I.R. 345). In a like manner, the Directives of Social Policy in Art.45, although non-binding in law, have been used to identify an unenumerated right to earn a livelihood protected by Art.40.3 (see *Murtagh Properties v Cleary* [1972] I.R. 330). The express right to vote by secret ballot has been said to support the existence of the unenumerated general right to privacy.

2. Christian and democratic nature of the State

In *Ryan v Attorney General*, Kenny J. suggested that these unenumerated rights flow from the "Christian and Democratic nature of the State". The fact that the State broadly springs from a Christian and democratic tradition necessary implies that certain rights and values enjoy constitutional protection. This approach was cited in *Kennedy v Ireland* [1987] I.R. 587, for example, to support a general right to privacy. Likewise in *State (M) v Attorney General*

[1979] I.R. 73, Finlay P. concluded that the right to travel flowed from the Christian and democratic nature of the State. He contrasted the restrictions on foreign travel in some authoritarian, non-democratic states with the general right to travel in democratic states.

3. Inherent rights

In *McGee v Attorney General* [1974] I.R. 284, Henchy J. speaks of unenumerated rights as rights that are "fundamental to the standing of the individual ... in the context of the social order envisaged by the Constitution". In *Norris v Attorney General* [1984] I.R. 36 the same judge remarked:

> "... [T]here is necessarily given to the citizen, within the required social, political and moral framework, such a range of personal freedoms or immunities as are necessary to ensure his dignity and freedom as an individual in the type of society envisaged. The essence of those rights is that they inhere in the individual personality of the citizen in his capacity as a vital human component of the social, political and moral order posited by the Constitution."

4. Natural rights

Some judges in the past have used the concept of natural law and natural rights to determine the content of various unenumerated rights. The concept of natural law embraces the idea that, through the observation of human nature and the use of reason, one may discern certain universal principles of right and wrong. From such an exercise, one may thus identify certain natural rights that all humans enjoy. The text of the Constitution itself references the concept of natural rights. Both Arts 41 and 43, for instance, make express reference to natural rights that are "antecedent [prior to] and superior to" positive law, that is, laws enacted by humans. These are rights, then, that exist independently of human-made law; rights that inhere in us by virtue of a higher universal law superior to the State. These rights, moreover, exist in each human regardless of the content of positive law.

GREATER RETICENCE AROUND IDENTIFYING NEW UNENUMERATED RIGHTS AND USING NATURAL LAW

In *McGee v Attorney General* [1974] I.R. 284 Walsh J. relied heavily on the concept of natural law as a source of constitutional rights. In more recent decisions, however, the courts have rowed back from reliance on natural law. In particular, in *Article 26 and the Regulation of Information (Services Outside the State for Termination of Pregnancies) Bill 1995* [1995] 1 I.R. 1, the Supreme Court rejected the proposition that the natural law or any "higher law" prevailed over the will of the people as expressed in a constitutional referendum. The people are constitutionally sovereign and supreme, and not subject to any higher law. Indeed, that case seems generally to have heralded a demise in the courts' willingness to identify new rights under the unenumerated rights doctrine and to use natural law as a source of such rights. The Supreme Court pointed out that in previous cases identifying unenumerated rights,

> "the Court in each such case had satisfied itself that such personal right was one which could be reasonably implied from and was guaranteed by the provisions of the Constitution, interpreted in accordance with its ideas of prudence, justice and charity."

This suggests that the courts nowadays will not readily resort to identifying new rights unless they are reasonably implicit in the constitutional text.

It is difficult to escape the conclusion that widely framed tests give judges too much leeway to "create" rights where none existed before, or to deny them, in accordance with the judges' own personal perspectives. In *Riordan v An Tánaiste* [2005] 3 I.R. 62 Budd J. observed that the natural law approach to interpretation "permits reliance on standards which are often subjective and nebulous and which may not give reliable guidelines in dealing with actual constitutional problems". Although the decision in *IO'T v B* [1998] 2 I.R. 321 gave rise to a new unenumerated right (the right to know one's identity), Keane J. (dissenting) heralded an emerging reticence around identifying new rights when he commented, "[i]t is sufficient to say that, save where an unenumerated right has been unequivocally established by precedent ... some degree of judicial restraint is called for in identifying new rights of this nature ...". (See, also, *TD v Minister for Education* [2001] 4 I.R. 259). Certainly, the courts have moved away from reliance on natural law as a source of rights.

SOME IMPORTANT EXAMPLES OF UNENUMERATED RIGHTS

Since the decision in *Ryan v Attorney General* [1965] I.R. 294, the courts have determined the existence of many unenumerated rights. Here are some of the more important rights that have been identified to date.

THE RIGHT TO BODILY INTEGRITY/RIGHT TO HEALTH

The first "unenumerated" right to be identified by a court was the right to bodily integrity. This right was first established in *Ryan v Attorney General* [1965] I.R. 294, where the courts were asked to consider the constitutionality of a law allowing the fluoridation of public water supplies by the State. Although the courts concluded that there was no proven danger from such fluoridation and no breach of the Constitution, both the High Court and the Supreme Court were satisfied that the plaintiff had a right to bodily integrity under the Constitution. That right entailed that "no mutilation of the body or any of its members may be carried out on any citizen under authority of the law except for the good of the whole body and that no process which is or may, as a matter of probability, be dangerous or harmful to the life or health of the citizens or any of them may be imposed (in the sense of being made compulsory) by an Act of the Oireachtas". The courts concluded, however, that there was no violation of the right in this case. In *State (C) v Frawley* [1976] I.R. 365, Finlay P. confirmed that where a person is lawfully imprisoned the State cannot "without justification or necessity, expose the health of that person to risk or danger" and has a general duty to safeguard prisoners' health. The court found, in that case, that the detention of a prisoner with serious mental health problems in solitary confinement and under physical restraint was lawful because of the serious risk of harm to himself and others. The court also dismissed the applicant's claim to be entitled to a rare, highly specialised form of treatment for his condition.

In *State (Richardson) v Mountjoy Prison* [1980] I.R. 82, a prisoner successfully argued that the insanitary conditions of the "slopping out" facilities at Mountjoy Prison constituted a breach of her right to health. The High Court ruled that the State had failed to protect the applicant's health while she was incarcerated, particularly as there was a risk of cross-contamination of facilities used for disposing of human waste. The Constitution required that, while in prison, she was entitled to appropriate facilities to maintain hygiene.

One aspect of the right to bodily integrity relates to the entitlement of a person to refuse medical treatment, even where this will inevitably lead to the death of that person. In *Re a Ward of Court (Withdrawal of Medical Treatment)* [1996] 2 I.R. 79, the Supreme Court ruled that the right to bodily integrity presupposes that a person cannot ordinarily be made to undergo medical treatment to which he or she has not consented.

In *Kinsella v Governor of Mountjoy Prison* [2011] IEHC 235, Hogan J. noted that the State is obliged to protect not only bodily integrity but also that of the mind and human personality.

THE RIGHT TO EARN A LIVELIHOOD

It is unconstitutional for the State, arbitrarily and without good reason, to prevent a person from earning a living through a legitimate trade or profession for which that person is qualified. This does not, of course, mean that the State is obliged to give everyone a job, still less to guarantee all citizens that they may work in whatever field they so desire. Nor does it prevent the State from placing proportionate restrictions on the practice of various professions, with a view to protecting consumer rights and the public good.

The first case to establish this right to earn a livelihood was *Murtagh Properties v Cleary* [1972] I.R. 330. There Kenny J. held that a proposed union picket, protesting the employment of female bar staff at a pub, was in breach of the constitutional right of the female staff to earn a livelihood. Kenny J. determined the existence of this right by reference to the (non-binding) Directive Principles of Social Policy, outlined in Art.45 of the Constitution. One of these principles noted that "men and women equally" have the right to an adequate means of livelihood. This implied, he said, a right to earn a livelihood, protected under Art.40.3.1° as an unenumerated personal right. The union thus could not legally picket the pub with a view to preventing the female bar staff from earning a livelihood on account of their sex. To condone such activity, Kenny J. concluded, would be in breach of the women's right to make their living free from unjust restrictions.

Similarly in *NHV v Minister for Justice and Equality* [2017] IESC 35, O'Donnell J. spoke of "... a freedom to seek work which ... implies a negative obligation not to prevent the person from seeking or obtaining employment, at least without substantial justification". The Supreme Court in that case found that an absolute prohibition on all asylum seekers working infringed the constitutional right to seek employment. Although the Court acknowledged that limitations might be placed on the entitlement of non-EU nationals to work in the State, the absolute bar in this case, with no time limit, infringed the right. O'Donnell J. noted that "a right to work at least in the sense of a freedom to work or seek employment is a part of the human personality and accordingly the Art.40.1 requirement that individuals as human persons are required [to] be held equal before the law, means that those aspects of the right which are part of human personality cannot be withheld absolutely from non-citizens."

Nonetheless, as Costello J. remarked in *Attorney General v Paperlink Ltd* [1984] I.L.R.M. 373 at 384, the "... freedom to exercise this constitutional right is not an absolute one, however, and it may be subject to legitimate legal restraints". Therefore where the State can show a good reason to prevent a person from working in a particular profession, no right will have been breached. Thus, laws that restrict children from working, with the aim of protecting children from exploitation and ensuring they get a proper education, are unlikely to be found unconstitutional. (See the Protection of Young Persons in Employment Act 1996.) In *Landers v Attorney General* (1973) 109 I.L.T.R. 1, the High Court ruled that a law preventing a young boy from singing in pubs for money was not unconstitutional, the rationale being that the Oireachtas was entitled to consider that such an environment was not a suitable place for a child to be employed.

Laws may also prevent a person from working in his chosen profession where this would pose a danger to the public (or, for instance, to children or vulnerable people) or where the person has broken the law in the course of his employment. In *Hand v Dublin Corporation* [1991] 1 I.R. 409, for instance, the Supreme Court upheld legislation preventing a street trader from obtaining a casual trading licence, the reason being that the trader had twice been convicted of trading without such a licence.

In *Attorney General v Paperlink Ltd* [1984] I.L.R.M. 373 at 384 Costello J. remarks, "[i]t is clear that the constitutional right to earn a livelihood is not a right to earn a livelihood in whatever manner a person chooses. Obviously a person must be adequately qualified to do that work." Likewise, in *White v Bar Council of Ireland* [2016] IECA 363 the Court of Appeal noted that this right "does not extend to a right to earn a livelihood by any particular means or through the exercise of any particular occupation". In *Kenny v Dental Council* [2004] IEHC 29, for instance, Gilligan J. ruled that the State was entitled to restrict the practice of dentistry to persons who met certain requirements as to training and competency.

In summary, provided the State can offer a legitimate and sufficiently serious reason for such restriction, it is always possible to curtail the right to earn a livelihood. Such penalties or restrictions must, however, be fair and proportionate. In *Cox v Ireland* [1992] 2 I.R. 503 a measure preventing a convicted person from working for the State for seven years following a conviction was declared disproportionate. The severe consequences far outstripped the relatively minor nature of some of the crimes to which the measure was applied. (See also *Lovett v Minister for Education* [1997] I.L.R.M. 89.)

THE RIGHT TO PRIVACY

A person has the general right to privacy, especially in relation to his or her personal and family affairs. The right to privacy first arose in *McGee v Attorney General* [1974] I.R. 284, a case concerning a legislative ban on the importation of contraception. In that case, the Supreme Court ruled, by a majority, that this prohibition infringed the marital privacy rights of a married couple. By banning access to contraceptives, the State was unjustifiably interfering in what was essentially a family decision, a matter of marital privacy.

In *Kennedy v Ireland* [1987] I.R. 587, Hamilton P. ruled that by tapping the phones of two journalists without good reason, the State had infringed their individual right to privacy. A key element of this decision was that the State had no legitimate security interest in the conversations of these reporters; the tapping was "deliberate, conscious, and unjustified". The tapping was allegedly effected merely for political purposes. This not being a good reason for tapping a phone, the State was ordered to pay damages to the journalists for the breach of their constitutional right to privacy. (Phones can, however, be tapped for national security reasons and to prevent serious crime, subject to procedural safeguards laid down by law.)

In *Simpson v Governor of Mountjoy Prison* [2017] IEHC 561 White J. concluded that there had been a breach of a prisoner's right to privacy in circumstances where he was required to share a cell without in-cell sanitation. This meant that he had to use a chamber pot, without a privacy screen.

It appears the right to privacy can be applied horizontally, against parties other than the State. In *Herrity v Associated Newspapers* [2009] 1 I.R. 316 the defendant had published phone conversations secretly tape-recorded in breach of legislation. The conversations concerned an affair between a married woman and a Catholic priest. Dunne J. concluded that, even though the defendant was a private organisation, it could be sued for a breach of the right to privacy. Given that the phone conversations were recorded illegally, Dunne J. concluded that there had been a breach of the right, awarding the plaintiff €90,000 for that breach.

The right to privacy, however, is not an absolute right. The State may, where it has good reason to do so and in accordance with law, impinge upon the privacy of a citizen, where for instance it is necessary to protect the security of the State or to vindicate the constitutional rights of others. The right to privacy, in particular, has to be balanced against the right to free expression, and the common good. In *Cogley and Aherne v RTÉ* [2005] IEHC 180 the High Court refused to restrain the broadcast of a television programme including the secret recording of conditions within a nursing home, with a view to exposing alleged abuse of patients at the home. Citing the right to freedom of expression and the public interest in the rights of the patients, the court declined to prevent the broadcast of the programme. In fact, due to the right of free expression, the courts generally are very reluctant to impose prior restraint on publications and broadcasts.

THE RIGHT TO HAVE CHILDREN AND THE RIGHT TO IDENTITY

In *Murray v Attorney General* [1991] 1 I.L.R.M. 465, the Supreme Court ruled that, ordinarily, married couples have the right to bear children. In that case, however, the plaintiffs were both prisoners, jailed for life for the murder of a Garda. The court ruled, therefore, that the requirements of prison security meant that their right could be restricted insofar as its exercise would compromise prison security and place unreasonable demands on the prison authorities. There is also an unenumerated right for a child to know his or her identity and origins, though this right must be balanced against parents' right to privacy. (*I.O'T v B.* [1998] 2 I.R. 321)

THE RIGHT TO MARRY

In *Ryan v Attorney General* it was first suggested (though it was not relevant in that case) that Art.40.3 protected the right to marry. This point was confirmed later in *O'Shea v Ireland* [2007] 2 I.R. 313. There the High Court declared a law preventing a woman from marrying her former husband's brother (the woman having divorced her former husband) to be unconstitutional. Laffoy J. agreed that the State had infringed the plaintiffs' right to marry, further concluding that this infringement was not necessary to protect the institution of marriage, the family, or the common good. The right to marry, she noted, was not unlimited or absolute, but could be regulated in the common good.

In *Zappone and Gilligan v Revenue Commissioners* [2006] IEHC 404 the High Court ruled that a lesbian couple who had married in Canada was not entitled to be treated as married for tax purposes. There was, at that time, no constitutional right to marry a person of the same sex. The right to marry, however, now extends to same-sex as well as opposite-sex couples. Article 41.4 of the Constitution (as inserted by the Thirty-fourth Amendment) states: "Marriage may be contracted in accordance with law by two persons without distinction as to their sex." The Marriage Act 2015 now permits the marriage of same-sex couples. This means that marriage, under the Constitution, is open to same-sex and opposite-sex couples alike, provided they comply with the normal legal requirements for entering into marriage.

THE RIGHT OF ACCESS TO THE COURTS (THE RIGHT TO LITIGATE)

A person cannot normally be refused access to justice. In *Macauley v Minister for Posts and Telegraphs* [1966] I.R. 345, Kenny J. declared unconstitutional a rule that prevented a case being taken against a Government Minister without the Attorney General's prior approval. Similarly, in *Byrne v Ireland* [1972] I.R. 241 the Supreme Court declared that the State is not immune from being sued for negligence. Both cases confirm the general right of the citizen to access the courts of law and to litigate (take cases).

In *Murphy v Greene* [1990] 2 I.R. 566 the Supreme Court ruled that requiring the leave of the High Court to start proceedings under s.260 of the Mental Treatment Act 1945 was a curtailment of the constitutional right of access to the courts and thus should be strictly construed. Similarly, in *Blehein v Minister for Health* [2004] IEHC 374, [2008] IESC 40 a provision of the Mental Treatment Act 1945 restricting legal challenges to a decision to incarcerate mentally ill persons was declared an infringement of the right to litigate. The legislation required the patient to seek leave from the High Court prior to litigation, which would be granted only where a substantial case could be made to the effect that the decision to incarcerate was made in bad faith or without reasonable care. Declaring the provision to be unconstitutional,

Carroll J. ruled that the permitted grounds for challenge set out in the Act were so narrow as to deny the patient the right to litigate. On appeal, the Supreme Court agreed, ruling that while restrictions may be placed on the right to litigate, the restrictions in this case were disproportionate in that they were arbitrary and did not restrict the plaintiff's rights as little as possible. (See also *Grant v Roche Products* [2009] 4 I.R. 679.)

It is not, however, unconstitutional generally to restrict a person's access to court on the grounds that there has been an inordinate delay in the taking of proceedings. The Statutes of Limitations 1957–2000 (as amended), for instance, set out certain periods of limitation for the taking of cases. In *Tuohy v Courtney* [1994] 3 I.R. 1, the Supreme Court ruled that, provided they were not unreasonably short, periods of limitation were not unconstitutional. The right to litigate, the court reasoned, was subject to the defendant's right to certainty and finality in respect of his or her potential legal liability. Nonetheless, where a period of limitation is unreasonably short it may be unconstitutional, especially where there is no provision for the extension of the time limit by a judge. (See *White v Dublin City Council* [2004] 1 I.R. 545 and *Brady v Donegal County Council* [1989] I.L.R.M. 182, though see also *Re Article 26 and Sections 5 and 10 of the Illegal Immigrants (Trafficking) Bill, 1999* [2000] 2 I.R. 360.)

THE RIGHT TO LEGAL REPRESENTATION

It is well established that a person is entitled to legal representation in both criminal and civil cases before the courts. This is a necessary corollary to the right to litigate and to access the courts.

The right to legal representation extends also to situations in which a person is required to give evidence to an inquiry or administrative body, where the good name and reputation or other personal rights of the person giving evidence are potentially in jeopardy as a result of such investigation. This right was emphasised in *Re the Commission to Inquire into Child Abuse; the Commission v Notice Party A* [2002] 3 I.R. 459. There, the court found that a restriction on the number of legal representatives accompanying a witness before the Commission, to one barrister and one solicitor only, infringed the witness's constitutional right to be represented by counsel of his choice. The Commission could not, on its own initiative, curtail the attendance of the legal representatives of the witness's choosing.

A key barrier to court access, however, is arguably not legal, but financial. Court cases tend to be extremely expensive. Thus the question arises whether a person has a constitutional right to free legal aid in taking a case.

It is clear that free legal aid is certainly constitutionally required in criminal cases for those who cannot afford legal representation, this being an aspect of the accused's right to defend himself or herself adequately. In *State (Healy) v Donoghue* [1976] I.R. 325, the Supreme Court ruled that a poorly educated and deprived young man was entitled under the Constitution to free legal aid in his defence against charges of criminal wrongdoing. Without such aid, the court reasoned, the accused might well be denied his constitutional right to legal representation at trial, and to mount an adequate defence of his innocence. The extent of State-funded representation to which a person is entitled depends on the seriousness and complexity of the case but may (depending on the circumstances) include a right to both a solicitor and a barrister, so that the accused will not be at a disadvantage in court in complex or serious cases. (See *Carmody v Minister for Justice* [2010] 1 I.R. 635.)

In civil proceedings, however, the courts have proved less generous. In *Magee v Farrell* [2009] I.R. 703, the Supreme Court concluded that the constitutional right to legal aid generally extended only to criminal proceedings, and did not entitle a woman to legal aid for the purpose of being adequately represented at a coroner's inquest into her son's death. Where a person's liberty is at stake, constitutional fairness requires such a right be extended (see *Kirwan v Minister for Justice* [1994] 2 I.R. 417, where the applicant was seeking release from the Central Mental Hospital), but otherwise it would appear that the scope for a constitutional right to civil legal aid is very limited. There is, however, a *legal* right to civil legal aid in certain circumstances under the Civil Legal Aid Act 1995. Where civil legal aid is made available by statute, there is a constitutional duty to ensure that it is administered fairly such that very long delays in obtaining civil legal aid may be unlawful (see *O'Donoghue v Legal Aid Board* [2004] IEHC 413).

THE RIGHT TO TRAVEL

In *State (M.) v Attorney General* [1979] I.R. 73, the High Court ruled that a law preventing the removal of certain children from the State, even with the consent of both parents, was unconstitutional. The denial of a passport in this case to an Irish-born infant (whose parents wanted her to travel to live with her grandparents in Nigeria) infringed her constitutional right to travel outside the State. Similarly, in *Lennon and Ganly v Fitzgerald* [1981] I.L.R.M 84, O'Hanlon J. declined to prevent the Irish rugby union team from travelling to South Africa in the apartheid era, reasoning that to do so would infringe the constitutional right to travel.

The right to travel, however, is not absolute. It may be lawfully restricted, for instance, to prevent criminal suspects from escaping justice, or to prevent the unlawful removal of children from the custody of their parents. Similarly, the right to travel only guarantees the right to leave the State, with no necessary guarantee that a person will be granted permission to enter another State. (As EU citizens, however, Irish citizens have rights of free movement within the European Union).

The right to communicate

In *Attorney General v Paperlink* [1984] I.L.R.M. 373, Costello J. ruled that citizens have a constitutional right to communicate ideas and information. In *Holland v Governor of Portlaoise Prison* [2004] 2 I.R. 573, McKechnie J. declared invalid a decision of the prison governor refusing a prisoner permission to be visited by members of the media. The prisoner was seeking public support for his claim that he had been wrongly convicted. The prison governor, however, applied a blanket policy which prevented contact between any prisoner and a member of the media. While acknowledging that there might be good reason to limit such access in specific cases, McKechnie J. ruled that the imposition of a blanket ban on media contact disproportionately infringed the right of the prisoner to communicate, as well as his freedom of expression. The judge ruled that the governor was required to consider each request for contact on its merits. Moreover, he could restrict contact only where this was necessary to safeguard the security and good order of the prison.

Fair procedures

The courts have concluded on a number of occasions that Art.40.3 entitles citizens to be treated fairly by the State. In particular, it is well established that citizens have a right to have fair procedures (sometimes called "natural justice" or "constitutional justice") applied by State bodies making decisions that impact on citizens. (See *Glover v BLN Ltd.* [1973] I.R. 388, *Garvey v Ireland* [1981] I.R. 75.) Fair procedures include a right to be heard in cases where a person's rights are at stake and a right to an independent and impartial decision-maker. (See, for instance, *Maguire v Ardagh* [2002] 1 I.R. 385.)

Limitations and restrictions on constitutional rights

Few constitutional rights are ever absolute. Most rights are subject to limitations and qualifications, whether on the grounds that the right conflicts with another person's superior rights or that the common good demands that one's rights be curtailed. The Constitution necessarily permits individual constitutional rights to be limited by reference to certain social or economic priorities and, in particular, by reference to the "common good" (the collective interest of society as a whole). The Preamble to the Constitution, for instance, while guaranteeing the "dignity and freedom of the individual" insists also that "true social order [be] attained". Similarly, the rights to free expression and association in Art.40.6 are expressly stated to be subject to limitation where "public order or morality" so demand. Article 9.3 emphasises that citizens have duties as well as rights. Personal rights under Art.40.3 are to be defended and vindicated "as far as practicable".

For instance, where a person is lawfully imprisoned, his or her right to liberty is necessarily curtailed. In *Creighton v Ireland* [2010] IESC 50 the Supreme Court noted that "[a] sentence of imprisonment deprives a person of his right to personal liberty". Nonetheless, it added "the prisoner may continue to exercise rights 'which do not depend on the continuance of his personal liberty...'". In *Murray v Ireland* [1985] I.R. 332, [1991] 1 I.L.R.M. 465, the High Court and Supreme Court alike ruled that a married couple's right to have children could be limited in certain cases. The husband and wife in this case were both serving prison sentences for the unlawful killing of a Garda. Although the courts accepted that the couple had a right to bear children, the requirements of prison security, and the duty to safeguard the general public, justified the refusal to facilitate the plaintiffs' aspirations to procreate. As Costello J. explained, "[w]hen the State lawfully exercises its power to deprive a citizen of his constitutional right to liberty many consequences result, including the deprivation of liberty to exercise many other constitutionally protected rights, which prisoners must accept". (Prisoners, nonetheless, continued to enjoy those rights that do not conflict with the requirements of prison security and good order). The conflicting rights of other persons may also be used to justify the curtailment of lesser rights in certain situations. For instance, in *People (DPP) v Shaw* [1982] I.R. 1, the Supreme Court ruled that an accused's right to liberty could be curtailed with a view to vindicating the right to life of a young woman.

The courts have regularly acknowledged that the Oireachtas is entitled, in making laws, to restrict the exercise of rights and balance conflicting rights with a view to promoting the collective interest (common good). In considering the extent to which a right may be curtailed, the courts have laid down a number of tests. In *Tuohy v Courtney* [1994] 3 I.R. 1, Finlay C.J. in the Supreme Court noted that the Oireachtas was entitled to balance constitutional rights and duties. It was not the function of the courts "to impose their view of the correct or desirable balance in substitution for the view of the legislature". Instead the court's role was to determine "whether the balance contained in the impugned legislation is so contrary to reason and fairness as to constitute an unjust attack on some individual's constitutional rights". This is called the "rationality test".

A somewhat more robust test—that of proportionality—was set out in *Heaney v Ireland* [1994] 3 I.R. 593 (a case concerning permitted restrictions on the right to silence):

- The objective (or reason) behind the restrictive measure must be "of sufficient importance to warrant over-riding a constitutionally protected right".

- The reasons for the restrictions on rights must be "pressing and substantial".
- The restrictions must, moreover, be proportionate in that they:
    (1) "are rationally connected to the objective ...;
    (2) are not arbitrary, unfair or based on irrational considerations;
    (3) impair the right as little as possible and
    (4) their effects on rights are proportional to the objective."

The proportionality test suggests that rights may be validly curtailed by law for legitimate and pressing reasons relating to the common good. Nonetheless, the courts require that the steps taken to achieve this purpose should be connected to the legitimate state purpose, should be broadly justified by the seriousness of that objective, and should be no more restrictive than is necessary to achieve the purpose. The measure should "intrude into constitutional rights as little as is reasonably possible" (in *Re Article 26 and the Employment Equality Bill 1996* [1997] 2 I.R. 321). A colloquial way of putting this might be to say that one need not use a sledgehammer to crack a nut.

17 The Right to Life

Arguably the most important right in the Constitution, the right to life, is guaranteed protection generally by Art.40.3.2°. The courts place a high value on the right to life, which generally prevails over other rights. (See *In the Matter of Baby AB* [2011] IEHC 1 and *People (D.P.P.) v Shaw* (1982) I.R. 1).

The right to life arguably ranks above other rights, but it is not absolute. The right to life of each individual is subject to the right to life of every other individual. Thus, Irish criminal law acknowledges that a homicide may be justified on the grounds that one person killed another person in of reasonable self-defence. In the *People (Attorney General) v Dwyer* [1972] I.R. 416, Walsh J. observed: "A homicide is not unlawful if it is committed in the execution or advancement of justice, or in reasonable self-defence of person or property, or in order to prevent the commission of an atrocious crime, or by misadventure."

THE BAN ON THE DEATH PENALTY

The Criminal Justice Act 1990 abolished the death penalty in Ireland. Since 2001, moreover, the Constitution contains an express prohibition on the reintroduction of the death penalty, preventing a sentence of death being imposed for any crime. Article 15.5.2° (introduced by the Twenty-first Amendment) prevents the Oireachtas from ever prescribing death as a penalty for an offence, even in times of war or emergency under Art.28.3.

RIGHT TO REFUSE MEDICAL TREATMENT

A person with sufficient mental capacity generally has the right to refuse medical treatment or surgery, however necessary it may be, even if this may result in the death of that person (see *Re a Ward of Court* [1996] 2 I.R. 79). This is an aspect of the constitutional rights to bodily integrity and autonomy/privacy. A person of sound mind and sufficient capacity may request the withdrawal of treatment and thus allow nature to take its course, even if this leads to death. Ordinarily, where a person forces another to undergo medical treatment against his or her will, this would amount to a breach of that person's rights to privacy and bodily integrity. (On the test for capacity, see *Fitzpatrick v*

FK [2009] 2 I.R. 7.) In a similar vein see *Governor of X. Prison v P.McD.* [2015] IECH 259, though see also *A.B. v C.D.* [2016] IEHC 161.

In *Re a Ward of Court* [1996] 2 I.R. 79, this right was extended to its logical conclusion, with the Supreme Court ruling that citizens generally have a right to die a *natural* death. That case involved a severely brain-damaged woman who had remained in a near-persistent vegetative state for nearly 23 years, with no prospect of recovery. Her family, distressed at their relative's condition, wanted a tube supplying food to her stomach to be removed, so that she could, as they saw it, die with dignity.

The Supreme Court agreed that a person had the right to refuse such medical treatment even if this resulted in the death of the individual. Where an individual, moreover, lacked the mental capacity to make such a decision, the court itself would decide based on the "best interests" of the person. The Court concluded that the withdrawal of treatment was in the ward's best interest. The Court emphasised, however, that this did not permit a person actively to take another's life. The constitutional right is confined to death by natural means. (See also *In the Matter of S.R. (A Ward of Court)* [2012] IEHC 2.)

There is, in particular, no constitutional right to die by artificial means, or through the active intervention of another party. In *Fleming v Ireland* [2013] IESC 19 the Supreme Court rejected a challenge to the ban on assisted suicide, concluding that there was no constitutional right to end one's life by active means, or to have another person assist in taking one's life. While suicide itself is no longer a crime, the Supreme Court concluded that the ban on assisted suicide was constitutional.

THE RIGHT TO LIFE OF THE UNBORN

From 1983 to 2018, the Constitution greatly restricted the termination of pregnancy in Ireland. The Eighth Amendment to the Constitution 1983 inserted a new Art.40.3.3° into the Constitution expressly confirming the "right to life of the unborn", subject to the equal right to life of its mother. It guaranteed "as far as practicable" to defend and vindicate the right to life of the unborn.

According to the Supreme Court decision in the *Attorney General v X* [1992] 1 I.R. 1, under the Eighth Amendment, deliberate action that resulted in the ending of unborn life was not constitutionally permitted in Ireland unless "... it is established as a matter of probability that there is a real and substantial risk to the life, as distinct from the health, of the mother, which can only be avoided by the termination of her pregnancy ...". The risk need not have been immediate or imminent, but it had to be a risk to life rather than just health. The defendant in *X*, a 14-year-old girl, had become pregnant following an alleged rape and was, as a result, suicidal. The High Court had imposed an injunction preventing her from travelling outside the jurisdiction or otherwise making arrangements for an abortion. The Supreme Court, however, lifted this injunction. It agreed that the likelihood that the girl would commit suicide constituted a real and substantial risk to her life such that she was entitled to an abortion in Ireland. (See also *A and B v Eastern Health Board* [1998] 1 I.R. 464.) The procedures for determining whether an abortion is permitted in Ireland were legislated for in the Protection of Life During Pregnancy Act 2013.

A risk to life included, for this purpose, a risk that the woman would commit suicide unless she had a termination. In 1992 and again in 2002, the people rejected referendums proposing to confine the right to an abortion to cases where the risk to life did not arise from the mother's suicidal state. (These were the failed Twelfth and Twenty-fifth Amendments.)

In *M v Minister for Justice and Equality* [2018] IESC 14 the Supreme Court concluded that provisions of the Constitution other than the original Art.40.3.3° do not offer constitutional protection to the unborn. It ruled that the unborn had (until birth) no constitutional rights other than the right to life under the former Art.40.3.3°. In particular, it said, Art.42A (the children's rights provision of the Constitution) does not apply to the unborn, who is not a child for this purpose. Thus, by removing the Eighth Amendment, it would appear the unborn no longer enjoys constitutional protection (though the Oireachtas is entitled to legislate to restrict abortion with a view to protecting foetal life).

What was the "unborn" for this purpose?

In *Roche v Roche* [2006] IEHC 359, the Supreme Court ruled that embryos created and stored outside the womb for the purpose of IVF treatment did not attract the protection of the Eighth Amendment until they were implanted in the womb. Some of the judges looked, in particular, to the context in which the Eighth Amendment was passed, the aim being to prevent the legalisation of abortion. Notably, the Protection of Life During Pregnancy Act 2013 defined unborn life as "a life during the period of time commencing after implantation in the womb of a woman and ending on the complete emergence of the life from the body of the woman". This meant that, under that Act, legal protection commenced only from the point at which a fertilised egg attached itself to the wall of the womb.

Where the unborn has little chance of survival

The 2013 Act did not permit abortion in Ireland in cases of fatal foetal abnormalities, where the unborn has a condition affording little or no prospect of its being born alive or of surviving after birth. The *X* case test did not address this point and did not permit abortion in such cases (unless, exceptionally, there was also a risk to the life of the mother). In *PP v HSE* [2014] IEHC 622 the High Court found that it was not in the best interests of an unborn to continue providing life support to its mother. The mother had suffered a brain stem death 15 weeks into her pregnancy. Doctors were keeping her alive in the hope that the child in her womb might be saved. The High Court concluded, however, that the unborn in that case had no prospect of survival or safe delivery and that it was not in its best interests to keep the mother alive.

THE FREEDOM TO TRAVEL AND TO INFORMATION

In the 1980s, a series of decisions relied on the Eighth Amendment to prevent people in Ireland from providing information that might help a woman obtain an abortion outside Ireland. (See for instance *Attorney General (S.P.U.C.) v Open Door Counselling* [1988] I.R. 593, *S.P.U.C. v Coogan* [1989] I.R. 734, and *S.P.U.C. v Grogan* [1989] I.R. 753.) The argument accepted in these cases was that the distribution of information (such as the contact details for foreign abortion clinics) could be curtailed if that was necessary to protect the superior right to life of the unborn. Similarly, some of the Supreme Court judges in the *X* case had suggested (albeit obiter) that the right to travel could potentially have been restricted in order to protect unborn life where there was no risk to the mother's life.

The Thirteenth and Fourteenth Amendments, passed in 1992, prevented the State from relying on the Eighth Amendment to restrict, respectively, freedom to travel and the dissemination of information on foreign abortions.

- The Thirteenth Amendment prevented the Eighth Amendment from being invoked to inhibit a woman's freedom of travel for the purpose of an abortion. (See *A and B v Eastern Health Board* [1998] 1 I.R. 464 and *D. v Health Service Executive (HSE)* unreported, McKechnie J., 9 May 2007.)
- The Fourteenth Amendment guaranteed a right to access information on abortions lawfully available abroad, subject to the conditions laid down in the Regulation of Information Act 1995. Under that Act, a person could provide information on abortions lawfully available abroad (such as contact details for clinics) but could not promote abortion and was obliged to provide information on alternatives to abortion.

THE REPEAL AND REPLACEMENT OF THE EIGHTH AMENDMENT

In 2018, the People approved the Thirty-sixth Amendment to the Constitution, repealing the Eighth, Thirteenth and Fourteenth Amendments. The Thirty-sixth

Amendment replaced the former provisions of Art.40.3.3° with a statement: "Provision may be made by law for the regulation of termination of pregnancy". This effectively leaves it to the Oireachtas to determine in what circumstances a termination may or may not be permitted, such that the issue of abortion will in future be regulated by Act of Parliament rather than by the Constitution. In the wake of the *M.* decision and the Thirty-sixth Amendment, the unborn has, it appears, no rights under the Constitution, though it is open to the Oireachtas to regulate and restrict the circumstances in which a termination of pregnancy is possible. At the time of going to print, legislation is proposed that would allow abortion in Ireland at the pregnant woman's request, up to 12 weeks into the pregnancy. Beyond 12 weeks, the proposed legislation will allow terminations in cases where there is a risk to a woman's life, a serious risk to her health, or where there is a condition likely to lead to the death of the foetus before or shortly after birth.

Freedom of Expression, Association and Assembly

Article 40.6.1.i of the Constitution guarantees the right of the citizen freely to express his or her convictions and opinions. The State, in other words, is not generally entitled to penalise a person for speaking his or her mind. It is said also that from freedom of expression arises a corollary right to silence, that is the right of an accused person not to have to convey certain facts to the Gardaí or to a court (see *Heaney v Ireland* [1994] 3 I.R. 593; [1996] 1 I.R. 580). This right to free expression, however, is not absolute. It is, in particular, according to the terms of the Constitution itself, "subject to public order and morality". Indeed, the right to free expression (and the right to silence) can be restricted where there are legitimate reasons for so doing, provided such restrictions are proportionate.

Freedom of expression applies not only to views and opinions that are mainstream and conventional, but most particularly to views that are unpopular or unconventional, that may shock, offend or disturb. The right of free expression, additionally, is not confined to publications that are considered worthy or in the public interest. In *Mahon v. Post Publications* [2007] IESC 15, Fennelly J. remarked: "The right of freedom of expression extends the same protection to worthless, prurient and meretricious publication as it does to worthy, serious and socially valuable works."

OVERLAP WITH THE RIGHT TO COMMUNICATE

A distinction has sometimes been made between freedom of expression, which is said to protect the expression of opinions (what one believes), and the right to communicate under Art.40.3, which concerns the dissemination or communication of facts or information. (See, for *instance, Attorney General v Paperlink* [1984] I.L.R.M. 373.) In more recent cases, however, the courts have generally played down this distinction, concluding that the level of protection is the same regardless of the Article invoked. In *Irish Times v Ireland* [1998] 1 I.R. 359 Barrington J. observed that the press had a right not only to comment on the news but also to report facts on which such opinions might be based. As O'Flaherty J commented, "... freedom of the press is guaranteed under Article 40.6.1 and that the protection in the constitutional provision is not confined to mere expressions of convictions and opinions". (See also *Murphy v Independent Radio and Television Commission* [1998] 2 I.L.R.M. 360.)

FREEDOM OF THE PRESS

Encompassed in this right is the concept of the "freedom of the press", the right of media organs to communicate and comment on certain phenomena, in particular those relating to the formation of Government policy. This right, however, is not unlimited. The Constitution declares, for instance, that the freedom of the press "shall not be used to undermine public order or morality or the authority of the State". The Constitution is clear in that it guarantees the "rightful liberty" of the organs of public opinion including the radio, the press and cinema, to free expression and, in particular, the right to criticise government policy. In *Mahon v Post Publications* [2007] IESC 15, the Supreme Court emphasised "the cardinal importance of press freedom". Any restriction on it "must be proportionate and no more than is necessary to promote the legitimate object of the restriction". In *Cullen v Tóibín* [1984] I.L.R.M. 577, O'Higgins C.J. remarked: "The freedom of the press and of communication which is guaranteed by the Constitution ... cannot be lightly curtailed." (See also *Foley v Sunday Newspapers Ltd.* [2005] 1 I.R. 89.)

The freedom of the press was emphasised, for instance, in the *Irish Times v Ireland* [1998] 1 I.R. 359. This case concerned the permissible limits on the requirement that justice be administered in public, the presiding judge having excluded most contemporaneous media reporting of a criminal trial. While acknowledging that restrictions could be permitted in order to protect the accused's right to a fair trial, the Supreme Court ruled that the facts of the case did not justify so broad a restriction on publicity in this case. In the course of their judgments, three of the Supreme Court judges referred to the importance of a free press under Art.40.6.

EXAMPLES OF THE RIGHT

In *Dillon v DPP* [2008] 1 I.R. 383 DeValera J. declared unconstitutional a provision of the Vagrancy Act 1847, which penalised the act of begging in public. The judge agreed that the measure in question disproportionately interfered with the accused's right to free expression and his right to communicate. Some proportionate restrictions (such as a ban on aggressive begging or a law preventing begging by children), however, would be valid.

Freedom of expression also formed the basis for the decision in *Holland v Governor of Portlaoise Prison* [2004] 2 I.R. 573. There McKechnie J. declared invalid a ruling of the prison governor refusing permission to a prisoner seeking approval for contact with and visits by members of the media. While acknowledging that free speech was not an absolute right, and might validly be restricted for the purpose of preserving good order in a prison, McKechnie J. ruled that the imposition of a blanket ban on media contact disproportionately infringed the prisoner's right to communicate as well as his freedom of expression. The judge ruled that the governor was required to consider each request for contact on its merits, and that he could only restrict contact where this was necessary to safeguard prison security and good order.

FREEDOM OF EXPRESSION IS NOT ABSOLUTE

There are various limitations upon the exercise of free expression that reflect the delicate balance between leaving people free to speak their mind, and protecting the public against speech that may undermine public security, order or morality. Indeed, Art.40.6 expressly states that the exercise of free expression, free assembly and association is "subject to public order and morality". Thus, in several respects the constitutional right to free expression has been qualified by the superseding interests of the common good and the conflicting rights of other persons. Such restrictions are permissible if they are designed to achieve a legitimate objective and are proportionate.

In *Murphy v IRTC* [1999] 1 I.R. 12 the Supreme Court found that restrictions on paid religious advertisements on radio and television stations were constitutional. The Court reasoned that the Oireachtas was entitled to consider that such advertisements might offend religious sensitivities. The ban might also be justified, the court reasoned, by concerns that richer religious denominations would gain an advantage over poorer denominations by flooding the airwaves with religious adverts. The Supreme Court also noted that the ban was limited in that it was confined to broadcast advertisements only, and did not prevent general discussion of religion on radio and television, or the placing of religious advertisements in other places, such as newspapers or magazines.

Some examples follow of the circumstances in which such free expression can be validly restricted:

TO PROTECT OTHER PEOPLE'S RIGHTS

The Constitution contains an express guarantee of the right to one's good name (Art.40.3.2°). For instance, the Defamation Act 2009 allows litigants to sue for the tort of defamation, which entails making a statement that "tends to injure a person's reputation in the eyes of reasonable members of society", unless it can be shown to be true or privileged. Similarly, it appears that the State may legislate to protect people's privacy, which of necessity may limit the right of free speech. Certain laws also protect confidential information from public disclosure.

TO PROTECT PUBLIC ORDER AND PUBLIC MORALITY

The law generally prohibits speech that is likely to incite a breach of the peace or otherwise to incite others to commit a crime. In particular, s.6 of the Criminal Justice (Public Order) Act 1994 makes it an offence to use "threatening, abusive or insulting words or behaviour" in a public place where such words or behaviour are intended to provoke a breach of the peace. It is also constitutional to limit the right to free expression with a view to upholding public morality by, for instance, censoring or otherwise restricting access to material that is indecent or obscene.

TO PROTECT THE SECURITY OF THE STATE

It is generally constitutional to restrict "seditious" speech (inciting rebellion), or speech that is otherwise liable to undermine the authority or security of the State. In *State (Lynch) v Cooney* [1983] I.L.R.M. 89, for instance, the Supreme Court had to consider a Government order under s.31 of the Broadcasting Act 1960 banning members of Sinn Féin from being interviewed on Irish radio or television. The Court concluded that both s.31 and the specific order in respect of Sinn Féin were constitutional, as they were both considered necessary in order to protect the order and authority of the State (though the courts can review such orders to ensure they are not irrational or unjust).

TO ENSURE RESPECT FOR THE COURT PROCESS

While freedom of expression generally allows citizens to criticise the courts, it is unlawful to pour scorn on the courts in a manner that brings judges into disrepute ("scandalising" the court). Where, for instance, a person suggests that a judge has behaved illegally or improperly, it is open to the court to find that person in "contempt of court" for such comments. (See for instance *Re Kennedy and McCann* [1976] I.R. 382.) Likewise, the law may restrict free speech with a view to protecting the right to a fair trial and preventing comment that may influence the jury's decision in a criminal trial.

TO PREVENT BLASPHEMY AND PROTECT RELIGIOUS SENSITIVITIES

Uniquely, the Constitution expressly stipulates that the publication or utterance of blasphemous, seditious or indecent matter shall be a criminal offence.

Section 36 of the Defamation Act 2009 makes it an offence to publish or utter blasphemous matter. The latter is defined as "matter that is grossly abusive or insulting in relation to matters held sacred by any religion, thereby causing outrage among a substantial number of the adherents of that religion". The person must intend "by the publication or utterance of the matter concerned, to cause such outrage". This resolves the legal gap identified in *Corway v Independent Newspapers* [2000] 1 I.L.R.M. 426, where the Supreme Court found that, in the absence of legislation defining blasphemy, there was no workable legal definition of blasphemy. The prior common law understanding of blasphemy related to the formerly established Church of Ireland and to so confine the definition would not be compatible with the constitutional guarantee of freedom of religion and non-discrimination. (A referendum to remove the blasphemy ban is proposed for 2018).

FREEDOM OF ASSEMBLY

Article 40.6 guarantees the right to assemble peaceably and without arms. Read alongside the right to free expression, this appears to imply a right to gather to engage in peaceful protest. This right is subject to public order and morality and may be proportionately limited with a view to protecting public order and preventing violence. The Constitution, in particular, allows for legislation to prevent and control meetings calculated (in accordance with law) to cause a breach of the peace or to be a danger or nuisance to the public. Legislation may also control meetings within the vicinity of the Houses of the Oireachtas.

FREEDOM OF ASSOCIATION

Article 40.6 also guarantees a right to free association, subject to public order and morality and to state regulation. The State is generally not entitled to restrain people from associating together or from forming unions or associations based on a common interest or concern. By the same token, the State is generally precluded from forcing individuals to be part of an organisation of which those individuals disapprove. As a corollary to the right to associate and to form unions, citizens also enjoy a right to dissociate, that is, not to be a member of a union or association. The State thus cannot support or condone steps taken to force a person to be a member of a union against his or her will. For instance, in *Meskell v C.I.É.* [1973] I.R. 121, the defendant, a State-run transport company, attempted to sack all its workers, readmitting them to employment only on condition that they agreed to join one of four specified unions. The Supreme Court ruled that this infringed the constitutional right of the plaintiff not to be a member of a union, i.e. to dissociate. (See also *Educational Co. v Fitzpatrick (No. 2)* [1961] I.R. 345.)

Freedom of association is not absolute. Article 40.6 expressly allows the State to enact laws regulating and controlling the exercise of this right in the public interest. The State may also curtail such freedom where the curtailment is necessitated by considerations of public order or morality, a point that arguably justifies the banning of various organisations engaged in terrorist activities with a view to undermining the authority or security of the State. Notably, however, laws regulating free association and free assembly may not discriminate on the basis of politics, religion, or class.

The Family, Children, and Education

THE FAMILY

The Constitution places a very strong emphasis on the Family. Articles 41 and 42 guarantee to the "family" certain "inalienable and imprescriptible rights", special rights that cannot (generally) be given away, taken away or lost. The rights involved are "collective" rights, enjoyed by the family as a unit, though they may be invoked by an individual family member. (*Murray v Ireland* [1985] I.R. 532, *DPP v J.T.* (1988) 3 Frewen 141). The family, in particular, enjoys a right to autonomy, broadly remaining free from government interference in its internal affairs, outside of exceptional circumstances. It is important to note, however, that the courts have consistently ruled that the family that is protected by these Articles is exclusively the family based on marriage. Thus, for instance, an unmarried cohabiting couple enjoys no constitutional rights under Arts 41 and 42, as the parties are not married to each other.

MARRIAGE AND THE DEFINITION OF "FAMILY"

The Constitution sees marriage as the essential foundation of the family. It requires the State "to guard with special care the institution of Marriage, on which the Family is founded, and to protect it against attack" (Art.41.3.1°).

In *State (Nicolaou) v An Bord Uchtála* [1966] I.R. 567, the Supreme Court ruled that an unmarried father (Mr Nicolaou) and his child were not part of a family recognised by Art.41. The child's mother had placed her child for adoption without Mr Nicolaou's knowledge or consent. In response to the father's objection that this infringed his family rights under Art.41, the Supreme Court ruled that the father could not plead any of the rights afforded by Art.41, as he was not a member of a constitutionally recognised family. This outcome derived, the Court argued, from the wording of Art.41 itself. In Art.41.3.1° the State pledges to guard with special care the institution of marriage on which, it says, "the Family is founded". As Walsh J. noted in the Supreme Court: "… [i]t is quite clear … that the family referred to in [Art.41] is the family which is founded on the institution of marriage …". According to *G v An Bord Uchtála*

[1980] I.R. 32, even a mother of a child born outside marriage is not part of the child's family within the meaning of Art.41, although a majority of the Supreme Court recognised that an unmarried mother has a personal constitutional right to the custody of the child under Art.40.3. As O'Higgins C.J. observed, Art.41 "refers exclusively to the family founded and based on the institution of marriage".

In *W.O'R. v E.H.* [1996] 2 I.R. 248, the Supreme Court noted that whatever legal rights an unmarried father might have, "the effect of the Constitution grounding the family for the purposes of Article 41 on marriage was to exclude natural fathers from that institution". Most recently, in *JMcD v PL and BM* [2010] 2 I.R. 199 the Supreme Court again confirmed that for the purpose of Art.41 the family is the family based on marriage alone. Thus, an unmarried lesbian couple and their child were not a family for the purpose of the Constitution. (See also *C. O'S. v Judge Doyle* [2013] IESC 60.)

A married couple, same-sex or opposite-sex, with or without children, is treated as a family for the purpose of Art.41, as are widows, widowers, separated spouses, and orphans (where their parents were married to each other while alive). Unmarried couples and households not based on marriage, however, are not families for the purpose of Art.41.

THE SPECIAL POSITION OF MARRIAGE

Generally, marriage enjoys a privileged position under the Constitution. Under Art.41.3 of the Constitution, the State "pledges itself to guard with special care the institution of marriage, on which the Family is founded, and to protect it against attack". It is generally unconstitutional, therefore, for the State to treat a non-marital family more favourably than one based on marriage, thereby penalising the married family. In *Murphy v Attorney General* [1982] I.R. 241, for instance, the Supreme Court declared certain provisions of the tax code unconstitutional, on the ground that they potentially placed a higher tax burden on a double-income married couple than on a similarly placed cohabiting non-marital couple, contrary to Art.41. Similarly, in *Greene v Minister for Agriculture* [1990] 2 I.R. 17, the Supreme Court ruled that a farm support scheme that discriminated in favour of unmarried farmers was unconstitutional. In means-testing farmers for the purpose of this scheme, the off-farm income of a farmer's spouse, but not of a farmer's cohabiting non-marital partner, was to be considered as part of the income of the farmer. This meant that a married farmer might not qualify for farm support in a case where a similarly placed unmarried (but cohabiting) farmer would.

This constitutional preference for marriage has been used to justify measures that discriminate against members of the non-marital family. In

O'B. v S. [1984] I.R. 316, for instance, a daughter of a deceased man claimed that parts of the Succession Act 1965 were unconstitutional because they discriminated against a child of unmarried parents. Under that legislation, at that time, a child whose father had died without making a will could claim from her father's estate only if his or her parents had been married to each other. The Supreme Court concluded that the provisions of Art.41 favouring the institution of marriage constitutionally justified this difference of treatment. There was thus no breach of Art.40.1 (the equality guarantee) as Art.41 permitted (though it did not mandate) preferential treatment for marital families. (The Status of Children Act 1987 has since equalised the position of non-marital children in respect of inheritance law.)

It is not, however, unconstitutional to have regard to certain practical differences between one-parent and two-parent families, in particular, the extra burden that is placed on lone parents by virtue of their situation. In *MhicMhathúna v Ireland* [1995] I.L.R.M. 69, the Supreme Court ruled that special social welfare and tax allowances for lone parents did not constitute an attack on marriage. The court considered that the State was entitled to recognise the more difficult plight of the single parent relative to that of a couple with children.

EQUALITY AND MARRIAGE

Article 41.4 of the Constitution, inserted by the Thirty-fourth Amendment in 2015, states that "[m]arriage may be contracted in accordance with law by two persons without distinction as to their sex". This means that the Constitution guarantees the right of both opposite-sex and same-sex couples to marry, subject to meeting certain requirements laid down by law. The Marriage Act 2015 removed the pre-existing bar on couples of the same sex marrying each other. This effectively overturns the earlier decision in *Zappone and Gilligan v Revenue Commissioners* [2006] IEHC 404 in which the High Court found that there was (prior to 2015) no constitutional right to marry a person of the same sex.

Likewise, in *Re Tilson* [1951] I.R. 1, the Supreme Court ruled that, notwithstanding any contrary rule of law or social practice, spouses are equal in law, in particular in relation to the upbringing of their children. Thus the court held that a father could not depart from an agreement made with his wife regarding the religious upbringing of their children. Similarly, in *State (DPP) v Walsh* [1981] I.R. 412 the Supreme Court had to consider the legality of an old presumption that a wife who commits a crime in the presence of her husband did so under coercion by him. This presumption was unconstitutional, the Court ruled, it being inconsistent with the principle that husband and wife (or spouses) were equal in law.

THE AUTONOMY OF THE CONSTITUTIONAL FAMILY

The constitutional family is considered to enjoy a strong measure of independence from government interference. The family enjoys a general "autonomy", that is, a right to make decisions as to its best interests generally without being overruled by the State. The State cannot, for instance, tell a family how many children it may (or should) have, or where its children should attend school.

In *McGee v Attorney General* [1974] I.R. 284, a landmark decision of the Supreme Court, legislation prohibiting the importation of contraception was declared unconstitutional on the ground that it infringed a married couple's right to privacy and their right to make decisions about family size. In *Re Article 26 and the Matrimonial Home Bill 1993* [1994] 1 I.R. 305, the Supreme Court had to consider a Bill that was designed to split the beneficial ownership of the family homes of all married couples between the spouses jointly and equally. The Court ruled that the legislation was unconstitutional as it threatened to upset long-standing family agreements about the ownership of the matrimonial home in contravention of the family's right to autonomy.

In *North-Western Health Board v H.W.* [2001] 3 I.R. 622, the Supreme Court prevented the State from interfering with the privileges of the marital family. In that case the Court ruled that the State could not, without the consent of his parents, perform a relatively simple "pin-prick test" on a child to test for certain conditions and disorders, notably PKU, which affect a disproportionate number of Irish people. This case establishes that (particularly in the absence of legislation) the State may not generally override family decisions unless there are exceptional circumstances or some exceptional failure of duty. (Though see Art.42A, which now places greater emphasis on the child's best interests).

In *McK v Information Commissioner* [2006] IESC 2, the Supreme Court again emphasised the strong constitutional position of married parents, even when they have been separated. In this case, the Supreme Court ruled that there was a presumption, flowing from Arts 41 and 42, that parents should normally be entitled to access information on their child's medical state. The presumption could be displaced by evidence that it was not in the best interests of the child to release the information but the correct test is to presume that such access is in the child's best interests until the opposite is established. In so ruling, the Supreme Court stressed the importance of the parent-child relationship under the Constitution.

Notably, Art.42 prevents the State from limiting parental choice by instructing parents to send their children to a particular school or type of school. Article 42 states clearly that the primary educator of the child is to be its parents. Thus the parents of a child are afforded considerable freedom in determining how their children are to be educated. For instance, the State is not permitted to instruct parents to send their children to particular schools or types of schools (e.g. State schools as opposed to private schools). Nor can the State or a school force a child to undergo religious education in a school funded by the State (see Art.44.2.4°).

LIMITATIONS ON FAMILY RIGHTS

While family rights enjoy a privileged status in the Constitution, it is clear that the rights of the family are not absolute. In *Murray v Ireland* [1991] 1 I.L.R.M. 465, for instance, the Supreme Court ruled that the rights of an imprisoned married couple to engage in sexual intercourse while in prison, with a view to having children, could legitimately be curtailed in the interests of prison security. Similarly, in *Foy v Governor of Cloverhill Prison* [2010] IEHC 529, Charlton J. noted that imprisonment of a family member does not infringe family rights "if the order to imprison is validly made and the conditions of detention humanely recognise such rights as the prisoner retains within the context of the reasonable management and governance of a lawful place of detention". In that case, the High Court found that a prison governor was therefore entitled to prevent physical contact during visits by prisoners' family members, provided a decision to do so reasonably relates to the management of a prison and is not arbitrary, discriminatory or wholly unreasonable.

The autonomy of the family can be validly curtailed in exceptional cases where a child's welfare is at risk. In *The Matter of Baby AB: Temple Street Hospital v CD* [2011] IEHC 1, the High Court gave doctors permission to administer a blood transfusion to a seriously ill three-month-old child, notwithstanding his parents' religious objections to such treatment. Hogan J. reasoned that the transfusion was urgent and necessary and that, in these circumstances, the child's right to life prevailed over the family's rights. There is no doubt, he concluded, "that the court can intervene in a case such as this where the child's life, general welfare and other vital interests are at stake".

Article 42A of the Constitution also envisages that parental rights may be curtailed by State intervention, where, in exceptional cases, parents have failed in their duty towards their children to such an extent that the safety or welfare of the children is likely to be prejudicially affected. For instance, under the Child Care Act 1991, children may be taken into emergency or long-term care if neglect, ill-treatment or abuse has occurred or is likely to occur. Such interventions, however, must be proportionate. Article 42A also mandates the Oireachtas to legislate to ensure that the child's best interests will be the paramount consideration in litigation involving the child, a principle that arguably shifts the emphasis in the Constitution from the integrity of the family to the interests of the child.

In addition, the right to a family life cannot be used absolutely to preclude the State from enforcing immigration law, for instance by deporting a parent or spouse who is not an EU citizen. In *Osheku v Ireland* [1987] I.L.R.M. 330, the High Court ruled that the fact that the plaintiff, a non-Irish national, was married to an Irish citizen did not prevent his removal from the State. The rights enjoyed by the family, while significant, were not absolute and could be curtailed where this was necessary to achieve the common good. (See also *Pok Sun Shum v Ireland* [1986] I.L.R.M. 593 and *Margine v Minister for Justice, Equality and Law Reform* [2004] IEHC 127.) The State is entitled to control entry at its borders and to manage immigration in an orderly fashion and to preserve the orderly operation of the asylum regime, provided always that it acts reasonably and proportionately.

In *Lobe, Osayande v Minister for Justice, Equality and Law Reform* [2003] 1 I.R. 1, the Supreme Court confirmed that the non-EU national parents of an Irish-citizen child can be removed from the State, even if this has the practical effect of requiring the citizen also to leave. A majority concluded that the Minister was entitled to uphold the integrity of the State's asylum and immigration systems. The Court thus ruled that it is legally and constitutionally possible for the State to deport the non-Irish national parents of an Irish child, if the Minister forms the view that there were grave and substantial reasons related to the common good that so required. Although the State is obliged to give due consideration to the effect of any adverse immigration decision on family and children's rights, family rights do not override the State's entitlement to administer an effective immigration system.

WOMEN AND MOTHERS

Article 41.2 of the Constitution recognises the particular contribution to the common good by the woman working within the home. It indicates that the State "shall, therefore, endeavour to ensure that mothers shall not be obliged by economic necessity to engage in labour to the neglect of their duties in the home". Although this clause does not require women and mothers to work solely in the home, the implication that the burden of childcare and housework should fall on one sex alone has been criticised. Several reviews of the Constitution have recommended modifying this clause to make it gender neutral (see, for instance, the recommendations of the Constitution Review Group and of the Constitutional Convention). A constitutional referendum to remove Art.41.2 is planned for late 2018.

Divorce

Prior to 1995, it was not possible to obtain a divorce from a court in the Republic of Ireland. This was because of the prohibition on divorce in Art.41.3.2°, which formerly stated that "[n]o law shall be enacted providing for the grant of a dissolution of marriage." This prohibition was removed by a referendum held in November 1995 (the Fifteenth Amendment of the Constitution). Today it is possible to secure a divorce, and thus to remarry, under the terms of the new Art.41.3.2°. This provision entrenches the conditions for divorce within the Constitution. It requires that a court may grant a dissolution of marriage only where:

- the parties have been living apart from one another for a period or periods amounting to at least four of the previous five years;
- there is no reasonable prospect of rehabilitation between the parties; and
- the court is satisfied that proper provision has been or will be made for both spouses and for any children of the parties or of either of the parties.

The requirement of "living apart" presupposes more than mere physical separation. It also requires a mental element, a resolve on the part of one or both parties that the marriage has come to an end. Thus, two parties may be living in separate places (for instance, for work) but not be "living apart" for this purpose if they regard their relationship as intact. Equally, it is possible for spouses to share the same house and nonetheless be living apart, provided that they live largely separate and independent lives (see *McA. v McA.* [2000] 2 I.L.R.M. 48).

The Rights of Non-Marital Parents and Families

Families not based on marriage do not enjoy the constitutional rights guaranteed by Art.41. Nevertheless, the courts have found that mothers of children born outside marriage (but not unmarried fathers) enjoy certain personal constitutional rights to the custody of their children as a result of Art.40.3.1°. Under the Status of Children Act 1987, children born outside marriage enjoy broadly equal rights with their marital counterparts. The Thirty-first Amendment inserted a new Art.42A, brought into force in 2015, guaranteeing the rights of *all* children, including children born outside marriage. Yet, even before Art.42A came into force, non-marital children were recognised as having personal constitutional rights to be cared for and to have their welfare safeguarded under Art.40.3 of the Constitution. (*G. v An Bord Uchtála* [1980] I.R. 32.)

A mother who is not married to the father of her child enjoys the constitutional right and duty, under Art.40.3.1°, to care for and have custody of her child (*G. v An Bord Uchtála* [1980] I.R. 32). In sharp contrast, a father who is not married to the mother of his child enjoys no *constitutional* rights to guardianship or custody of that child. The Supreme Court has consistently ruled that, while an unmarried father has certain rights conferred by legislation, he has no constitutional rights to the care and custody of his child either under Arts 41 or 40.3. (See *State (Nicolaou) v An Bord Uchtála* [1966] I.R. 567, *K. v W.* [1990] 2 I.R. 437 and *W.O'R v E.H.* [1996] 2 I.R. 248.) Nonetheless, in *Kl v Minister for Justice and Equality* [2014] IEHC 83 the High Court observed that children have rights under Art.40.3 deriving from their relationship with their natural parents such that the father-child relationship must be considered by a decision-maker where there is a proposal to deport a father.

The guardians of a child born inside marriage are both its married father and mother, jointly and equally. With a non-marital child, however, only the mother is automatically deemed to be a guardian. The non-marital father may apply to court to be made a guardian, or may acquire guardianship by agreement with the mother, or after a period of cohabitation with the mother, but he has no automatic entitlement either to succeed in the court application (see *K. v W.* [1990] 2 I.R. 437) or to gain the mother's consent to a guardianship agreement. Where an unmarried father applies for a court order for guardianship, the court must decide based on the best interests of the child. In *K. v W.* [1990] 2 I.R. 437 the Supreme Court noted that, in relation to the father of a child born outside of marriage, "although there may be rights of interest or concern arising from the blood link between the father and the child, no constitutional right to guardianship in the father of the child exists". An unmarried father has only a legal right to *apply* for guardianship and no automatic right to be granted it. In such applications, the extent of the father's legal rights depend on the circumstances, and the weight to be placed on the blood link between father and child depend on the extent of his input in the child's life. If the father has had minimal input in the life of his child and little contact with the mother, the rights of the father may be quite minimal. On the other hand, if the child is being raised by the child's mother and father as part of "a stable and established relationship" and the child has been "nurtured at the commencement of his life by his father and mother in a situation bearing nearly all of the characteristics of a constitutionally protected family", the legal rights of the unmarried father "would be very extensive indeed". In all such cases, however, the court will grant guardianship to the father where satisfied that it is in the best interests of the child to do so. (See also *W.O'R v E.H.* [1996] 2 I.R. 248.)

While the unmarried father of a child has no constitutional right to object to the adoption of his child, an unmarried father (under the Adoption Act

2010) must be consulted in respect of a proposal to adopt his child. If he has been appointed a guardian of his child, his consent is required to a voluntary adoption of the child and he may veto such an adoption.

ARTICLE 42 AND THE EDUCATION OF CHILDREN

Article 42 acknowledges parents to be the natural and primary educators of their children. The parents to whom this provision applies are, as in Art.41, the parents of children born within marriage.

- Thus married parents have both a right and a duty "to provide, according to their means, for the religious and moral, intellectual, physical and social education of their children".
- These parental rights and duties are described, moreover, as "inalienable" and "imprescriptible". In other words, they cannot generally be given away, taken away or lost. (Though see Art.42A.2.1°.)
- The parents of children, in principle, enjoy freedom of choice in relation to the education of their children. Parents cannot, in particular, be forced to send their children to schools designated by the State.
- The State is, however, entitled to require that children obtain a "certain minimum level [of] education, moral, intellectual and social". Failure to provide "suitable elementary education" for a child may, indeed, lead to the prosecution of parents as in *DPP v Best* [2000] 2 I.L.R.M. 1.

Article 42.4 obliges the State to provide for free primary education. The right also extends to children with disabilities, who are entitled to an education to make the best use of their capabilities. The right to benefit from this, however, is confined to "children", being persons under the age of 18. In *Sinnott v Minister for Education* [2001] 2 I.R. 545, the Supreme Court ruled that a 23-year-old intellectually disabled man was not, as a matter of constitutional right, entitled to continuing State provision for his primary education. In doing so, the Supreme Court overruled the High Court decision of Barr J., who had concluded that the right to free primary education lasted for so long as the education was needed by the disabled person.

Article 42.4 does not place any obligation on the State itself to educate children. The language used here is important: the State is essentially obliged to provide for such education, in other words to fund its provision by either the State or by private groups. The primary responsibility to educate in this context is that of the parents. The State in this regard is essentially expected to cater for parental choice, in short, to support and facilitate the provision of free primary education by funding its delivery. As Kenny J. observed in *Crowley v*

Ireland [1980] I.R. 102, the State itself "... is under no obligation to educate". Instead, the State supports and facilitates the delivery of education by parents in their local communities, usually, though not exclusively, acting through their churches. Effectively, then, the State is obliged to "provide the buildings, to pay the teachers ... to provide the means of transport to the schools if this is necessary to avoid hardship, and to prescribe minimum standards". This view appears to have been endorsed in *Campaign to Separate Church and State v Minister for Education* [1998] 2 I.L.R.M. 81, where the Supreme Court upheld State funding for religious chaplains in community schools. They did so partly on the basis that the funding was required to vindicate the rights of parents under Art.42.4 to an education of their choice, which education might feasibly include matters of religious and moral formation. In other words, the funding facilitated parental choice.

CHILDREN'S RIGHTS

Under Art.42A of the Constitution, "the State recognises and affirms the natural and imprescriptible rights of all children ...". The Article, inserted by the Thirty-first Amendment and brought into force in 2015, requires the State, by its law, to protect and vindicate those rights, as far as practicable. The clause is notable in that it applies to *all* children, whether born inside or outside marriage. Even before Art.42A was enacted, it had been recognised that a child born to unmarried parents enjoyed, under Art.40.3.1°, constitutional rights similar to those enjoyed by a marital child. These rights included the right to be cared for and to have his or her welfare safeguarded, and the right to an adequate education and upbringing (*Re M., an infant* [1946] I.R. 334, *G. v An Bord Uchtála* [1980] I.R. 32). Under legislation, a child born outside marriage is generally to be treated the same as a child born inside marriage (Status of Children Act 1987).

In general, the Constitution envisages that parents will play the primary role in raising a child and making decisions about the child's life and welfare. Nonetheless, Art.42A.2 requires the State, in exceptional cases, to step in to "endeavour to supply the place of the parents". This may only happen, however, where parents have "failed in their duty towards their children to such extent that the safety or welfare of any of their children is likely to be prejudicially affected". Such steps as taken by the State, moreover, must be "proportionate" (no more than is necessary to achieve the child's welfare and appropriate in the circumstances), and must be provided by law.

The reference in Art.42A to "all children" includes children born inside and outside marriage, as well as children who are not citizens of Ireland. According to the Supreme Court in *M v Minister for Justice and Equality* [2018] IESC 14, however, the unborn is not a "child" for the purpose of Art.42A and does not enjoy rights under that Article until born.

Article 42A also requires the following:

- That provision shall be made by law to ensure that, in proceedings relating to adoption, guardianship, custody and access to any child, or proceedings taken by the State for the purpose of child protection, the best interests of the child shall be the paramount consideration. This constitutionalises the best interests principle, which requires that in cases concerning children, their best interests shall be the primary consideration.
- In such proceedings, Art.42A also requires that where a child is capable of forming his or her views, those views shall be ascertained in such proceedings and given due weight having regard to the age and maturity of the child. This effectively requires the courts to hear the voice of the child, though any decision made must be made in the best interests of the child. (See *F.N. v C.O.* [2004] IEHC 60).
- That provision be made by law to allow the adoption of children where the best interests of the child so require, where parents have failed for such period of time as may be prescribed by law in their duty towards the child. Section 54 of the Adoption Act 2010 (as amended by the Adoption (Amendment) Act 2017) allows a child to be adopted without the consent of parents in exceptional circumstances, subject to certain strict conditions and with the approval of the High Court.
- That provision be made by law for the voluntary placement for adoption and adoption of any child. Prior to the Adoption (Amendment) Act 2017, it was only possible to adopt the children of married parents where the child was an orphan or in the exceptional circumstances envisaged by s.54 of the Adoption Act 2010. The 2017 Act allows a child to be adopted with the consent of his married parents.

Formerly, in custody disputes involving married parents and third parties, a constitutional presumption arose that the child's welfare would generally be best served in the custody of his or her marital parents. This preference for the child's marital parents was most heavily underlined in *Re J.H.; K.C. v An Bord Uchtála* [1985] I.R. 375 and *N. and N. v Health Service Executive* [2006] IESC 60 (commonly known as the "Baby Ann" case). These cases involved custody disputes between the natural, married parents of children and prospective adopters with whom these children were placed, in cases where the proposed adoptions did not proceed. In each case, the Supreme Court ruled that there was a constitutional presumption that the child's welfare would be best served by returning the child to its constitutional family. This presumption, moreover, could only be displaced where there were exceptional circumstances or compelling reasons justifying such a move. In light of the passage of Art.42A, however, it is unclear to what extent such a presumption remains in place, given the emphasis in Art.42A on the child's best interests as the paramount consideration in custody cases. The courts may still lean in favour of the child's birth family, although the emphasis on best interests means that it is no longer a foregone conclusion.

Property Rights

Articles 40.3.2° and 43 of the Constitution concern the right to own property, and to have that property protected from unjust attack. The term "property" in this context has been interpreted quite widely. In *Dellway v NAMA* [2011] IESC 4, Hardiman J. observed that property rights were not confined to land, goods and money, but extended to established contractual rights, to the right to earn a living, to the right to one's entitlements under a contract of employment, and to pensions, gratuities or other emoluments which one had earned. Shares also are treated as property in this context. It is clear also that a right to sue for the recovery of money or land may be a property right for these purposes. For instance, in *Re Article 26 and the Health (Amendment) (No. 2) Bill 2004* [2005] IESC 7, the Supreme Court ruled that a right to sue to recover monies collected in breach of the law was a property right protected under Art.40.3. (See also *O'Brien v Keogh* [1972] I.R. 144.) On the other hand, a milk quota is not property for this purpose (see *Maher v Minister for Agriculture* [2001] 2 I.R. 139.)

THE SCOPE (AND LIMITS) OF PROPERTY RIGHTS

While Art.43 protects the general right to own and transfer property, Art.40.3.2° concerns the personal property rights of individuals in respect of specific items of property belonging to them. The distinction is explained by O'Higgins C.J. in *Blake v Attorney General* [1982] I.R. 117, where he noted that Art.43 "prohibits the abolition of private property as an institution" and guarantees the general right to pass property by will and to buy, sell, transfer and inherit property. Article 40.3, on the other hand, protects "the citizen's right to a particular item of property" belonging or bequeathed to him.

These rights are not, however, without limits. Article 43.2, for instance, expressly contemplates that a property owner's rights may be lawfully restricted where it is necessary to do so to promote the interests of the community as a whole. The exercise of property rights is said to be subject to regulation in accordance with "the principles of social justice". The State may thus "delimit" the exercise of such rights "with a view to reconciling their exercise with the exigencies [requirements] of the common good".

For instance, in *Central Dublin Development Association v Attorney General* (1975) 109 I.L.T.R. 69, the High Court ruled that the requirement to obtain planning permission for development was not unconstitutional. The State was entitled to restrict and regulate building with a view to protecting the environmental amenity of an area and the common good. In *Madigan v Attorney General* [1986] I.L.R.M. 136, the Supreme Court concluded that a tax imposed on residential property was constitutional. Likewise, in *Clinton v An Bord Pleanála* [2005] IEHC 84, the High Court ruled that legislation may allow the State compulsorily to purchase land without the consent of the owner, where such land is necessary for important public projects. Finnegan P. remarked, however, that "[t]he delimitation of private ownership to be valid must be reconcilable with the exigencies of the common good and with the principles of social justice. There must be a sufficient and proper public purpose for the acquisition and which purpose cannot be achieved by lesser means."

An "unjust attack" on property rights

While the Constitution permits interference with property rights where the public interest so demands, Art.40.3.2° generally purports to protect these rights from "unjust attack". This means that, while the State may restrict property rights in order to achieve social justice and/or promote the common good, the property rights of an individual cannot ordinarily be taken away in a manner that is objectively unreasonable, unfairly discriminatory, or arbitrary.

As Keane J. remarked in *Iarnród Éireann v Ireland* [1996] 3 I.R. 321: "If the State elects to invade the property rights of the individual citizen, it can do so only to the extent that this is required by the exigencies of the common good. If the means used are disproportionate to the end sought, the invasion will constitute an 'unjust attack' within the meaning of Article 40.3.2." In that case, the plaintiff had been found 30 per cent responsible for an accident for which another party was 70 per cent responsible. The latter, however, was unable to pay. By s.12(1) of the Civil Liability Act 1961, where two or more people are jointly found to be responsible for wrongdoing they "are each liable for the whole of the damage in respect of which they are concurrent wrongdoers". The plaintiff claimed that this constituted an unjust attack on property rights, though the Supreme Court concluded that the restriction of property rights was proportionate and just. The Court noted, in particular, that to rule in favour of the plaintiff would be to exonerate "the blameworthy at the expense of the blameless".

Where the State can show that the restrictions on property rights are rational and serve an important purpose, it is likely they will be found constitutional. The Article 26 reference of *Part V of the Planning and Development Bill 1999* [2001] 1 I.L.R.M. 81 concerned a proposal that, as a condition for obtaining planning permission, builders would have to give up to 20 per cent of the building development land (or the value thereof) to local authorities for social and affordable housing. Builders would receive compensation for this land but at a significantly lower rate than the market value of the land with full planning permission. Noting its important purpose (to provide affordable housing) the Supreme Court held that this restriction on property rights was just and proportionate. The fact that the land's value was enhanced by the State's grant of planning permission was a factor in the judgment.

On the other hand, in *Re Article 26 and the Health (Amendment) (No. 2) Bill 2004* [2005] IESC 7, the Supreme Court declared that a Bill that attempted to prevent older people from suing for recovery of the money paid in breach of the law was unconstitutional. The State had previously charged nursing home residents for care to which they were legally entitled free of charge. The 2004 Bill sought to prevent them from suing to recover these charges. The Supreme Court agreed that there was no general constitutional right to free health care, and that provisions levying charges on residents prospectively (i.e. for care provided from 2004 onward) were constitutional. It concluded, nonetheless, that the attempt retrospectively to validate the illegal payments made before 2004 constituted an unjust attack on the property rights of vulnerable older people. The Court's view was that the right to sue to recover monies collected unlawfully was a property right protected under Art.40.3. As the Bill purported to remove this right, it was unconstitutional. While the Court acknowledged that this would have an impact on the finances of the State, such an intrusion could only be justified to avoid "extreme financial crisis", which was not the case in this situation.

Buckley v Attorney General (the "Sinn Féin Funds" case) [1950] I.R. 67 concerned the ownership of trust monies held in the name of Sinn Féin. In the midst of a court case where the rightful ownership of the monies was being considered, the Oireachtas passed an Act purporting to terminate the case and requiring that the money be distributed in a particular manner. The Supreme Court concluded that the Oireachtas, in addition to interfering in the administration of justice, had breached the plaintiffs' property rights. By its actions, the Oireachtas had removed the plaintiffs' right to assert ownership of the monies and ultimately to obtain access to the funds. This constituted a breach of Art.43, there being no legitimate state interest to justify the intrusion in this case.

Laws that interfere with property rights in an arbitrary and unjust manner have been declared unconstitutional. In *Brennan v Attorney General* [1984] I.L.R.M. 355, the Supreme Court ruled that a system for the collection of rates from landowners based on valuations that were over 100 years old amounted to an unjust attack on property rights. The system gave rise to significant anomalies, with some relatively poor land attracting much higher rates than more fertile properties. Given the arbitrary and irrational system for determining rates, the law amounted to an "unjust attack" on the plaintiff's property rights, and was found to be unconstitutional.

Likewise, in *Blake v Attorney General* [1982] I.R. 117, the plaintiff challenged rent control legislation that broadly sought to control rental prices and to protect tenancy rights in respect of certain properties. This legislation applied only to properties built before 1941 (with no sound reason for this restriction) and did not take into account the financial circumstances of tenants (who may well have been able to afford higher rents). No review of rent was permitted and there was no compensation for landlords, who bore the full burden of these restrictions. In these circumstances, the Supreme Court concluded that the rent controls were unfair and arbitrary and thus constituted an unjust attack on property rights. (See also *Article 26 reference of the Housing (Private Rented Dwellings) Bill 1981* [1984] I.L.R.M. 246.)

While an outcome may be socially just, placing an excessive burden on a narrow segment of society alone to fund that outcome may be deemed unconstitutional. In the Article 26 references of the *Employment Equality Bill 1996* [1997] 2 I.R. 321, and the *Equal Status Bill 1997* [1997] 2 I.R. 387, employers and service providers respectively were called upon to equip their premises to make them fully accessible to people with disabilities. Although this was a worthy aim, the Supreme Court ruled that the requirements placed on employers and businesspersons by this legislation (without compensation or State supports) constituted an unjust attack on the property rights and right to earn a livelihood of those individuals. The Court agreed that providing such facilities for people with disabilities was a socially just outcome, but noted that the legislation had unfairly cast the potentially heavy burden and cost of achieving and paying for this general duty of society on a narrow segment of society. Nonetheless, as *Part V of the Planning and Development Bill 1999* illustrates, requiring builders to subsidise social and affordable housing in exchange for planning permission is not per se unconstitutional.

Restrictions on property rights must be proportionate. In *Cox v Ireland* [1992] 2 I.R. 503 a law sought to deprive a person convicted of certain crimes of the right to work for the State and to receive a pension and other annuities to which he was entitled on foot of his past employment. This mandatory provision, the court concluded, constituted a disproportionate infringement of property rights, given the relatively minor nature of some of the crimes to which the law applied. Likewise, in *Lovett v Minister for Education* [1997] I.L.R.M. 89, a measure that sought to nullify the pension of a retired teacher on imprisonment for more than 12 months was disproportionate in that the severe penalty far outstripped the relatively minor nature of some of the crimes to which it was applied.

THE RIGHT TO COMPENSATION

The Constitution expressly mentions the right to compensation only in Art.44.2.6°, where property is being compulsorily purchased from a religious order. Nonetheless, in other cases, while compensation is not always required, confiscation of one's rightful property without compensation (otherwise than as the penalty for a crime) may be treated as an unjust attack on property rights. In *Central Dublin Development Association v Attorney General* (1975) 109 I.L.T.R. 69 Kenny J. suggested that, as a general rule, state acquisition of the full ownership rights in a property without compensation "would in all cases be such an [unjust] attack". Similarly, in *Re Article 26 and Part V of the Planning and Development Bill 1999* [2000] 2 I.R. 321, Keane C.J. notes: "There can be no doubt that a person who is compulsorily deprived of his or her property in the interests of the common good should normally be fully compensated at a level equivalent to at least the market value of the acquired property." In *E.S.B. v Gormley* [1985] I.L.R.M. 494, the Supreme Court ruled that a property owner had a right to be compensated by the ESB for the routing of large electricity pylons through her land.

This right, however, is not absolute. The absence of compensation at full value does not automatically give rise to an unjust attack (see *Dreher v Irish Land Commission* [1984] I.L.R.M. 94). For instance in *Re Article 26 and Part V of the Planning and Development Bill 1991*, the Supreme Court found that compensation at less than market value was permissible and just in the circumstances. Likewise, in *LB v Ireland* [2015] IESC 1 the Supreme Court ruled that a man required by a court to make financial provision for and to transfer property to his former wife following divorce (as required by Art.41.3.2°) was not entitled to compensation from the State. There is also no constitutional entitlement to compensation when planning permission is denied or when restrictions are imposed on the use of land in the interests of social justice or the common good (see *O'Callaghan v Commissioners of Public Works* [1985] I.L.R.M. 364).

It is notable, however, that compensation on its own does make an interference with property rights constitutional if the restriction is not justified by the requirements of the common good or in the interests of social justice (*Clinton v An Bord Pleanála* [2005] IEHC 84).

21 Freedom of Religion

Religious conflict has been a regular feature of our island's history. To this end, Art.44 broadly guarantees freedom of religious conscience, profession and practice. A person is free, therefore, to adopt religious beliefs, to practise the religion of his or her choice, and to express his or her religious perspective. Equally, a person is free to reject religious teaching and may choose not to practise a religion. These rights are not absolute, however, and are subject to public order and morality.

The Constitution leans heavily in favour of religion. Article 44 begins by stating that "the homage of public worship is due to Almighty God" whose Name shall be held "in reverence" (Art.44.1). The Preamble also invokes the "Most Holy Trinity" and "our Divine Lord, Jesus Christ". On investiture, the President and judges are required to take oaths containing references to "Almighty God".

As enacted, the Constitution acknowledged the "special position" of the Roman Catholic Church as the church of the majority of the population. This reference, however, has since been removed by the Fifth Amendment (1972) alongside references to other specified religions.

The courts, however, are reluctant to involve themselves in disputes between different moral and religious perspectives, preferring to maintain, in their deliberations, a strict separation of civil and religious matters. In *T.F. v Ireland* [1995] 1 I.R. 321 for instance, the High Court refused, in a case challenging the constitutionality of judicial separation laws, to hear testimony from a Catholic priest regarding matters of Roman Catholic canon law. Similarly, in *M.R. v T.R.* [2006] IEHC 359, McGovern J. noted that the concern of the courts is to enforce the law, and not morality. The courts moreover had no role in "weigh[ing] the views of one religion against another" or in resolving conflicts on points of morality (as opposed to law).

LIMITS ON THE FREE PRACTICE OF RELIGION

In the *Matter of AB: Temple Street Hospital v CD* [2011] 1 I.R. 665 two parents objected to a blood transfusion being administered to their three-month-old child, on the basis that it infringed their religious beliefs as Jehovah's Witnesses. Doctors had warned that the child was in serious danger unless the blood transfusion was administered. Hogan J. concluded that the State was entitled to intervene to protect the right to life and the person of the child: "[I]t is incontestable but that this court is given a jurisdiction (and, indeed, a duty) to override the religious objections of the parents where adherence to these beliefs would threaten the life and general welfare of their child." That said, Hogan J. noted also that an adult with full capacity and full information has a constitutionally protected right to refuse medical treatment—whether for religious or other reasons: see *Fitzpatrick v FK* [2009] 2 I.R. 7.

In *Murphy v IRTC* [1999] 1 I.R. 12 the Supreme Court found that a law banning religious advertising on radio and television did not infringe Art.44. The Court concluded that the ban applied equally to all religions and addressed advertisements attacking religion as well. It was not, therefore, an attack on the right to practise. While it limited the right to profess religion, the Court found that the restriction was justified and proportionate. It aimed to protect the religious sensitivities of others and to prevent wealthier religions monopolising the airwaves. It applied, moreover, only to paid advertisements on radio and television, and did not preclude discussion of religion in other types of broadcast. It did not apply, moreover, to print media or the internet.

THE ESTABLISHMENT OF RELIGION

An "establishment" of religion involves making a particular religion the religion of a state and making financial provision for that religion out of the state funds. Although the Constitution does not expressly address this point, it would appear that the State may not establish a religion. Such establishment would arguably involve the type of religious discrimination prohibited by Art.44.2.3°.

THE ENDOWMENT OF RELIGION

The "endowment" of religion is prohibited by Art.44.2.2°. In the *Campaign to Separate Church and State v Ireland* [1998] 2 I.L.R.M. 181 Keane C.J. defined endowment for this purpose as "the vesting of property or income in a religion as such in perpetual or quasi-perpetual form". The Supreme Court thus concluded, in that case, that the State was entitled to fund the employment of religious chaplains in community schools. A number of principles arise from this case:

- It is permissible for the State to fund the provision of education in schools run by religious groups and orders. The Constitution appears implicitly to allow this when it states that the funding of schools shall not discriminate between schools run by different religious denominations (Art.44.2.4°).

This suggests that the Constitution anticipated that the State would fund schools run by religious denominations (which would have been the norm in 1937). Because religious education is a fundamental part of the curriculum in religious-run schools, and the State is entitled to fund education in such schools, the Court concluded that the State was also allowed to fund religious instruction in denominational schools.
- It is permissible, moreover, for the State to pay the salaries of school chaplains, that is, ministers of religion charged with the religious formation and general moral welfare of students in a particular school.

Nonetheless, Art.44.2.4° of the Constitution states that "[l]egislation providing State aid for schools shall not discriminate between schools under the management of different religious denominations ...". Such legislation, moreover, cannot "affect prejudicially the right of any child to attend a school receiving public money without attending religious instruction at that school". This means that, where the State funds a school, no child may be forced to attend religious instruction in such a school.

THE BAN ON RELIGIOUS DISCRIMINATION

It is generally unconstitutional for the State, in its laws, to differentiate between people on the basis of their religious profession, status or belief (Art.44.2.3°).

In *Quinn's Supermarket v Attorney General* [1972] I.R. 1, the Supreme Court declared unconstitutional a Government order that exempted Jewish kosher shops from restrictions on the opening hours of meat shops. The Court concluded that the exemption discriminated on the basis of religion, and went further than was necessary to protect the free practice of religion. This case illustrates that discrimination for this purpose can include positive as well as adverse discrimination. The Supreme Court nonetheless indicated that discrimination may be possible where the purpose is to support or facilitate the free practice of religion provided that the differential treatment goes no further than is necessary to protect religious freedom.

The State may not discriminate between persons on the grounds of their status within a particular religious grouping. In *Mulloy v Minister for Education* [1975] I.R. 88, a priest who had taught for some time in a school in Nigeria was, when he returned to Ireland, denied incremental salary credits (i.e. extra pay) in respect of his experience teaching in Nigeria. Had the plaintiff been a layperson teaching abroad, he would have been given incremental credit. This discriminatory treatment centred on his status as a priest, and thus constituted a breach of Art.44.2.3°.

The State cannot penalise a person for marrying outside his own religion. In *M. v An Bord Uchtála* [1975] I.R. 81, the High Court found that a provision of the Adoption Act 1952 that prevented a married couple of mixed faith from adopting the wife's own child was unconstitutional as it imposed a disability based on religion and discriminated based on religion.

SUPPORT FOR THE PRACTICE OF RELIGION

The decided cases on freedom of religion seem generally to indicate a strong preference for the State support of religion, even where this may involve apparent infringements of the requirement of non-discrimination noted above. In particular, the Supreme Court has indicated that discrimination may be permissible where this is necessary to support or buttress the free practice of religion.

In *Quinn's Supermarket v Attorney General* [1972] I.R. 1, the Supreme Court declared unconstitutional a Government order that exempted Jewish kosher shops from restrictions on the opening hours of meat shops. (Kosher shops are facilities that prepare food in accordance with Jewish religious laws.) In doing so, however, the court noted that had such an exemption been fully necessary to facilitate those of the Jewish faith in the free practice of their religion, the measure would have been constitutionally permissible. The majority felt that the exemption went further than was necessary to protect the free practice of the Jewish faith (i.e. it was disproportionate). It did, however, agree that a less extensive exemption, designed to ensure that Jewish people would not be forced to purchase meat during their Sabbath, would have been permissible. This was despite the fact that such a measure would technically have involved discrimination between different religions.

In *McGrath v Maynooth College* [1979] I.L.R.M. 166, two lecturers were dismissed from their jobs at a State-funded Catholic third-level college because they had broken certain religious rules imposed by the Roman Catholic Church. The Supreme Court ruled that the dismissals were valid despite the fact that such a ruling involved an endorsement of the discriminatory rules of a particular religion. The Court's reasoning in this regard again seemed to suggest that the State was entitled, even obliged, to support the free practice of religion, even where this involved turning a blind eye to what some people might see as the unfair practices of such religions. The Court also relied on the right of religious denominations to manage their own affairs (see Art.44.2.5). (See also *Flynn v Power* [1985] I.R. 648, where the High Court endorsed a decision of a religious order to dismiss a teacher who had become pregnant outside marriage.) Likewise in *Re the Employment Equality Bill 1996* [1997]

2 I.R. 321, the Supreme Court found that a power to discriminate to protect a school or hospital's religious ethos was constitutionally permissible.

Similarly, in *Campaign to Separate Church and State v Minister for Education* [1998] 2 I.L.R.M. 181, the Supreme Court ruled that it was not unconstitutional to fund the salaries of religious chaplains working in State-run community schools. The reasoning of the court was that the State, in doing so, was merely supporting the free choice of parents regarding the religious formation of their children, as guaranteed by Art.42.4 of the Constitution.

Amending the Constitution

How is the Constitution amended?

Only the People of Ireland may amend the Constitution, and only at the invitation of the Oireachtas. They do so in referendums proposed by the Houses of the Oireachtas (see generally Arts 46 and 47). Such proposals are put to the People in the form of a "Bill" initiated in Dáil Éireann and passed (or deemed under Art.23 to have been passed) by both the Dáil and the Seanad. If the referendum proposal succeeds in attracting a majority of the votes cast in the referendum, the Amendment is deemed to have passed. In such a case, the President will sign and promulgate the Act as having amended the Constitution.

The power of initiating a referendum lies solely with Dáil Éireann. The People have no power to initiate a referendum; they must in all cases act on a proposal from Parliament. Their role in that sense is passive; they can only vote on proposals made by the Oireachtas.

Between 1938 and 1941, it was possible for the Oireachtas on its own to amend the Constitution, without resort to the People. It did so on two occasions, once in 1939 and again in 1941. The Constitution, however, expressly prevented the Oireachtas from extending the period during which it enjoyed this exclusive power. Thus, this power to amend the Constitution is no longer available to the Oireachtas alone. Since 1941, only the People may make an amendment to the Constitution, though only when invited to do so by a proposal from the Oireachtas.

What kind of amendments can the People make?

There are no restrictions or limits on the types of amendment that may be put to the people or made to the Constitution (see the decision of the Supreme Court in *Re Article 26 and the Regulation of Information Bill 1995* [1995] 1 I.R. 1). The People, for instance, could pass an amendment that did little more than clarify the meaning of the Constitution. (See *Finn v Attorney General* [1983] I.R. 514.)

The courts have consistently stressed that the content of a proposed amendment to the Constitution is a matter for the People alone. The courts will not, moreover, entertain a request to clarify the meaning of a proposed amendment before it is passed by the People.

In particular, judges are extremely reluctant to prevent a referendum proposal duly passed by the Oireachtas from being put to the People. In a series of cases, the courts have refused to stop a referendum proposed by the Oireachtas from being put to the People. The rationale is that the People are entitled to vote on any proposal that the Oireachtas puts to them (see, for instance, *Finn v Attorney General* [1983] I.R. 514, *Slattery v An Taoiseach* [1993] 1 I.R. 286 and *Riordan v An Taoiseach (No. 2)* [1999] 4 I.R. 343, *Morris and Ó Maoldhomhnaigh v Minister for the Environment* [2002] 1 I.R. 326.)

CAN AN AMENDMENT BE MADE CONTINGENT ON EVENTS OCCURRING?

An amendment may contain a contingency or condition precedent to its activation. For instance, the Nineteenth Amendment stated that new Articles 2 and 3 of the Constitution (removing the legal claim over Northern Ireland) would only come into force when an order of Government was made (in this case, following the establishment of the bodies agreed under the Good Friday Agreement.) The Supreme Court upheld this approach as legally valid in *Riordan v An Taoiseach (No. 2)* (1999). Similarly, it appears that a constitutional amendment may refer to, and thus approve and give constitutional protection or status to, a text that is external to the text of the Constitution itself (see *Morris and Ó Maoldhomhnaigh v Minister for the Environment* [2002] 1 I.R. 326.).

THE CONDUCT OF A REFERENDUM

While the courts generally will not interfere in relation to the substance of a proposal to amend the Constitution, they have, on several occasions, acted in relation to the manner in which a referendum is conducted. In particular, the courts have stressed the importance of equal treatment by the State of the campaigns for and against an amendment. It is unconstitutional, according to the Supreme Court in *McKenna v An Taoiseach (No. 2)* [1995] 2 I.R. 10, for either the Government or the Oireachtas to spend public monies with a view to promoting a particular referendum result (i.e. to promote only one side of a referendum campaign). In that case, the Supreme Court ruled that the allocation by the State of nearly €650,000 to promote a "Yes" vote in the divorce referendum of 1995 (with no funds for the "No" side) was unconstitutional, as it breached the guarantee of equality, the right to free expression and infringed the democratic nature of the State. (This does not, however, prevent Government Ministers from personally advocating for a particular result, provided State money is not used to fund their campaign).

Likewise, in *McCrystal v Minister for Children and Youth Affairs* [2012] IESC 53 a government-funded advertising campaign providing information on the proposed children's referendum was found to be unconstitutional on the basis that it implicitly encouraged voters to favour the proposed amendment and was not sufficiently impartial and unbiased.

Therefore:

- Public funds cannot be used to promote one side only of a referendum debate to the detriment of the alternative.
- In a similar vein, according to *Coughlan v RTÉ* [2000] 3 I.R. 1, public sector broadcasters (such as RTÉ and TG4) must be balanced in their treatment of the "yes" and "no" sides of a referendum campaign.

Under the Referendum Act 1994 it is possible to challenge the result of a referendum if it has been conducted in an unlawful manner, but such a challenge will succeed only if the petitioner can demonstrate that the wrongful conduct had a material effect on the referendum outcome. Such challenges have been rejected in *Hanafin v Minister for the Environment* [1996] 2 I.R. 321 and *Jordan v Minister for the Environment* [2015] 4 I.R. 232, as the plaintiffs were unable to demonstrate that unlawful spending on referendum campaigns materially affected the referendum results. The test to be applied here is whether "a reasonable person would be in doubt about, and no longer trust, the provisional outcome of the election or referendum" (*Jordan*).

THE AMENDMENTS EXPLAINED

To date, since 1937, there have been 30 Amendments made to the Constitution, two by the legislature and the remainder by the People in referendum. These include:

- the Third, Tenth, Eleventh, Eighteenth and Twenty-eighth Amendments allowing Ireland to join what is now the European Union and to ratify various EU treaties;
- the Fifth Amendment removing the special place of the Roman Catholic Church from the Constitution;

- the Eighth, Thirteenth, Fourteenth and Thirty-sixth Amendments on the issue of abortion;
- the Fifteenth Amendment, which removed the former constitutional ban on divorce;
- the Nineteenth Amendment, which dropped the former legal claim over Northern Ireland and replaced it with an aspiration to unity through peaceful and democratic means;
- the Thirth-first Amendment affirming the rights of children; and
- the Thirty-fourth Amendment allowing couples of the same sex to marry.

THE FAILED AMENDMENTS

Eight proposals to amend the Constitution have proved unsuccessful, having been rejected by the People. These include two failed attempts to abolish the system of proportional representation in Irish elections, one in 1959 and the other in 1968; two amendments seeking to restrict abortion on grounds of a suicide risk (1992 and 2002); a referendum proposing the abolition of the Seanad (2013); and a proposal to reduce the minimum age for the Presidency to 21 (2015).

As a result of the people voting against these changes, there is no Twelfth, Twenty-fourth, Twenty-fifth, Thirty-second or Thirty-fifth Amendment, the proposals for these changes having been turned down. A proposal for a Twenty-second Amendment, regarding the removal and censure of judges, was proposed but withdrawn before referendum in 2001.

There is no restriction, however, on the topic of a failed referendum being put to the People a second time. The constitutional ban on divorce and the Nice Treaty, for instance, have both been put to People twice, with the second referendum succeeding on each occasion.

Index

Abbeylara inquiry, 69–70, 118
abortion
    constitutional interpretation, 7, 8, 11
    distribution of information, 87, 135
    Eighth Amendment, 7, 11, 133–134
    embryo outside womb, 134
    freedom to travel, 135
    little chance of foetus surviving, 134–135
    proposed legislation, 136
    repeal and replacement of Eighth Amendment, 135–136
    right to life of unborn, 7, 133–134
    suicide risk, 133–134
access to court, 126–127
access to lawyer, 97, 105–106
actio popularis, 23
administration of justice in public, 90
adoption
    child of married parents, 153
    mixed-faith couple, 14, 163
    unmarried father's position, 143, 150–151
    widower, 112
amendment of Constitution
    conduct of referendum, 166–167
    contingent on event, 166
    failed amendments, 168
    list of amendments, 167–168
    procedure, 165
    types of amendments, 165–166
appeal
    acquittal, against, 6
    appellate jurisdiction, 85–86
    leap-frog appeal, 85
arrest
    member of Oireachtas, 69
    suspect's rights, 96–97

assisted suicide, 115–116, 133
Attorney General
    appointment, 83
    independence, 83
    proceedings by, 83
    prosecution of offences, 84
    resignation or removal, 83
    role, 83

bail, 100–101
begging, 138
Bill
    definition, 17
    Art.26 reference, 16–19
    legislative power *see* law-making
    Money Bills, 75–76
    presumption of constitutionality, 17–18
blasphemy, 140–141
blood transfusion, 147, 160–161
bodily integrity, 121–122
bona fide interest group, 22–23
by-election, 73

Cabinet confidentiality, 47, 81–82
carried over laws, 20
Censorship Board, 94
challenging constitutionality
    Bill, 16–19
    declaration of invalidity, 28
    EU law, 24–25, 43
    High Court jurisdiction, 86
    immunity from challenge, 23–25
    injunctive relief, 28
    locus standi, 21–23
    post-1937 law, 20
    pre-1937 law, 20
    retrospective effect of finding, 25–28
    severance of provision, 25, 28

children
    adoption *see* adoption
    best interests, 153–154
    constitutional rights, 152–154
    custody and guardianship, 150, 153–154
    deportation of parents, 148
    education *see* education
    employment, 123
    non-marital *see* non-marital child
    parental autonomy, 146–147
    right to have, 125, 130
    views to be considered, 153
    welfare at risk, 147, 152
    witnesses, 105
Christian ethos, 3, 160
communication, 129, 137–138
commutative justice, 49
compulsory purchase
    compensation, 159
    constitutionality, 156
    discrimination, 115
constituencies, 72
Constitution of Ireland 1937
    amendment *see* amendment of Constitution
    background, 2–3
    commencement date, 1
    ethos, 3
    evolving nature, 3–4, 11–12
    interpretation *see* constitutional interpretation
    purpose, 1–2
    rights under *see* constitutional rights
Constitution of the Irish Free State 1922, 2
constitutional interpretation
    broad or purposive interpretation, 6–7
    constitutional issue last, 15
    double construction rule, 14–15
    harmonious interpretation, 8–9
    hierarchical interpretation, 9–10
    historical interpretation, 10–11
    Irish or English text, 5
    literal interpretation, 6
    natural rights approach, 12–13
    precedent, 5
    updating interpretation, 11–12
constitutional rights
    children, 152–154
    enumerated personal rights, 117–118
    equality *see* equality
    family *see* family
    freedom of assembly, 141
    freedom of association, 141–142
    freedom of expression/press, 137–141
    hierarchy, 9–10
    life *see* life
    limitations and restrictions, 129–131
    property, 155–159
    religion, 160–164
    unenumerated rights *see* unenumerated rights
contempt of court, 88, 110, 140
contraception, 4, 12, 124, 146
controlled drugs, 60–61
Council of State, 56
Court of Appeal, 86
courts
    assessment of evidence, 88–89
    determination of guilt or innocence, 88, 92
    imposition of sentence, 92–93
    judges *see* judges
    public and media access, 90
    role, 47–48
    structure, 85–86
criminal intent, 107–108
criminal matter, 94
cross-examination of witnesses, 105
customary international law, 38

Dáil
    elections *see* elections
    Government responsibility to, 76–77, 78
    membership, 73–74
    money matters, 49–50
De Valera, Éamon, 2

death penalty, 24, 132
debt collection, 118
declaration of incompatibility, 41
declaration of war, 38, 77
declaratory theory, 57–58
delay in proceedings, 101–102
delegated legislation
    changing, amending or repealing legislation, 62–63
    implementation of EU law, 63–64
    principles and policies test, 59–62
democracy, 32
deportation, 148
Derrynaflan Hoard, 35
detention, 96
discrimination *see* equality
distributive justice, 49
divorce, 4, 149
double construction rule, 14–15
double jeopardy, 6
DPP, 84
dualist state, 39–41

earning a livelihood, 122–124
education
    choice of school, 146–147
    free primary education, 151
    parental rights and duties, 151–152
    school run by religious denomination, 161–164
    State funding for religious chaplains, 152, 161–162, 164
    State obligations, 151–152
elections
    by-elections, 73
    constituencies, 72
    deposit, 72
    dual mandate, 73
    fairness and equality, 72–73, 114
    non-party candidates, 73
    spending cap, 114
    voting, 71–72
emergency powers, 23–24
equality
    compulsory purchase, 115
    constitutional rights, 111–112
    criminal context, 114–115
    gender, 112–113
    justification for discrimination, 115–116
    political process, 72–73, 114
EU law
    automatically part of Irish law, 43–44
    direct applicability/effects, 44
    exemption from constitutional challenge, 24–25, 43
    generally, 42
    regulations implementing, 44, 63–64
    supremacy, 43
    treaties, 44–45
European Convention on Human Rights, 41–42
European Stability Mechanism, 34, 37, 81
evidence
    assessment by court, 88–89
    unconstitutionally obtained evidence, 106–107
    video link, 105
Executive *see* **Government**
extra-territoriality, 42

fair procedures, 129
fair trial
    access to lawyer, 105–106
    bail, 100–101
    constitutional right, 98
    criminal intent, 107–108
    defence, 105
    impartial judge and jury, 103–104
    offence certain and clear, 98–99
    presence at trial, 102–103
    presumption of innocence, 99–100
    reasonably expeditious trial, 101–102
    retrospective offence, 99
    right to silence, 104–105
    unconstitutionally obtained evidence, 106–107
    understanding proceedings, 103
family
    autonomy of constitutional family, 146–147
    constitutional rights, 143

family *(continued)*
   limitations on rights, 147–148
   non-marital families, 143–145, 149–151
flag, 31
fluoridation of public water, 121–122
forcible entry, 98
foreign relations
   Art.29 not conferring individual rights, 38–39
   Dáil powers, 37–38
   exclusive power of Government, 36–38, 47, 80–81
   President's role, 36
   State sovereignty, 34, 37
freedom of assembly, 141
freedom of association, 141–142
freedom of expression
   begging, 138
   blasphemy, 140–141
   constitutional right, 137
   defamation, 139–140
   limitations, 139–141
   prisoners, 139
   public order and morality, 140
   right to communicate and, 137–138
   scandalising the court, 140
   seditious speech, 140
freedom of the press, 137–138

Garda prosecution, costs, 9
Garda questioning
   access to lawyer, 97
   oppressive questioning, 97
   right to silence, 104–105
gender equality, 112–113
Good Friday Agreement, 29–30
good name, 117–118, 139–140
Government
   Cabinet confidentiality, 47, 81–82
   delegated legislation, 59–62
   foreign relations, 36–38, 47, 80–81
   Ministers, 79–80
   money matters, 49–50
   responsibility to Dáil, 76–77, 78
   role, 47, 78
   structure, 78
   Taoiseach, 76, 78–79
guardianship, 150

habeas corpus proceedings, 22
harmonious interpretation, 8–9
health rights, 121–122
hierarchy of rights, 9–10
High Court, 86
historical interpretation, 10–11
homosexuality, 21–22, 40, 112–113

illegitimacy *see* non-marital child
independence of state, 33
insanity, 92
interpretation of Constitution *see* constitutional interpretation
interpreter, 103
investigative committees, 69–70, 118
inviolability of the dwelling, 97–98
Irish Free State, 2
Irish Human Rights and Equality Commission, 22
Irish Nation, 29–30
ius tertii, 21

Jewish faith, 162, 163
judges
   appointment, 87
   bias, 87
   independence, 87–89
   judicial function, 91–93
   reduction in remuneration, 7, 87
   reluctance to engage in law-making, 57–59
   removal from office, 89
   role, 47–48
judicial function
   characteristics, 91
   exercise by other bodies, 93–95
jury trial
   exceptions, 108
   fair cross-section of society, 110

impartiality of jury, 103–104
purpose, 110
right to, 108
women jurors, 110, 112

law-making
Dáil role, 74–75
delegated legislation, 59–64
judicial reluctance, 57–59
legislative power, 46–47, 57
Money Bills, 75–76
reference, by, 64–65
Seanad opposition to Bill, 74–75
legal aid, 127–128
legal representation, 105–106, 127–128
legislation
commencement, 65
delegated legislation *see* delegated legislation
law-making power *see* law-making
unreasonable delay in commencing, 65
legislature *see* Oireachtas
liberty, 96, 130
life
constitutional right, 132
death penalty, 24, 132
hierarchy of rights, 9–10
refusal of medical treatment, 122, 132–132
self-defence, 132
unborn's right, 7, 133–136
limitation periods, 127
literal interpretation, 6
litigation right, 126–127
locus standi, 21–23

mandatory orders, 48–49, 78
marriage
constitutional protection, 143–144
equality of spouses, 145
right to have children, 125, 130
right to marry, 126
same-sex couples, 4, 126, 145

medical treatment, refusal, 122, 132–132
membership of illegal organisation, 99–100
mentally ill person, 126–127
Ministers
appointment, 79–80
delegated legislation *see* delegated legislation
number, 78
portfolios, 80
resignation or removal, 80
unelected person, 80
minor offence, 11, 108–109
Money Bill, 75–76
moot issue, 23

name of Irish State, 31
nation, 29
natural law, 12–13, 120–121
nemo iudex in causa sua, 103
neutrality, 38, 77
non-citizen, right to work, 115, 123
non-marital child
adoption, 143, 150–151
constitutional rights, 149, 152
custody and guardianship, 150
succession, 10, 115, 144–145
Northern Ireland, 29–30
nursing home
conditions, 125
recovery of charges, 157

official languages, 31
Oireachtas
control of internal operation, 66–67
Dáil *see* Dáil
investigative committees, 69–70, 118
legislative role, 46–47, 57
parliamentary privilege, 65–69
privilege from arrest, 69
Seanad, 74
structure, 57

parliamentary privilege
    generally, 65–66
    private papers, 66–67
    sources of information, 68–69
    utterances, 67–68
passport, 128
personal rights, 117
pin-prick test, 146
precedent, 5
President
    accountability and impeachment, 55
    Art.26 reference, 16–19
    Art.27 referendum, 54–55
    ceremonial role, 36, 51
    death or resignation, 51
    discretionary powers, 54–55
    election, 51
    eligibility for office, 51–52
    foreign relations role, 36
    inability or unwillingness to act, 56
    limited powers, 52–53
    nomination, 52
    salary, 55
    term of office, 51
presumption of constitutionality, 13–14, 17–18
presumption of innocence, 99–100
pre-trial publicity, 103–104
principles and policies test, 59–62
prisoner
    breach of prison discipline, 194–95
    conviction under unconstitutional law, 26–28
    extradition, and equality, 114–115
    heath, 122
    media contact, 129, 139
    prison conditions, 118, 122
    privacy, 125
    right to have children, 125, 130
    solitary confinement, 122
    voting rights, 71
privacy, 124–125
property rights
    compensation, 159
    compulsory purchase *see* compulsory purchase
    harmonious interpretation, 9
    property concept, 155
    scope and limits, 155–156
    unjust attack, 156–158
proportional representation, 72
proportionality test, 130–131
prosecution of offences, 84
protection of the person, 118
public spending, 49–50
purposive interpretation, 6–7

reading down, 14–15
referendum
    amendment of Constitution, 165
    Art.27, 54–55
    conduct of, 166–167
    EU treaties, 44–45
    public funding, and equality, 114, 166–167
religion
    adoption of child, 14, 163
    advertising, 139, 161
    ban on discrimination, 162–163
    endowment, 161–162
    establishment, 161
    freedom of religion, 160
    limits on free practice, 160–161
    school run by religious denomination, 161–164
    State funding for religious chaplains, 152, 161–162, 164
    State support for free practice, 163–164
rent control, 158
republic, 2–3, 32
retrospective offence, 99
reverse-onus provisions, 99–100
Roman Catholic Church, 3, 160
royal prerogative powers, 34–35

same-sex marriage, 4, 126, 145
scandalising the court, 140

school *see* **education**
Seanad
    composition, 74
    rejection of Bill, 74–75
search warrant, 97–98
seditious speech, 140
self-defence, 132
self-incrimination, privilege against, 104
Senators, 74, 76
sentencing
    judicial function, 92–93
    mandatory penalty, 93
    maximum and minimum penalties, 93
    proportionality, 104
separation of powers
    checks and balances, 48
    executive role, 47
    judicial role, 47–48
    legislative role, 46–47
    mandatory orders, 48–49
    money matters, 49–50
    principle, 46
    regulations implementing EU law, 63–64
    republican state, 32
sexual offences against minors, 27–28, 58, 108, 113, 117
Shannon stopover, 38–39, 77
Sheehan **principle**, 65
silence, right to, 104–105
social welfare payments, 13
socio-economic rights, 50
solicitor
    access to lawyer, 97, 105–106
    striking off, 91, 94
sovereignty, 33–34, 37
Special Criminal Court, 86, 109–110
State
    definition, 31
    democratic nature, 32
    independence, 33
    legal personality, 31
    no immunity from suit, 35
    republic, 32
    royal prerogative powers, 34–35
    sovereignty, 33–34, 37
street trading, 124
Supreme Court, 85

Taoiseach
    appointment, 76, 78
    powers and duties, 78–79
    resignation, 76, 79
tax laws
    discrimination against married couples, 25, 115, 144
    presumption of constitutionality, 13
    recovery of overpaid taxes, 25–26
telephone tapping, 124–125
termination of pregnancy *see* **abortion**
transgender person, 41
travel, 128, 135
treasure trove, 35
tribunal of inquiry, 91–92

unborn
    definition, 11
    right to life, 7, 133–136
unconstitutional legislation
    challenging *see* challenging constitutionality
    vagueness, 98–99
unconstitutionally obtained evidence, 106–107
unenumerated rights
    access to courts, 126–127
    bodily integrity/health, 121–122
    children, 125
    Christian and democratic nature of state, 119–120
    communication, 129
    court recognition, 118–119
    earning a livelihood, 122–124
    fair procedures, 129
    implied rights, 119

unenumerated rights *(continued)*
  inherent rights, 120
  legal representation, 127–128
  marriage, 126
  natural rights, 120–121
  privacy, 124–125
  travel, 128
updating interpretation, 11–12

vicarious liability, 107–108
video link evidence, 105
voting, 71–72

women
  constitutional position, 148
  earning a livelihood, 123
  gender equality, 112–113